ACCLAIM FOR BARRY WERTH'S

The Scarlet Professor

"Absorbing. . . . Werth tells his story with dramatic flair, and he's especially good at fleshing out the political and cultural background of Arvin's drama. . . . A well-written, engaging book."   —*The Boston Globe*

"Lively, well-researched. . . . Werth . . . takes the reader rather deep inside Arvin's shell. . . . In the history of sex and intellectual life in America, Arvin's is a fascinating chapter."   —*The New York Times Book Review*

"Perceptive. . . . A human story. . . . Werth has told this gifted but unhappy man's story with sympathy but utterly without sentimentality or special pleading. His research . . . is thorough and surprising. . . . Werth writes about Arvin's sexual torments with refreshing and instructive dispassion, and eschews any temptation to turn Arvin's story into gay-rights propaganda."   —*The Washington Post Book World*

"Heartrending. . . . Harrowing. . . . [*The Scarlet Professor*] freshens our memory of yesterday's superstition and casts valuable if veiled light on today's evasions. . . . At the climax terror is palpable."
—*The New York Review of Books*

"Barry Werth has brought to vivid life a crucial episode in the history of American repression that is little known. The 'Smith College Homosexual Scandal of 1960,' centrally involving the famed literary critic Newton Arvin, has never before been researched and reported in such fascinating, horrifying detail. Barry Werth has a marvelous narrative gift, and he tells his tale with spellbinding skill."   —Martin Duberman

"Compelling. . . . A penetrating and compassionate look at one of the more prominent victims of [a] 'hidebound, old-fashioned, and darkly repressive' era." —*Brill's Content*

"Werth vividly chronicles how Arvin, a mentor of Carson McCullers and Truman Capote's one-time lover, was nearly destroyed in the now-forgotten 'Smith College Homosexual Scandal of 1960.' He also shines a light on one of the darker chapters in America's history of intolerance." —*The Providence Sunday Journal*

"Superb. . . . *The Scarlet Professor* may help restore the personal reputation of this flawed, fascinating and largely forgotten man." —*Courier-Post* (Cherry Hill, New Jersey)

"Insightful, compassionate. . . . Expansive and fascinating. . . . The greatest epilogue [for Newton Arvin] may be Werth's own book. *The Scarlet Professor* manifests precisely the traits that Arvin's literary biographies did: acute insight, deep compassion and an utter respect for language." —*Chicago Tribune*

"What a beautiful book. What I so admired about it is that it falls outside of any kind of easy definition or classification. It's biography. It's history. It's a book of quiet outrage at our mixed-up (and in this case just plain wrong-headed) cultural morality. I couldn't put the damn thing down." —Alex Kotlowitz, author of *The Other Side of the River* and *There Are No Children Here*

"Rewarding. . . . That Barry Werth, a married man with two children, could write such a sympathetic, nonjudgmental book about Arvin is testimony to a great depth of understanding. . . . [His] detailed life of a homosexual man will generate much belated understanding. . . . The rendering of the background of Arvin's life is first-rate—the 1930s, '40s and '50s." —*Houston Chronicle*

BARRY WERTH

The Scarlet Professor

Barry Werth is the author of *The Billion-Dollar Molecule* and *Damages*. His articles have appeared in *The New Yorker*, *The New York Times Magazine*, *GQ*, and *Outside*. He lives in Northampton, Massachusetts, with his wife and two children.

The Billion-Dollar Molecule

Damages

The Scarlet Professor

Anchor Books

A DIVISION OF RANDOM HOUSE, INC.

NEW YORK

The
Scarlet
Professor

NEWTON ARVIN

A LITERARY LIFE SHATTERED

BY SCANDAL

Barry Werth

For Emily and Alex

FIRST ANCHOR BOOKS EDITION, MARCH 2002

Copyright © 2001 by Barry Werth

All rights reserved under International and Pan-American Copyright Conventions. Published in the United States by Anchor Books, a division of Random House, Inc., New York, and simultaneously in Canada by Random House of Canada Limited, Toronto. Originally published in hardcover in the United States by Nan A. Talese, an imprint of Doubleday, a division of Random House, Inc., New York, in 2001.

Anchor Books and colophon are registered trademarks of Random House, Inc.

An encapsulation of this book has appeared in *The New Yorker.*

"Two Smith Professors Held in Vice Case," September 4, 1960 (copyright by United Press International) is reprinted with permission of United Press International.

The Library of Congress has cataloged the Nan A. Talese/Doubleday edition as follows:
Werth, Barry.
The scarlet professor : Newton Arvin : a literary life shattered by scandal / Barry Werth.—1st ed.
p.   cm.
ISBN 0-385-49468-8
1. Arvin, Newton, 1900–1963. 2. Capote, Truman, 1924–1984—Friends and associates.
3. American literature—History and criticism—Theory, etc. 4. English teachers—United
States—Biography. 5. Biographers—United States—Biography. 6. Gay men—United States—
Biography. 7. Smith College—Faculty—Biography. I. Title.
PE64.A78 W47 2001
810.9—dc21
[B]
00-060918
CIP

Anchor ISBN: 0-385-49469-6

Book design by Gretchen Achilles

www.anchorbooks.com

Printed in the United States of America
10   9   8   7   6   5   4   3   2   1

The Scarlet Professor

Prologue

NEWTON ARVIN AWOKE alone, as always. He pulled off his eyeshades, rubbed the exhaustion from his sallow face, reached for his gold wire-rim glasses, and pitched himself, slowly, upright in bed. Arvin fretted the cold, and the heat in his apartment was set so high that even in late summer tall cast-iron radiators, painted silver, clanged on cool mornings. The pings and steam hisses soothed him, like murmurs in a crowded restaurant. When he couldn't sleep, which was often, he imagined himself on an alien planet, the only soul from horizon to horizon. The radiators recalled him to the world. So did the intermittent clamor of church bells echoing off the wooded hills.

Arvin was weary as usual, though for no good reason, since he'd been sleeping better lately, and not drinking too much. Ten days earlier he had turned sixty, and he was feeling soft-bodied, depressed, edgy, and prey to a familiar seasonal lassitude. In a few weeks the students would be returning to Smith College, where he had taught for thirty-seven years and was the Mary Augusta Jordan Professor of English, the most distinguished professor in his department. The freedom and quiet of summer, his prime consolation for a lifetime of academic servitude, were about to be shattered.

"The thought of the semester beginning again," he had written two days earlier in his journal, "makes me think of an old plowhorse being hitched up to the plow once more when he ought to be put out to grass, or an old miner after a lifetime in the pits, wearily getting in the car again to descend the shaft."

Arvin was a writer and, until the benighted 1950s, a radical. For nearly forty years his views on American literature had been highly acclaimed in literary circles, even though Arvin himself was shy, retiring, and exceptionally reclusive. His top-floor apartment under the eaves of a once-grand house a half-block from campus was his carapace, his shell. Cross-shaped, the apartment looked out safely in all directions, but no one could see in. It was like living atop a watchtower, unbreachable save for two narrow sets of steeply twisting stairs, front and back. Though climbing the stairs exhausted him, leaving him struggling for breath as he fumbled with his key and then burst, huffing, heart palpitating, into his foyer, he couldn't imagine living elsewhere.

He padded to the foyer now, across two-inch oak floorboards stained a dull coffee-brown. On one side, neatly stacked and dusted, stood his Loeb Library leather-bound Greek and Latin classics. Arvin read seven languages, and the books were well-leafed, their spines lightly worn and faded. Behind him, facing the front door, hung a framed Leonard Baskin woodcut called *Tormented Man*, a gift from the artist. The image reminded the young poet Sylvia Plath, who visited occasionally, of Arvin. "Last night, weary, up the odd Gothic blind stairwell to Arvin's for drinks," she had written in her journal in 1957, three years earlier. "Arvin: bald head pink, eyes and mouth dry slits as on some carved rubicund mask."

Arvin dressed, carefully. Besides books, his other extravagance was clothes. He had two closets filled with $150 suits and nourished a fetish for linen shirts and cashmere sweaters, which he kept in great stacks in his wardrobe. In recent years, his once nimble face frequently wore a capsized expression, his skin wan, features pasty, and eyes heavy and troubled, the residue of a lonely, inward, deeply shadowed life. Alcohol and sleeping pills hadn't helped. But he never stopped dressing to perfection. This fussiness—he wore rubbers at the least hint of rain and seldom went out without a hat, which he tipped assiduously to passersby—had always made him seem older than he was, but now he *felt* old, too. The times were a part of it. Both presidential candidates, John Kennedy and Richard Nixon, were more than a decade younger than he. He found the recent political conventions "a ghoulish business," devoid of any real interest in social progress or the common man. Hoping Congress would push through legislation to improve the lives of—a new term he hated—"senior citizens," he wished there were a Greenback Party or a Free Soil Party to vote for.

All this made Arvin feel, as an American and a scholar, that his life was overdrawn and that nothing could change it. During the summer, he appeared to resolve, with some relief, no longer to try. He wrote in his journal, "Emerson is right about old age: one of its blessings is the knowledge that there cannot be so very much more of all this." But Arvin also lived a second life, in his apartment and elsewhere, a surreptitious sexual life less easily tamed.

His faded warren under the eaves sheltered that life, too. In the years after World War II, shortly after he'd moved in, he and young Truman Capote, still all but unknown outside publishing circles, fell headlong in love. Though Arvin was forty-six, staid, balding, scholarly, and nervous, and Capote was twenty-one, glittering, blond, uneducated, and bold, it was the most formative intimacy either would ever have. Twice a month for two years, Capote traveled by train from New York to Northampton, then scurried from the station to Arvin's apartment, up the steep stairs, and into his arms. "Newton was my Harvard," he would later say.

Arvin kept a nude bodybuilder photo of Capote on his bedroom bureau, and other keepsakes of their relationship were placed throughout the apartment: folders containing their faded love letters; a colorful wooden box Capote had brought back from the West Indies for the Broadway production of his play *House of Flowers*; a hidden cache of homoerotic pictures Capote had sent from Greece, including nude photos of Athenian boys and an amusingly illustrated *Robinson Crusoe*. Arvin's first great theme as a literary critic and biographer was the secrecy that marks so many public lives. As he got older, much of his own furtive life involved collecting erotica and discreetly inviting others to view it. His apartment was a haven for younger men, including several junior faculty members, with whom he could relax over drinks, talk freely, and, occasionally, have sex.

On this September morning, Arvin thought of venturing out. He'd never learned to drive, but cool, fair weather was forecast, and in this season, and at this point in his life, his errands tended to be small ones. Whatever its privations, this was the other great benefit of perching innocuously at the edge of small-town life—location. Arvin's apartment was situated at almost the precise geographic center of his world. When he was in his thirties, forties, and early fifties, with his literary career at its zenith, that world stretched far beyond Northampton. But as his "tether," as he called it, had shortened during the past few years, so had his prospects—literally. He could now see from his four eaves nearly all of the stations of his life: the campus, the town, the barricading hills. Those he couldn't see receded just beyond view, in memory and imagination. Arvin could head out on his bike, a Roadmaster with head- and taillights and a frog-like little horn that, on rare carefree mornings, he couldn't resist tooting, and go anywhere he needed to—his office, the library, the bookshop, the post office, the tavern—in less than five minutes.

He decided to stay in and try to read a little before his eyes, endlessly strained, gave out and idled him completely. Arvin had all but surrendered hope of producing any large work at this stage, but he still had pending a few small editing projects and book reviews, although he wasn't optimistic about finishing those, either. Yesterday, after taking some notes at the office and getting a manuscript wrapped by a "very nice boy" at the bookshop, he'd been so fatigued that he went to bed in the afternoon and remained there the rest of the day. Arvin was used to such days and nights. He'd routinely suffered them—and much worse—ever since he was a twelve-year-old boy growing up in Indiana in the years before World War I. With the noise and tumult of the long Labor Day weekend looming—the annual Three-County Fair would start on Saturday, clogging Northampton with cars, people, exhibits, and livestock from throughout western New England—he planned to spend a quiet Friday alone, indoors, which is how, with fewer and fewer exceptions, Arvin now preferred to be.

Sergeant John Regan of the Massachusetts State Police drove the first of the two unmarked squad cars, holding five officers in all. Big, burly, and loquacious, Regan, an Irish Catholic, was a former Marine with a blustery laugh who had been hired off the street after World War II to help meet a shortage of "boots"; he had risen to become a star of the force, the first recipient of the former troopers' association's Outstanding Public Service Award. The state, having recently made it a felony to possess obscene pictures with the intent of showing them to others, had created a new unit to enforce the law and had put Regan and his partner, Gerald Crowley, in charge. Since May, Regan and Crowley had made more than forty arrests, placing them in the vanguard of a national crusade that was now cresting with the adoption of broad new federal powers to fight mail-order filth. Troopers in Massachusetts, as elsewhere, thought themselves a special breed, though they lived like conscripts, stationed away from their families, working shifts measured in weeks, not hours. At Troop B Barracks in Northampton, "Dirty Pictures" Regan was already well known as the hard-charging vice investigator from Boston who kept barracks around the state supplied with pornography.

It was around 11 A.M. when the matching Ford coupes pulled up in front of the red brick house at 45 Prospect Street. From the quiet, maple-shaded sidewalk, the century-old residence brooded like a rectory; gloomy, stony, quasi-religious, the color of dried blood. Regan, wearing street clothes, led the four officers up the worn brownstone steps and into the building. He was forty-two, six feet tall, weighed 220 pounds, and exuded toughness—lumbering, bullnecked, bulging under his suit, up on the balls of his overburdened feet. He'd fought at Iwo Jima, and the other officers thought him fearsome.

Regan and Crowley had told the three other officers that the suspect was "a pretty important man on the Smith campus," a "fag," but otherwise, as Crowley put it, "just another flyspeck on the wall"—a routine suspect. Contrary to public opinion, they knew most obscenity suspects to be meek, educated, guilt-stricken loners. They anticipated no resistance now.

The air inside the stairwell was cool and still. The narrow stairs coiled tightly to the left, and the men had to file up singly, seventeen steps to the first landing, twelve to the next. The floors became shorter the higher they rose. Regan, who had flat feet and bad ankles, was out of breath by the time they reached the tiny third-floor landing, where, stopping, then climbing two more steps to the right, he stood and knocked. The door, with recessed panels and brass fixtures, was scarcely wider and higher than he was.

Arvin answered tentatively. He wasn't expecting anyone. His most intimate friend and frequent guest, the young classicist Ned Spofford, was out of town. After opening the door, Arvin saw on the landing only Regan and, positioned behind him, Crowley. The appearance of two large men in inexpensive suits could have meant anything or nothing. Perhaps they were door-to-door salesmen, missionaries, supervisors from the gas and light departments. When Regan introduced himself and asked whether they could come in, Arvin said they could.

Jammed in the foyer, the officers towered over Arvin, who was five feet seven inches, physically unventuresome, and slight. At least three of the police could touch the ceiling flatfooted. It was Regan who spoke. He told Arvin that his name had come to their attention as a result of a postal investigation and that police had evidence linking him to organized pornography traffic. Regan, looming over suspects, had a way of making them feel he knew everything about them. It was unclear whether he had a warrant, but he asked whether the police could search Arvin's apartment, and Arvin said yes to that request, too.

The officers fanned out, brusquely. In Arvin's study, near the neatly shelved copies of the celebrated biographies he had written of American classical writers, lay several issues of *One,* the Mattachine Society publication, which Arvin had picked up at a newsstand in New York and dismissed, disappointedly, in a letter to a friend as "pretty tame." There were muscle magazines, with titles like *Adonis, Tomorrow's Man,* and *Physique Pictorial,* that had black-and-white pictures of seminude male models, their genitals covered by posing straps. Arvin could hear the officers ransacking his furniture, turning over his mattress, couch, chair cushions; opening books and mail; rifling his drawers, closets, briefcase, even his wallet. He knew they would soon find harder evidence.

For Arvin, it was hellish, all of it. He had always known that something like this could happen, yet as four of the men penetrated his rooms, leaving him with Regan, he was paralyzed, beyond fear. *What would they do with him?* He had retreated to the far margin of life, and still they had found him out. He felt helpless, a mollusk without its shell. And yet he had been through so much unreality before this, ages of it. His panic was nothing new. And so although he was terrified, he maintained a certain well-developed detachment and resignation. His attitude, one of the arresting officers would recall, was "I'm caught." He answered quietly, cooperating with each of Regan's requests.

As the police kept searching, Regan told Arvin he was under arrest. Massachusetts's harsh new obscenity law, which made possession of pornography a felony punishable by up to five years in prison, distinguished between merely owning erotica and sharing it, but Regan was unlikely to have clarified the difference, nor would Arvin have been calmed by it. His whole life had been against the law. So whatever happened now would not, he felt, be a product of his possessing sexual pictures, but of what had led up to it, his entire history, starting with his "uniquely misbegotten" childhood and scrolling through his tumultuous adulthood in town and at Smith. Indeed, Arvin had forecast such a reckoning more than thirty years earlier, not long after moving to Northampton. Writing about Hawthorne's *The Scarlet Letter,* he observed that in America, particularly the Calvinist America in which Hester Prynne was branded with an embroidered A on her bosom, people were punished most severely not for their crimes but for their secrets. "It is not for the intrinsic flagrance of the sin she has committed, but for the waywardness and irregularity of all wrongdoing that she is punished," Arvin wrote, "and the penalty is made to suit the offense."

But what was the punishment when the sin was being oneself?

Just as he had come to accept that his life was all but spent and that nothing else could hurt him, Newton Arvin was about to learn.

Part One

A writer is, at very least, two persons. He is the prosing man at his desk and a sort of valet who dogs him and does the living.

—V. S. PRITCHETT

I have often thought that the best mode of life for me would be to sit in the innermost room of a spacious locked cellar with my writing things and a lamp. Food would be brought and always put down far away from my room, outside the cellar's outermost door. The walk to my food, in my dressing gown, through the vaulted cellars, would be my only exercise. I would then return to my table, eat slowly and with deliberation, then start writing again at once. And how I would write! From what depths I would drag it up!

—FRANZ KAFKA, TO HIS FIANCÉE

Chapter One

IT WAS NEAR dusk when Arvin entered the narrow, ill-lit walk-up next to Lambie's dry goods store on Main Street. Though he was still new in town, a shy, frail twenty-four-year-old Smith instructor, he affected a jaunty contempt as he hastened past the second-floor doorway of Dr. John C. Allen, President Calvin Coolidge's dentist and closest friend. As Arvin knew, Coolidge had started his political career as Northampton's mayor, and his homestead was a wood-frame duplex a few blocks from Arvin's six-dollar-a-week room in a boarding house. Anyone with an atom of love for Dear Old Hamp proudly supported Coolidge's re-election effort. Not Arvin. Like most members of his famously Lost Generation, he reviled Cool Cal *and* small towns. In August, he'd offered to lead the local campaign for seventy-four-year-old "Fighting Bob" La Follette, Coolidge's third-party opponent. Now, in the lingering heat, he continued upstairs to the International Order of Hibernians' hall to preside over the opening of Northampton's La Follette Boom Club.

Privately, Arvin leaned toward Bolshevism and dismissed La Follette as a relic of the trust-busting, pro-farm spirit that had exhausted itself before the Great War. Arvin's generation, F. Scott Fitzgerald wrote, had emerged from that war to "find all Gods dead, all wars fought, all faiths in man shaken." His peers were busy thronging to the profane cities, disdaining Great Causes, and baying after pleasure and art. Yet Arvin relished the subversiveness of becoming, as he would boast in his next Harvard Class Report, "president of the La Follette Club in the President's hometown." Haunted by wanting other men, doubting his ability ever to fit in, he embraced the role of political outcast. He could champion progress but not his real self.

He took the podium and, with surprising vehemence—glee, even—flayed the two major political parties. The Democrats, he said in a high-toned, punctilious Midwestern voice—a voice the critic Alfred Kazin would call "larger than the man"—stood for "sectionalism, bossism, and watchful wobbling." He reserved harsher words for Coolidge and the Republicans, whom he called "incurably identified with economic privilege of the darkest kind."

As a radical with no local roots—and no desire for any—Arvin ably proved his impertinence. But as a political organizer trying to enlist a conservative, nostalgic citizenry, his instincts were—and would be—less keen.

Paddle fans beat indolently overhead as seventy-five men and women fanned themselves in the hard wooden folding chairs. With his slight build, Arvin was scarcely the picture of a rabble-rouser. He had a gentle, inviting face, pale as milk. His gray-green eyes glinted anxiously behind gold wire-rim spectacles, his prim lips hid several teeth in need of removal, and, receding above a domish, lightly pocked forehead, his soft brown hair, already thinning, lay flat. Only his clothes—a sturdy three-piece suit, soft-collared shirt, and silk tie—announced greater temerity than would have been expected of the mild young clerk who inhabited them. He raised his voice and his rhetoric. Only through the independent candidacy of La Follette, he told the crowd, could the left "lay the basis for a Progressive Party with a kick in it, and put the fear of God in the hearts of the politicians."

Afterward, as he returned home, Arvin was reminded how much the darkened town belonged to Coolidge and the past, not to him. Directly across Main Street, past the trolley tracks and overhead wires, stood the pinnacled, rock-faced county courthouse, the fifth on the site, where Coolidge had begun his law career. Just to its left rose the stolid beaux arts façade of the Northampton Institution for Savings, where, as a young man, Coolidge, who preached hard thrift and frugality, had served as vice-president. Beyond the bank soared the ninety-foot soot-blackened brownstone spire of the First Congregational Church, on the ground where, two centuries earlier, the fiery Protestant divine Jonathan Edwards had launched the apocalyptic frontier revival known as the Great Awakening, in which the mass fervor for combating Satan rose to such a pitch that Edwards's cousin slit his own throat in an anguished attempt to cleanse an impure conscience and appease an angry God.

Indeed, Northampton, a lovely if fading county seat and farm center of twenty thousand, cupped against the foothills of the Berkshires, could not have stood more proudly for the catchpenny puritanism that Coolidge promised to the country and that Arvin's generation reviled—what the Massachusetts-bred writer Robert Benchley called that "old time New England streak . . . that atavistic yearning for a bad time if a bad time is possible." To the right of the courthouse, across King Street, glittered the town's grand new vaudeville house, originally to be named the Mayflower but earlier in the year—with no intended irony for a town that, until seventy-five years earlier, banned stage plays because they fostered "immorality, impiety, and a contempt for religion"—renamed the Calvin.

And yet Arvin, who came from Valparaiso, Indiana, felt flushed with a sense of purpose, of belonging. He was intoxicated by the challenge of *living* in the enclosed, forbidding social world around him, something that as recently as a year ago he doubted he would be able to do. All he wanted was to be a literary critic. But even the most bookish scholar had to be a man of action, a citizen. In the new world, passivity was the gravest crime, and it was necessary for those who saw the truth about America to tell it, in word and deed.

Far from being discouraged by the weak turnout, Arvin relished his status as leader of the town's anti-Coolidge renegades. Not only had he got himself in the trenches; he was in back of enemy lines, pinned down by barrages, his position hopeless. A few days earlier he had written to his best boyhood friend, a young Chicago labor lawyer named David Lilienthal, about his decision to stump for La Follette: "I think it will possibly save me from the kindnesses of a lot of respectable (and very dull) people who rather enjoy a literary radical but gag at a political one." Now, the day after the rally, he wrote to Lilienthal again, boasting—and joking—about his newest success.

Coolidge, famously parsimonious, was known, even during Prohibition, to like bourbon, pouring shots for himself and visitors from a bottle he kept in the lower compartment of his washstand. There was a famous story about him, which Arvin must have known, that on the night in 1918 when he was elected governor of Massachusetts, a guest noticed an old friend sitting on the bed in Coolidge's dollar-and-a-half room in a boarding house—without a drink. "Bill's already had hisn," Coolidge had snapped at the visitor.

Writing to Lilienthal, Arvin reported; "The movement is promising well here in the seats of the sot." Whatever his intentions, they excluded staying in Northampton long enough to care whether its patriotic citizens disliked his lampooning their favorite son as a cheap drunkard.

Everything in Arvin's recent past pointed to his being here, despite himself.

He had been a sickly Harvard junior when Coolidge became an overnight hero to an anxious, pent-up nation in the fall of 1919. All that summer America had seemed on the brink of class warfare. Strikes, lockouts, bombings, the Palmer Raids, deportations, violent nativism, Red scares, and calls for a proletarian revolt were everywhere, especially in Massachusetts, the most urban state in the country. Then, on September 9, the Boston police went on strike, the city's Central Labor Union threatened a general walkout, and fear succumbed to terror. Coolidge, in his first year as governor, stepped in after three nights of rioting and looting, and committed armed guard detachments to the city, as well as mobilizing forty thousand reserves. The effect was galvanic. A week before, few people beyond Massachusetts knew Coolidge's name. Now, as order returned and labor retreated, he burst on the national consciousness as the flinty, nononsense Republican who had "defied Bolshevism and more."

Arvin was back in Valparaiso that fall with his parents, recuperating from severe anemia. A shy, solitary English major, he dreamed only of becoming a writer, a man of letters. He was desperate to get back to Cambridge, but years of reading up to ten hours a day had so strained his eyes that his mother had to read to him. Jessie, a parched Midwestern housewife of fifty-five, had long seemed to her son a bitter and distant woman. The fourth of six children and second and younger son, Arvin blamed his father for his mother's straitened emotions. Frederic Arvin was a stern, demanding businessman who had made something of himself as vice-president of a farm loan association in Indianapolis. Family life was distasteful to him, and he was seldom at home. When he did grudgingly return for a weekend once a month or so, he was short tempered and truculent, a remote figure but a daunting one.

Arvin's return home after two years on his own in the East had unsettled him. "Walking through a mausoleum," he called it. Valparaiso, where Arvin was born in 1900, was a town of fifteen thousand in the flat, featureless northern tier of the state, the sort of insular Midwestern farm town soon to be harshly memorialized in Sherwood Anderson's *Winesburg, Ohio* and Sinclair Lewis's *Main Street*. The presence of Valparaiso College, promoted by generations of Midwesterners as "the poor man's Harvard," elevated the town's cultural quotient, but not by much. Arvin had concluded years earlier that anyone who was sensitive or imaginative would be crippled and thwarted there. He also believed that his father, for whom he'd been named (he would drop his first name soon after college), thought him effeminate and weak and despised him for it.

The situation deteriorated sharply in November, when young Arvin wrote a letter to the editor of the local paper, the *Vidette*, protesting the library board's decision to remove all copies of *The New Republic*, a prickly, five-year-old left-leaning opinion magazine, from its shelves and burn them. Arvin's father, whom Arvin felt "capable of emotional brutality," reacted hostilely. The last time Fred Arvin's namesake had been featured in the *Vidette* was when he was sixteen and had had two poems published in the *Indianapolis Star,* the state's leading newspaper; the headline read VALPO BOY SHOWS RARE POETIC SKILL. That article concluded, "Young Arvin's rhythm is said to be perfect and his rhyming unusual. Friends predict a brilliant future for him." Now, having been drummed out of Harvard's Student Army Training Corps the previous fall for failing his physical, he suffered from vaguely feminine maladies and bleak prospects. Worse, he had become, as Fred Arvin would later say, "tinctured with Sovietism."

Arvin returned to Harvard in January 1920 at a low ebb. Although he regarded himself as dull and unattractive, he yearned for affection; he'd expressed the fierce longing even at thirteen, when he wrote in his diary, "I feel so lonesome for an intimate friend." Before then, his only real friend had been Lilienthal, one of the few other aspiring intellectuals in a town where most boys preferred games to books and normal boyish cruelty to sensitive discourse. The two put together political scrapbooks, cutting out articles and pictures of great events from magazines. They formed a political club and a magazine of their own in a clubhouse they built from packing crates in the Lilienthals' barn.

Until then, Arvin had felt "uniquely misbegotten," alone, unaccepted, derided, with an "insuperable chasm" between himself and other boys—surely the only boy of his kind in the world. "I was certainly a girlish small boy, not a virile one, even in promise," he would write. "I was timid, shrinking, weak, and unventuresome. I had no skill in boyish games and sports, and no interest in them, and I was quickly penalized as a result—by taunts, jeers, and sometimes, though rarely blows." Lilienthal, by comparison, was an excessively "normal" boy, outgoing, spontaneous, and unaffected. Arvin, gleeful to have such a gifted friend, credited Lilienthal with keeping him "in line with at least something like normality" at an age when he might well have withdrawn altogether from the world of boys.

But suddenly, a few months before Arvin's thirteenth birthday, Lilienthal's father, a Jewish dry goods dealer, failed in business, and the family moved to Missouri. Arvin and Lilienthal corresponded faithfully and swore allegiance to each other throughout high school and college. But now they were young men, and Lilienthal, a senior at DePauw College in Greencastle, Indiana, had plans to marry, which prompted Arvin to write jealously that his friend "need have no apprehensions" that he himself would ever wed. He would always be, Arvin wrote on his return to Cambridge, "the bachelor friend of the family, consoling himself for his loneliness by dropping in for tea every Monday."

Then, two weeks later, he wrote:

The past four or five days have been indescribably wonderful for me, and in point of fact I am not yet walking on common earth. To say it is one grand and glorious feeling to be back in Cambridge is to put it very mildly. After what I have gone through it is almost too good to be true . . . I wish I could express to you in words what I have to say, to give you an idea of the very beautiful, very fine, and very precious thing that has come into my life, and very nearly changed the whole seeming of existence to me . . . In one sense I am no longer quite the same person. (I could be concrete instead of so beautifully vague, but somehow I dislike to be. You will understand.)

Arvin ended by apologizing for his evasiveness; "Take it from me," he wrote, " 'there's a reason.' " What he dared not say was that he was in the thrall of his first adult crush, and that the object of his passion was his roommate in Thayer Hall, a tall, dark-haired, studious-looking drama major from Chicago with a full, sensual mouth and cleft chin named Harold Ehrensperger. Arvin joked in another letter about the possibility of "nuptial ties" between him and "Bud," but he seemed to be suggesting nothing more than that the two of them had become companionable. Even in the eroticized cities, homosexuality remained the forbidden province of pansies and fairies, and Lilienthal knew Arvin to be, if unmanly in appearance, a bold thinker with a masculine mind—epicene, yes, but if anything, asexual. In other words he hadn't yet found the right woman to arouse his manhood. Lilienthal misconstrued Arvin's vagueness; his relief at his friend's euphoria let him overlook its significance.

Arvin's ebullience had other factors: his returning health and his studies. In March he wrote to Lilienthal that his weight was up to $113^1/2$ pounds, an "appreciable gain," and that he was taking gym work daily, going for long walks, and sleeping eight or nine hours a night. To avoid overexertion, he'd taken a light course load, which left him plenty of time for "desultory reading of one sort or another . . . Freud's *Leonardo da Vinci, Aberrations of Sex, Sexology of Childhood*; Gamaliel Bradford's *Portraits of American Women*; Emily Dickinson's Letters and Poems; Wm. James's Talks to Students; William's *Lenin, the Man and His Work*; Conrad Aiken's *Scepticisms*; Philip Littell's *Books and Things*; Paul Elmer More's *Platonism*; etc." Arvin had always read expansively, quenchlessly, but now, a nineteen-year-old junior, he glimpsed within his obsession for books not only a prescription for a career but for a moral life.

"I want you to read a little book by Van Wyck Brooks, entitled *Letters and Leadership,"* he wrote to Lilienthal in May. Little known outside literary circles, Brooks was by then the oracle for the younger generation of artists and writers starting to make history in the cities. A stiff, slight, formal man of thirty-four, with searing eyes, a sharp nose, and a bottle-brush mustache, he had graduated from Harvard in 1907 and traveled widely in Europe. On his return to America, he wrote scathingly about the plight of its native artists, especially writers. Brooks, a socialist, believed that puritan materialism had crushed American culture. American writers, he observed, were forced either to compromise their art, as Mark Twain did, by becoming irredeemably commercial and "lowbrow"; or, like Henry James, to flee the country for a more civilized exile in Europe, rupturing their ties with American life. Brooks's call to arms for a new American literature that defied puritan commercialism while rising triumphantly out of native soil had ignited the left-leaning literary world of New York and, especially, Greenwich Village, which since the war had become the epicenter of American freethinking.

Brooks's manifesto was hotly debated in garrets, coffeehouses, and the offices of the lively new magazines. *Was it possible? Could America, godhead of business culture, produce great books and writers?* The answer was by no means clear. As irrepressibly modern as it was, the country was forever falling back upon the root contradictions of the past: freedom belied by conformity, liberty bound by suspicion and blame, talent yoked to utility. Like Arvin, countless young men and women dreamed of overturning the Babbittry of their parents' generation and writing great novels, poems, and plays. But even if they had the talent, most agreed the culture wouldn't let them. It would devour them first.

Arvin found in Brooks a "spiritual forebear," a hero. He explained to Lilienthal that although he still regarded creative writing as a "much more glorious aim" than criticism, "perhaps in a period like ours the man who does really first-rate criticism in the service of American letters will prove to be of more value in the long run than the men who content themselves with mediocre creative work . . . American art," he wrote,

> needs someone to formulate ideals, to erect standards that shall be
> living and valid and not just dug out of the tombs of French and

English literature, to study critically the American mind and American society and try to bring out the most valuable features in it.

Here was Arvin's credo: literary criticism was social criticism, a nobler calling. Two months shy of his twentieth birthday, he forswore the last of his family's hopes that he would straighten up after graduation and pursue a manly career; instead, he set his sights on an uncertain future as a standard-bearer, conscience, and champion of American literature, a neophyte in Brooks's priesthood.

Few career choices were less promising. There was no academic industry in American studies, as there is today, and little reason to expect one to emerge. Most of the classic writers of the nineteenth century—Hawthorne, Melville, Emerson—went unappreciated by critics and disregarded by the public. Melville's *Moby-Dick,* for example, had languished out of print for more than six decades, as neglected as its author, whose death in a tenement on East Twenty-fourth Street in New York, six years after he retired as a customs clerk, was, Arvin would write, "all but unregarded by the world," and whose books had only lately been rediscovered because of a vogue for stories about the South Seas. What's more, if Brooks was right, the sum of America's literary enterprise was a failure, inadequate to the needs of the great global power that the country was becoming. How could dedicating oneself to a devalued, superficial, inferior culture hold any promise? Brooks himself was tormented by doubts and frustration and worried endlessly how to make ends meet. Having recently moved east from a temporary teaching post at Stanford to take over as literary editor of *The Freeman,* one of a number of progressive journals to grow out of New York's postwar literary and political ferment, he was earning extra money editing a book of Harry Houdini's tricks.

Arvin stayed in Cambridge during the summer of 1920 to make up for the term he had lost, "obsessed (literally) with the desire to be psychoanalized," he wrote to Lilienthal. He returned to Valparaiso only in late August. The nation, tilting on the cusp of the Jazz Age, teemed with new crosscurrents. National Prohibition was in effect. The somber Republican ticket of Ohio senator Warren Harding and Coolidge was advancing toward the

White House after eight years of discredited Democratic idealism. After *The Little Review*, an avant-garde literary magazine, published, in its July-August number, an excerpt of James Joyce's *Ulysses* in which Leopold Bloom tamely fantasizes about a young girl's uncovered legs, its owners were arrested and convicted on obscenity charges, ensuring that no American publisher would bring out the book for another eleven years. Fitzgerald's first novel, *This Side of Paradise*, published before he was twenty-three, heralded the new era of youthful hedonism, sex, and drinking. In Massachusetts, two Italian-born anarchists, Nicola Sacco and Bartolomeo Vanzetti, were convicted for the murder of a payroll clerk and sentenced to die.

Arvin, roiled with the times, felt his oats. "I don't think I ever hated this burg so as I have since I got back this time," he wrote to Lilienthal on August 21. "I can't imagine any atmosphere more oppressive than a small town like this."

He could scarcely face his parents. His father, learning of his ambition to become a critic, lambasted him as a dreamer and a Red and told him he would do better washing dishes at Abbe's restaurant or windows at Szold's dry goods store, both in downtown Valparaiso. Frederic Arvin, born during the Civil War, could not have fathomed his son's homosexuality. But he was appalled nonetheless by what he considered Newton's deviancy and fecklessness. A man of staunch opinions and old-fashioned propriety, he'd once written the suitor of one of his four daughters, "Take the best care of her and for her. If a man does that and never wavers, he has done much." For Fred Arvin, manliness was duty and honor, life a struggle for constancy. Newton's heretical ideas about the world and his role in it simply disgusted him.

Only perhaps because Arvin had a letter of introduction to Brooks and hoped to meet with Brooks in New York on his return to Cambridge was he saved from being utterly shaken by the visit. As it was, he boarded the train in Chicago with a "dark-brown taste" in his mouth, once again grim and doubtful about his future.

It was Brooks who rescued Arvin and put him on the course that would take him to Northampton and the campaign against Coolidge. Now that

Brooks was at *The Freeman*, barricaded behind stacks of books in the magazine's hot, shabby, smoke-filled offices in a townhouse on West Twelfth Street, he intended to use his patronage power to develop a cadre of muscular young native critics. Arvin, who awkwardly delivered some student essays before racing up to Penn Station for the five o'clock train to Boston, seemed surprisingly well-suited to the task. Brooks was impressed by Arvin's learnedness, impeccable prose, and sure, firm style. What struck him most was the young man's literary fire and "most unusual craft and maturity," the sense of a full-blown talent ready to emerge. "You are a critic by nature," Brooks wrote to Arvin after reading three of his small pieces. "If you persist in your line you are certain to be what you wish to be."

Coming on the heels of Arvin's break with his father, Brooks's encouragement inspired Arvin with the confidence he so recently feared would always elude him. Going out for highest honors in his senior year, he achieved both Phi Beta Kappa and *summa cum laude,* one of only six in his class of 442. Harvard had taken him just three and a half years. Meantime, he began deluging *The Freeman*'s offices with near-flawless reviews, which Brooks, who complained often about having to rewrite the work of even seasoned critics, published without editing.

Brooks had advised Arvin after their first meeting to try his hand at a book, and Arvin had given the project much thought. But Brooks had also told him that he needed experience, and that his real life as a writer wouldn't begin until he was "thirty or so." Approaching graduation, Arvin mulled over his choices. He wanted nothing more than to move to New York and "do literary work." Brooks had told him there might be a job for him at *The Freeman*, but it fell through. Meanwhile, he received an offer to teach English at the Detroit Country Day School, a boys' school, for $1,600 for the 1921–1922 term. Arvin had no desire to teach, but he thought that the classroom job might enable him to save $500 to $600 and move to New York the next fall. Assuring him that he could continue to write for *The Freeman* if he took the job, Brooks urged him, "Take that position . . . If you have a little capital you can choose your own time, your own subjects, etc. and you will not have to write too much . . . Do it, by all means, however distasteful it may seem to you."

There was nothing in Arvin's world so desperate as a young man with a literary conscience forced to suspend a writing career in order to feed himself, especially in the early 1920s, when precocious novelists like Fitzgerald and Ernest Hemingway were becoming famous before they were twenty-four. Arvin resolved to make the best of it. He first went home, but he soon exploded at his father, and wrote the older man a series of letters so vitriolic that Lilienthal had to travel to Valparaiso to calm Arvin's mother, who was distraught over the episode. Then, when he met Lilienthal's fiancée, Arvin unaccountably broke down sobbing for the first time in years. He confessed shamefully to Lilienthal, "I am becoming, as to character, quite disgustingly flabby and flatchested. I've got to get myself better in hand."

Living on his own in Detroit only made matters worse. Lilienthal was in Cambridge, attending Harvard Law School, and Ehrensperger had moved to Evanston, Illinois, to teach drama at Northwestern University. Alone after four years of making a place for himself in Cambridge, and rejecting the only other hometown he'd known—that "accursed dump," he called Valparaiso—Arvin became sick and confused. "The boys are all right," he reassured Lilienthal about teaching. But nothing else was.

In fact, the strain of working with boys just a few years younger than he while concealing his ambiguous sexual longings unnerved him. Arvin worried incessantly about a mistaken gesture, a misunderstood word, his own undefinable and uncontainable feelings. He was agitated, verging on panic, unable to sleep, beset with dread, and without access to sedatives. He read the manuscripts Brooks sent from *The Freeman* but couldn't review them. All this took its toll on his health. When he had his lower left molars X-rayed in November, revealing an infected tooth, he wrote to Lilienthal, "It seems our worst fears are always more than justified." With winter arriving cold and bleak over the frozen Great Lakes, Arvin doubted he would make it through the semester.

He rallied, briefly, during winter break. "I finally realized how essentially cowardly a thing it would be to run away from anything just because it *was* hard and distasteful . . . ," he wrote to Lilienthal from Detroit on January 12, 1922, "how it would dog me all my life if I didn't live it down, in my own eyes, by going through many other things much harder; and how much good it might do me in some respects, to see something through, for once, even though I hated it like hell." Finding himself a "morbidly ego-centric person," Arvin chided himself, "Well, I really hope that sometime I shall get on my feet nervously, for I believe I have a fund of healthiness in me someplace if I can only get hold of it. It is a cinch that I shall *have* to accomplish this before very long, or I shall go to pieces entirely."

But Arvin by now was sinking, and his family and friends knew it. His older brother, Neil, believed that he should make peace with their father, and insisted that Arvin write home and apologize for his earlier letters. When he did, Fred Arvin took a train to Detroit and checked into the Hotel Statler, where he and his son spent the weekend awkwardly making amends while avoiding any mention of their past troubles. In the end, it was too late. Arvin lasted less than five more weeks before going to the school's headmaster and resigning.

> It is [he wrote to Lilienthal] a definite, immitigable defeat, and I
> am sorry for it—especially because it supplies hot water for so
> many other people—but the damage is done, and I think the part
> of wisdom now is to cover my retreat as strategically as possible. It
> is an unauspicious way to begin life, as you must concede, but if
> there is such a thing as making crutches out of one's defeats, I will
> try to do so with this one . . . the question is really, this time, to be
> or not to be, and also, where to be.

This was the Arvin—feeling himself a failure, lonely, flirting with thoughts of suicide, but also struggling to right himself and calculating how to avoid further collapses—who came to Smith the following September, at the age of twenty-two, to teach privileged young women to write term papers.

Smith was a bustling, nervous place, an island of youthful excitement grafted onto Northampton's rolling western ledge. It had been founded fifty years earlier by Amherst men, patriarchal Yankee evangelists like Coolidge, with money from Sophia Smith and sited illustriously on a knoll at the upper end of Main Street so that it would become part of the town. But as an all-female community, Smith was not assimilable and, as it attracted more and more young women of wealth, was beyond easy control, even by its own reform-minded administrators.

The college had two thousand students, whose parents were drawn to its mission of providing a protected, feminizing classical Christian education but who themselves were increasingly compelled by college "life" and one another. This had been the fear about women's colleges from the start—"The system is unnatural," an early opponent argued, "and not one young woman in ten can be subjected to it without injury"—and it had produced, even before the war, a daring expansion of sexual roles.

At Smith's all-female dances, sophomores squired freshmen like eager swains, sending them flowers, calling for them, filling out their dance cards, introducing their partners, and fetching them ices and frappes between dances. Smith pioneered the game of women's basketball, which taught the traditionally nonfeminine virtues of aggression and camaraderie, and the games were raucously attended. Since the war, armies of college men in automobiles and raccoon coats, bearing flasks and cigarettes and full sexual intentions, invaded the campus on weekends, transforming Smith and nearby Mount Holyoke into training schools for marriageable young society women. Smith's student newspaper now advertised fashion shows by Fifth Avenue retailers like Saks and Bonwit Teller at the Plymouth Inn, a privately owned five-story Romanesque off-campus dormitory with white marble floors and an indoor swimming pool.

Smith, to Arvin's surprise, delighted him. "I am very happy here . . . ," he wrote to Lilienthal in late September, "very cozily fixed and very eager to see what dents I can make in the skulls of Smith Freshmen." Back in his beloved New England, breathing Smith's liberal, high-minded, sensuous air, he felt free of the familial and sexual strains that had dogged him in Detroit. He liked the students—"a damn fine lot"—and although his teaching load of nine hours of classes, nine hours of conferences, and correcting seventy-three themes per week left him little time to read and write, he felt he was finally making progress. "I am willing to be reconciled to any way of life, for the time being, that gives me a chance to repair some of the defects of a very imperfect education," he wrote to Brooks, "and I'm not sure that the easy tempo of small-town life isn't very attractive to me."

He quickly met several other young faculty members whom he liked and who liked him; he even hinted to Lilienthal that he enjoyed going for walks and having lunch with a young assistant professor of economics, Miss Geraldine Jebb. After seeming prematurely old even to himself, Arvin experienced, probably for the first time, what it was like to be young, almost carefree.

He took up tennis. Then dancing. His wit, always sharp, became wicked and self-mocking. "These are things that, as a mere lawyer, you ought to know," he wrote to Lilienthal after quoting from an especially puerile student paper. "They will give you some idea why the ranks of suicides are filled chiefly with composition teachers—why every third nut in an asylum is an ex-composition teacher—why all the lurid and grotesque vices of our modern Babylons are committed by composition teachers—why composition teachers commit 20% of the murders in any given year." Mysteriously, he began to write aching, perfectly metered sonnets to nameless lovers, and he sent them to Lilienthal for review:

> Hiding the stubborn path my feet must take,
> My heart half sings, for it was I who kissed
> Your lips in inattentive sleep, and I
> Who once spent all my portion for your sake.

On Memorial Day 1923, Arvin attended his first Smith graduation, at which Coolidge, then the vice-president, delivered "a long, nasal and nasty oration about patriotism, prosperity, McKinley, and democracy," he reported to Lilienthal. On the subject of Cal Coolidge Arvin's blood was boiling. Two years earlier, less than six months after the inauguration, Coolidge had published three articles in *The Delineator*, a women's magazine, in which he characterized Arvin's ilk—faculty radicals at women's colleges—as predatory traitors. Entitled "Enemies of the Republic," and posing the question "Are the 'Reds' stalking our college women?" the series most likely was ghost-written by a public relations man named Bruce Barton, booster of a vulgarized Christianity and Coolidge's chief image-maker. But it was clear to Arvin that Coolidge somehow considered left-leaning "academic wage slaves" like him to be implacable foes in the war for America, and Arvin was only too happy to take him on. "Really, you know," he wrote to Lilienthal in disgust, "worms are all right, but vermin—"

Arvin continued to write for *The Freeman* until January 1924, when the magazine, losing money and torn by editorial disputes, ceased publication. "It has indeed gone to pieces," he wrote to Lilienthal, "and I am one of them." Fearful that the time was wrong "to make the break for New York next year," as he had hoped to do, he decided reluctantly to teach at Smith for another year, although he swore it would be his last.

Thus was Arvin living in Northampton for the fall election and Coolidge's ascension.

NOVEMBER 4, 1924
NORTHAMPTON

The Coolidge electoral landslide came as no surprise. Barton, Coolidge's chief handler, had revived the rhetoric of the Red scare early in the campaign, fanning fears that the country was again headed for chaos, perhaps even Bolshevik terror, if Coolidge lost. With the Democrats deeply divided, he coached Republicans to raise the specter of an election thrown to the House of Representatives, where La Follette and his forces might seize a share of power. It was the first election covered nationally on radio, and anxiety over domestic communism ensured that the message hit home. Though more voters now lived in cities than in small towns, nostalgia for a safer, less complex, more orderly America won out. Coolidge, the "most noble creation of God," as one local placard put it, was awarded the greatest plurality in the nation's history.

Northampton, draped in silk flags and butterfly-shaped bunting, celebrated with the grandest parade in its history. "Red fire, sky rockets and the glare of the myriads of automobile lights tooting their way down the streets of this sedate old town lit its Puritan gloom with a typical Cleveland glare," reported the *Daily Hampshire Gazette,* the local newspaper. At Smith, the student body snake-danced its way to the 2,100-seat John M. Greene Hall to hear the election returns on radio. As President William Allan Neilson announced returns state by state over a microphone, the crowd exploded with whistles, kazoos, rattles, cowbells, and waves of song. Ten o'clock curfew was happily overlooked.

Arvin spent the next few days too miserable with a flu-like reaction to a smallpox vaccination to care about the election results. When he recovered, he was calm and cerebral, appreciating the "overwhelming strength" of the Coolidge mandate and the extreme obstacles to launching a third party. "Yet I refuse to be soured by it all," he informed Lilienthal. "Four million votes throughout the country—and 713 votes in Hamp (about 10 percent)—do not seem to me a contemptible showing—especially in light of the money spent and the arguments used by the Republicans." He was more troubled by news from Bud Ehrensperger that he was studying for the ministry. "His trip to Europe seems to have made an extreme radical out of him, and he is taking this way of utilizing his impulse to reconstruction," he wrote in the same letter. "I confess to a certain dismay at the prospect."

The country had spoken, resoundingly, in more ways than one. Mainstream America had shown, by embracing Coolidge, that it wanted little to do with radical politics or freethinking; it gagged at political radicals *and* literary ones. The young metropolitans, most of whom had no interest in politics, moved on, hungover, to the next party. Hemingway and Fitzgerald decamped famously for Paris. Others, like Brooks, sought to rediscover a semblance of nineteenth-century New England in the ghost country beyond the New York suburbs, fleeing Greenwich Village to form leafy enclaves in places like Westport, Connecticut. Those few still concerned with Great Causes sought other channels; Lilienthal, for example, in regulating public utilities, the great engine of America's growth. But as the hedonism of the Jazz Age spread to the financial markets, the gay society of the early twenties veered, more and more recklessly, into mere excess.

Throughout a cold, lightless New England winter, Arvin again worked to gather his strength. His eyes were worse than ever, and he felt himself falling further behind in his reading. "I don't know what is really the matter with me," he complained grimly to Lilienthal in February 1925, three months after the election. "It is probably nothing physical and probably some psychic kink that after all these years I have not straightened out." He continued ominously:

What the end is I don't know. I have hopes of reaching shore some-time, and certainly have no idea of giving up the attempt to. Mean-while, I have no spiritual luxuries. I can't, for instance, allow myself to play with my immediate future as otherwise I should be wanting to. I accept a three-year appointment simply as the only solution for a practically insoluble problem. Graduate work is no longer even a possibility—and Brooks warns me away from New York . . . What an inglorious end for a promising "summa" man and an ex-member of the Freeman group!

Lilienthal normally was patient with Arvin's complaints. Now, he lashed back, inviting pity of his own. "I imagine if I had a visit with you there," he wrote, "I'd find you with a great lot of friends, interesting people; find you living in New England, in lovely country, with a fine background, with excellent library facilities, etc." By comparison, he wrote,

if you came out to see me you'd find me boarding a reeking train with hundreds of louts, riding . . . for 35 minutes *every* working morning past the most hideous sights in the world . . . then find me sitting in an office, at a desk, without contact with people most all the time, reading the outpourings of one of the most pompous class of men in the world, the judges.

Arvin was chastened, but only slightly. Though he knew Lilienthal was right, and said so in his return letter, there was much that he could not say. He couldn't discuss his confusion about wanting other men sexually, or the fact that he'd grown jealous of his best friend. Lilienthal, who had been a protégé of Felix Frankfurter at Harvard, was rapidly assembling credentials for an important career in public life. In the past year alone, he'd drafted two U.S. Supreme Court briefs while working on a series of public-interest suits against the most powerful man in Chicago, the utility baron Samuel Insull. Assigned by La Follette headquarters to dig up dirt on Charles G. Dawes, Coolidge's running mate, he'd written a raucous exposé in *The Nation* that got wide attention. With Arvin's help, he'd also begun writing for

The New Republic and was fast becoming known in liberal circles for his views on labor, law, and public policy.

Lean and strutting and angular and not yet twenty-six, prodigiously energetic and ambitious, Lilienthal lived life, as someone later said, at a "high trot." An amateur boxer in college, with a hawklike profile and casual good looks, he had a loving, supportive wife, Helen, a baby daughter, and, though still earning only a little more than Arvin, admiring friends and obvious prospects. Arvin, meanwhile, was bogged down in anguished excuse-making and brooding self-contempt. He apologized to Lilienthal for complaining, but his resentments were not easily let go. Replying contritely to Lilienthal's counter-complaints, he was philosophical, quoting Emerson: "Every obstacle to which we do not succumb is a benefactor."

If Lilienthal's progress failed to comfort him, neither, had Arvin fully known about it, would Van Wyck Brooks's. Approaching middle age, the fastidious Brooks was cracking up. *The Freeman*'s closing had allowed him more time to write, but had also compounded his worries about money and the fear that he had reached the limit of what he had to say, a crueler reckoning. He had finished a biography of Henry James so scathing that he had asked his brother, a lawyer, whether it was possible to libel the dead, and was now searching for a new subject, one that would show that it was possible to have a successful literary life in America after all. He considered writing about Walt Whitman, but was apparently so upset by Whitman's homosexuality that when the subject came up casually over lunch at the Harvard Club in New York, he turned deathly pale and fled the room. Finally, he decided on the transcendental philosopher Ralph Waldo Emerson.

Brooks had hoped that Emerson would end his despair over the plight of the American writer—a plight that Brooks, more than any other critic, had internalized. He now felt it doomed him, just as it had James. By the time his *Pilgrimage of Henry James* was published, in April, he was openly discussing suicide. "I saw every knife as something with which to cut one's throat and every high building as something to jump from," he would write.

Also despairing, Arvin would not have been surprised by the depth of Brooks's anguish. But at the time he knew little about it, other than that

Brooks was having trouble with Emerson and "wasn't well." It was an era of reticence and discretion, and of a code of conduct regarding personal crises: when at all possible, they were kept out of view; those which spilled over in public were ignored or treated with measured, if critical, silence. Edmund Wilson wrote that Brooks, in *Henry James,* "allowed his bitterness to overshoot its mark and to excoriate the victims of America along with the conditions from which they are supposed to suffer." Arvin, clear-eyed but still admiring of Brooks's earlier contributions, was more sympathetic. Reviewing the book in May in *Commonweal,* a new weekly, he wrote, "The pilgrimage of Henry James was a pilgrimage to an empty tomb, and having found it empty he could but flit about it in bewilderment . . . Mr. Brooks has not yet written a more beautiful book."

Whatever his sense of his own failings, and of America's, Arvin was determined to meet them head on, even if that meant staying on temporarily in the President's hometown; even if, as he now understood, he had announced himself an outsider, and could never hope to become more than that. James, too, had come to Northampton as a young man, and the experience had helped shape him at a similar juncture. He had journeyed from his patrician family's home in Newport, Rhode Island, to convalesce on Round Hill, a spa, in the summer of 1862, after a vague ailment, possibly diarrhea, had kept him from serving in the Civil War. He spent most of his time on his back in his room in a boarding house a few blocks from where Arvin now resided, reading and dreaming of moving beyond the short literary pieces he'd already had published. Occasionally he rode the dusty, unpaved road into town. Fourteen years later, living in London, James published his first novel, *Roderick Hudson,* the central theme of which is that American small towns, though morally upright and even charming, are ultimately fatal to the imagination. On the first page he described his heroine as having three misfortunes: "first, she had lost her husband; second, she had lost her money . . . and third, she lived in Northampton, Massachusetts."

In the weeks after his *Commonweal* review appeared, Arvin busied himself: grading papers, filling in for President Neilson at a lecture on Milton, writing more reviews, reading to exhaustion. He wavered between Nathaniel Hawthorne and James Fenimore Cooper as the more promising subject for his first book, flirted briefly with the notion of writing a novel, and made inquiries about the new Guggenheim Foundation fellowships, which allowed writers to study abroad. He had a quick, decisive love affair with a young Smith gym teacher whom he described to Lilienthal as having "shingled hair and a boyish figure and a Moon runabout." The idea of love with a woman intrigued him, as an agonizing rite of passage if nothing else, but by now he sensed that, no matter how he tried to resist, his real raptures were with men. Between his sexual ambiguity and his careful indirection with Lilienthal when the subject of women came up in their letters, he sounded relieved just to have the affair over, sooner rather than later. "I feel as if I had held my hand in the fire for an intolerable length of time," he wrote, "and am unspeakably glad to have it out again, as it would always have been just that."

Summer arrived in New England, sultry and oppressive, wetter than the year before. Arvin taught himself German. He took long walks through the vacant campus and around Northampton's neighborhoods, seeking shade under the towering wineglass-shaped elm trees that canopied lawns, porches, rooftops, and streets at more than seventy feet, topping everything but the church spires. In a sweltering courthouse in another small town, Dayton, Tennessee, near the poor mountains and still-unharnessed Tennessee River, a young biology teacher named John Scopes went on trial for violating a ban on teaching evolution. The trial was broadcast nationally on radio, the first time ever. America was the mightiest nation on earth, but its citizens were split bone-deep between science and superstition, past and future. Arvin, born with the century, a teacher by default, still didn't know whether there was a God but was staunchly on the side of science and reason, and he was riled by those who treated progressive ideas as un-American and slurs against the Bible as sin. He rooted for Scopes.

Chapter Two

"I CAN'T TELL you," Arvin wrote to Lilienthal on August 23, his twenty-fifth birthday, "how miserably unprepared I feel for being seriously twenty-five; how full I feel of all kinds of adolescent impulses and less than adolescent fears and uncertainties; how chagrined I feel to have defined for myself at this age no important clear-cut purposes, and outlined no approaches to them."

The thought of returning to Smith only deepened his anxiety. He had spent August writing reviews for *Commonweal*, the *New York Herald Tribune*, and the Massachusetts *Springfield Republican*; reading murderously, until his eyes wore out, as always; and in his idle hours doing what he called "herbarium work" on prose—painstaking aesthetic analysis. "I really think everybody who tends towards introversion should work up a little proficiency in the handling of some stanza form," he explained to Lilienthal. Arvin's mastery of language was prodigious—"One could almost build up a theory of sentence writing on the basis of those two periods," he advised on the use of punctuation in a short passage in *Pericles and Aspasia*. But his skills were those of the autodidact, the consultant; he knew a hundred ways to make love but no way to desire.

Convinced that nothing was worse for a writer than the drudgery of grading student themes, Arvin changed tack. Ten days before the fall term, he abruptly took a job in Boston as associate editor of *The Living Age*, an offshoot of *The Atlantic Monthly*. He took a leave of absence from Smith and moved back to Cambridge, to a rented room on the third floor of a house on Bond Street, near the grounds of the Harvard Observatory. The job involved no independent or original writing; the magazine was mainly a digest of modern European literature and opinion, and Arvin was essentially a rewrite man, doing quick translations of articles in French, German, and Italian. But it was a foothold in magazine work, perhaps a step toward more opportunities. As with his decision to stump for La Follette, he derived strength—"gusto," he called it—from breaking with his desultory pattern. He wrote to Lilienthal, "I have reached a point where a somewhat dangerous life holds out attractions to me."

Perhaps only someone who had been so scholarly in his youth would consider doing translations in an office adventurous, but Arvin had *acted impulsively,* and that in itself was evidence of a life lived. He began at *The Living Age* enthusiastically, working hard, in high spirits. He wrote twenty-five hundred words a week on deadline; became familiar with foreign papers, ideas, writers, and issues; and went to lunch with similarly aspiring low-level editors of the *Atlantic*. At night he studied alone in his room.

What he failed to do was creative, path-breaking work, nor did he advance his goal of finding a book subject. Within two months, although he continued to maintain that leaving Smith and Northampton "was the wisest thing I've ever done," he began to doubt whether magazine work was a surer route than teaching to a career as a critic. "My central passion," he wrote to Lilienthal in November, "is the pale passion of the scholar; the prurient craving of the incorrigibly bookish; and journalism, even of this type, is as much as an obstacle (in some ways) to the satisfaction of that passion as a means to it."

In truth, he missed the familiar and leisurely pace of college life in Northampton. And he was jealous of others moving ahead, especially Lilienthal, who, having recently assisted Clarence Darrow in gaining an acquittal for a Negro doctor in Detroit who had killed a white man, wrote about the case for both *The Nation* and H. L. Mencken's *American Mercury.* Fearing his best friend might well beat him to their common goal of writing a book, Arvin lectured, "Almost the whole purpose of composition should be to get the reader to forget the writer. When you swing into purple without much preliminary color-work, the reader at once begins to see *you*—and the jig is up. That was my experience in reading the Darrow article." He knew what he wanted to do, and it wasn't scut journalism.

By now Arvin was "coming to the conclusion that I am no more destined by God to be a journalist than a teacher" and that "perhaps any seven-hour-a-day job in a city would always be a little beyond me, temperamentally if not constitutionally." He had resigned himself to returning to Smith in the fall and "possibly spend the rest of my fleeting youth there, absorbing and absorbing and absorbing—and giving out, 'producing,' as little as possible." At the height of the so-called Coolidge Prosperity, amid unbridled optimism about America's future as the greatest nation, he resolved to plunge once again inward, since the world of experience still seemed no place for him. About social existence, Arvin still knew little.

As winter approached he studied Goethe, read several new French novels, delved into recent epic poetry, and surveyed Spanish literary criticism with an eye to learning something about "that language and that people." "I know no better remedy for the grouch than to tackle a new language," he advised Lilienthal, who had just been made partner in a prominent liberal law firm at a salary of $10,000 a year, four times what Arvin was earning. "I plan to do it every six months from now on until I liquify."

Arvin's book reviews and short essays continued to draw praise. Mencken himself grouped him with Edmund Wilson, Carl Van Doren, and Burton Rascoe. But he dreamed of becoming a major writer, and for that one had to write books on large subjects. Frustrated, Arvin redoubled his efforts to find what eluded him—the great topic that would match his learning and ambition—while working at jobs he disdained.

Brooks hoped privately that Arvin would choose to write about Hawthorne, even though a skilled biographer, Walter Fuller, recently had "taken him up." Writing from Westport on January 16, 1926, he urged Arvin not to be daunted by competition. "One's own angle of approach is the important thing," Brooks counseled. "But I shan't advise you. If I were you I would follow my impulse or interest, and get to work." When Arvin wrote back in

February that he was favoring Fenimore Cooper, Brooks applauded the choice as "a good thing." But Brooks was losing both patience and time. Then, suddenly, on April 20, as Arvin was finishing at *The Living Age* and anticipating his return to Smith, Brooks told him that Hawthorne was the better subject.

Brooks's urgency stemmed from the belief that he himself was coming apart. He was forty years old and had turned down several prestigious editorial positions that would have buttressed his position as America's most important literary critic; he was entangled in an intense love affair, about which he was deeply torn; he suffered from nightmares in which he shuddered before Henry James's "great luminous menacing gaze"; and he had all but given up trying to earn a living and was depending on his wife's relatives to support his family. "I have had to put my Emerson away for a while . . . ," he wrote to Arvin, "[a] subject so volatile that I have often felt I was trying to shape a mass of air."

Hawthorne, by comparison, was both flesh *and* spirit. The most inward and tormented of native writers, he invited discursive analysis, especially by someone like Arvin. A literary biographer must share an essential bond with his subject. Brooks was convinced that the retiring young Smith instructor was one of the few people knowledgeable about American literature who was capable of discerning the true Hawthorne, whom Brooks called "this most deeply planted of American writers, who indicates more than any other the subterranean history of the American character." He clinched Arvin's interest by adding, "I think you might be able to do something with the relations between Hawthorne and Melville."

Arvin, as Brooks seemed to anticipate, discovered himself in Hawthorne, even as he recoiled from what he found.

Like Arvin, Hawthorne had withdrawn as a youth into a world of books and solitude. "A shadowy figure even in a small college where shadows could not have been easy to maintain," he graduated from Bowdoin College, in Maine, and moved back to what he called his "dismal chamber under the eaves" of his mother's house in Salem, Massachusetts, where for thirteen years he lived in monk-like obscurity while writing little-read romance tales. "No other young man in New England in the 1820s was doing either of these things," Arvin would write, sympathetically, "yet Hawthorne did both."

Arvin saw within Hawthorne's self-exile elements not only of himself but of America's struggle with its young artists—the same struggle he'd had with his father. Hawthorne barely seemed cut from the same stock as his austere, black-bearded Puritan forebears, who had slain Indians, Quakers, and witches. His grandfather, Bold Daniel, had commanded a Revolutionary brig, and his father, a merchant ship captain, died of yellow fever when his only son was four. Nathaniel, by comparison, was a "queer changeling" who as a child pored over *The Pilgrim's Progress* and *The Faerie Queen* while other Salem boys made replicas of schooners and sailed them on the North River. As Arvin wrote with barely concealed personal urgency, the essential message Hawthorne received growing up was "that it was an ill thing to have a poetic imagination, and, in short, that to be a writer of storybooks was little better, little less degenerate, than to be a fiddler." No wonder he cloistered himself to write; as with Arvin, there was no other way.

But Arvin also sensed in Hawthorne's monasticism the seeds of a fatal destruction. Hawthorne became so isolated and lonely that the world's indifference felt like punishment. The question was: What was his crime? Arvin believed Hawthorne came to a single answer: The very act of withdrawing into himself. This was the great underlying theme of Hawthorne's most enduring work, Arvin believed. In Hawthorne's Calvinist America—the America of *The Scarlet Letter* and *The House of the Seven Gables*—people were punished most harshly not for their actions but for their secrets.

Here was Arvin's first great contribution as a critic—to reveal "the dark connection between guilt and secrecy" in Hawthorne's books as the solitary obsession of a young man choosing to live outside society. "Crime itself, no matter how monstrous, seemed to him less hideous than concealment," Arvin observed.

> The essential sin, [Hawthorne] would seem to say, lies in whatever shuts up the spirit in a dungeon where he is alone, beyond the reach of common sympathies and the general sunlight. All that isolates damns: all that associates, saves.

In reading Hawthorne, Arvin identified dark strains that perhaps only someone who cloaked unwanted desires could fully detect. He understood all too well how Hawthorne could write, at the age of sixteen, "Why was I not a girl that I might have been pinned all my life to my mother's aprons?" And how, a decade later, he could insist on taking his meals alone in his room while his mother and sister ate in theirs, venturing out only at night to walk through deserted New England streets. Arvin flirted dangerously with the ideal of such "perfect seclusion," though he fought against it. Nor did he fail to miss that Hawthorne was clearly asexual during this period and felt much the same sexual ambiguity as he did. "How fearfully," Arvin wrote knowingly, "he would have shrunk from intimate relations with a woman of large physical vitality and robust emotional needs!"

But viewing Hawthorne's life through the prism of his own torments forced Arvin to examine his own efforts to live in the world, and he found them wanting. The root sickness of America, as Hawthorne had posited, wasn't exploitation or deviancy. It was repression and self-hatred—shame. Smash them, Arvin seemed to sense, and the soul would flourish.

Returning to Smith for the 1926 fall term, Arvin was ever more re-solved to succeed in the social world around him, even if it meant going against his grain. He knew himself to be, as Hawthorne once described himself, "a mild, shy, gentle, melancholic, exceedingly sensitive, and not very forcible man." But he was determined to experience life on something like its own terms, so he set a course of renewed political action and heightened literary and social activity. Whatever his impulse to shrink from experience, he decided he would—must—push himself outward, lest he slowly dissolve in guilt and sorrow.

Despite the failure of its candidate, Northampton's La Follette Boom Club re-emerged during Arvin's year at *The Living Age* as the Hampshire County Progressive Club. It consisted mainly of liberal professors and their spouses, who, lacking a common ideology, essentially followed Mencken, on whom most Jazz Age radicals cut their intellectual teeth. Members ridiculed Coolidge, advocated free speech, defied Prohibition, winked at adultery, demonized politicians, scorned boobery, and exalted science, skepticism, and the aristocracy of ideas.

Arvin joined the club on his return and was immediately sought out by a second-year English instructor, Granville Hicks. Hicks, twenty-five, had studied at the Harvard Divinity School to become a minister, but, having decided that the liberal churches were no place to try to improve society, accepted a teaching job. He and his new wife, Dorothy, had arrived in Northampton the previous fall. A moralistic Yankee with a thin, lugubrious face and thick spectacles, he was suspected by other members of still being religious without realizing it. Hicks thought most of his colleagues shallow and snobbish, more interested in shocking American Legionnaires than fighting injustice. Having heard from them about Arvin's depth and freedom from cant, he hoped Arvin would become his ally in the Progressive Club.

Arvin, primed to take a larger role in events, quickly became much more than that; he took command of Hicks's political and literary education. Arvin was finally too reticent and insecure to lead in public, but his quiet fervor had begun to attract followers, and, as with his friendship with Lilienthal, he enjoyed the erotic charge, the profound intimacy, that came with infiltrating another mind. During the 1920s, intellectualism had become a movement in itself. Intellectuals saw themselves, and were seen, as a distinct subculture whose job it was to provide the nation with detached criticism and new ideas. Finding the other progressive faculty members a "grotesque exaggeration of the attitudes that isolate the intellectuals from the rest of society," Hicks thought Arvin exemplified what an intellectual ought to be, a scholar, but one who viewed knowledge and learning not as the property of a privileged elite but as "the foundation of a decent life for all the people."

Arvin and Hicks, much alike, were drawn to each other. Hicks, like Arvin, had been clumsy and weak as a boy, turning to stamp collecting and reading. At Harvard he had been a studious loner, uninvited into its clubs, unimpressed by his professors. Arvin, his first major intellectual influence, saw in him the makings of a fellow soldier in Brooks's army. During one of their first discussions, he urged Hicks to read Brooks's *Letters and Leadership,* the work that had inspired him to be a critic.

That fall, Dorothy Hicks became pregnant, and the Hickses moved into a seven-room duplex. Arvin, who had just moved up the street, visited almost every night. Still living out of a trunk, he had no home to speak of and little contact with his family, so his regular dinners at the Hickses' became the most domesticity he'd known since leaving Valparaiso. Arvin craved hospitality, and when he found it, he was an agreeable guest, helping with the dishes and brightening the conversation with gossip, especially about the eccentric, birdlike older women on the faculty who lived among their students in Smith's cottage-style "houses" and who, Arvin told Hicks, were lesbians.

After Dorothy had the baby, she often went to sleep early, and Hicks and Arvin took long, brisk, discursive walks around town—tutorials. They marched through Northampton's silk-stocking ward, past Coolidge's homestead, and over to the rose gardens in Wildwood Park; or they looped around Paradise Pond, beyond Smith's slate-roofed stables and up toward the leviathan state mental hospital that overlooked the college. Drunk with ideas, they feverishly discussed politics and books and what they ought to do. They agreed chiefly on two main points: the country was nearing a terrible reckoning, and when it came, they would have to be involved.

They were hardly alone. Under Coolidge, the country had grown wealthier but weaker, its people estranged and divided. The farm economy had been in a depression since 1920, yet Wall Street, encouraged by Coolidge's maxim that "the business of America is business," had soared on speculation. In September, the Florida land boom was wiped out overnight by a hurricane; in the aftermath, Coolidge optimistically reassured the country that American virtues and the American scene remained sound. And in January, as the Federal Reserve politely tried to rein in the stock market, Coolidge issued a statement predicting "continued healthy business activity and prosperity," fueling the frenzy for stocks and driving their prices still higher. Everywhere liberal intellectuals doubted that the old order of American stability and world leadership, set in place after World War I, would survive, and they were searching for a test of national morality and resolve in which to assert their leadership.

One episode above all focused their efforts. For six years, the Sacco-Vanzetti case had drawn scant notice outside eastern Massachusetts, where the crime took place, except among communists, who helped pay for the two anarchists' legal defense and urged their freedom at strikes, rallies, and demonstrations. Then, in March, Felix Frankfurter of Harvard published an article in *The Atlantic Monthly* that, as Arthur Schlesinger, Jr., wrote, abruptly made their scheduled execution "a world concern . . . [stabbing] through the indifference and gaiety of the twenties like a knife into the liberal conscience." In the article, Frankfurter accused Judge Webster Thayer, of Dedham, who'd boasted after the trial of what he had done to "those anarchist bastards," of deliberately prejudicing jurors still in the grip of war fever at the height of a Red scare. He also accused the state of falsifying ballistics evidence. Widely quoted and reprinted around the world, Frankfurter's denunciation suddenly inflamed a new audience. John Dewey, John Dos Passos, Mencken, and hundreds of other writers and academics decried the verdict. Sacco and Vanzetti were exalted as innocent martyrs—"dago Christs," the critic and poet Malcolm Cowley called them.

On their walks, Arvin and Hicks discussed how to organize in Northampton under the Progressive Club banner. Governor Alvan T. Fuller, a former bicycle mechanic who'd risen to become the state's largest Packard dealer, had appointed a panel, chaired by Harvard president Abbott Lawrence Lowell, to review the evidence in the case. Although Arvin argued for a more militant stand—immediate freedom for Sacco and Vanzetti—they opted to write a resolution urging Fuller to stay the executions until Lowell's committee finished its work. They then put the resolution to the town for a vote.

The Sacco-Vanzetti case taught Arvin and Hicks that Northampton had scant interest in their ideas *or* their leadership. Their "diplomatic little resolution—so tactfully, so politely, so meechingly worded," as Hicks wrote, provoked a near riot when it was presented at a citywide meeting in the high school auditorium. For three hours, irate townspeople denounced the organizers as disloyal subversives. "The old hometown of the President of the United States should not go on record in sympathy with the Reds of Union Square!" Judge Henry Field thundered, shortly before the police moved in and ushered both sides from the building.

Arvin, like liberals everywhere, was traumatized when Sacco and Vanzetti were electrocuted in prison on August 23, 1927, his twenty-seventh birthday. "Judicial murder," he called it. Politics for him was an imperative, to break the stranglehold of capitalism over American thought. That the executions had taken place in Massachusetts, the home of Emerson, Hawthorne, and Melville, and that Harvard, through Lowell, had played a role by concluding that Sacco and Vanzetti had received a fair trial caused him special shame.

As classes resumed in late September, he plotted ways to survive another year at Smith. He complained to Hicks that he now found it "quite unreal" to try to cure the world's ills and be an English professor at a "ladies seminary." "I cannot seem to get both things in anything like focus," he said. "I squint horribly when I try to." On one of their walks, he proposed that they jointly teach a new junior- and senior-level course in modern British and American literature, something perhaps no college in America had yet attempted. Arvin dazzled Hicks by offering on the spot an ambitious syllabus of poetry, fiction, drama, and criticism—all works he'd read and could discuss eloquently—and at the next department meeting the course was adopted. He and Hicks lectured on alternating weeks, and though Hicks was more popular with the students, Arvin noted with unexpected pleasure that the brightest girls seemed stimulated by him and sought him out after class.

Arvin still felt unprepared for life, yet he also recognized his inability to become too actively involved in anything other than literature. Dos Passos said famously that the murder of Sacco and Vanzetti proved that America was "two nations." The intellectuals had conscientiously led one nation—but what was the other? "Was it the rich and powerful of the state?" Hicks asked rhetorically. "Certainly it was. But it was also the doctors, the lawyers, the shopkeepers, the farmers, the workers. In Northampton—and it was not so different throughout the state—the battle was between the intellectuals and everybody else."

Arvin, deep in his estrangement, agreed.

In early July of 1928, Arvin rode a succession of trains to Saratoga Springs, New York, a fading upstate health resort near Lake George and the Adirondack Mountains. Fifty years earlier it had been favored by wealthy families as an ideal place to escape the stifling heat, dirt, dust, and fetid air of Manhattan in summer. The town boomed with mineral spas, grand hotels, Gilded Age mansions, and sprawling country estates, which begat both a class of rich, conservative citizens and a larger class of mostly young, immigrant domestic help. Now, Saratoga Springs was a wide-open city, with crap tables, speakeasies, horse racing (trotting and thoroughbred), cockfights, corner-store bookmakers, and relatively discreet high-class prostitution. Skidmore, a women's liberal arts college down a notch from Smith, flanked a bustling late-Victorian downtown that on summer nights overflowed with tourists.

One of the city's most splendid estates was Yaddo, built by the financier Spencer Trask for his wife, Katrina. Trask, a shrewd investor who made a fortune on Wall Street by backing Thomas Edison and helping Adolph Ochs to buy the *New York Times*, had had Yaddo constructed as a sumptuous palace for entertaining statesmen, moguls, captains of industry, and European royalty. An independent thinker, he offended local society by having Ochs, a Jew, to visit. In Yaddo's heyday, at the turn of the century, Katrina Trask ruled like an ethereal princess over what was nearly a baronial manor, magisterially maintained by a staff of a hundred and fifty, who at Christmastime lined up in the downstairs hall to receive purses filled with gold coins. It was said that Spencer Trask had a housemaid whose only job was to dust the upstairs hall and pluck lint from the pockets of his knee breeches.

The Trasks' four children had all died in childhood, two of them from diphtheria, which they contracted while visiting Katrina's room when she was recovering from the disease. Thus the couple was left to endure middle age in possession of a fifty-five-room granite, Tudor-style mansion inspired by the English manor house at Haddan Hall, cattle barns, formal gardens, terraced lakes, fountains, statuary, and four hundred acres of peaceful woods laced with winding roads over which Trask liked to race his coach-and-six—but with no direct heirs. Katrina, a romantic and amateur poet, dreamed in her grief of filling the place with poets and artists, and in 1900 Trask formed a nonprofit corporation to maintain Yaddo as a "residence and retreat" for people "usefully engaged in artistic and creative work." Rarely if ever in the history of arts patronage had a bequest been so selfless or open-ended. After the Trasks' deaths, Yaddo, maintained by their fortune, would exist solely to serve, house, feed, and nurture generations of writers, visual artists, and composers.

Traveling for the first time past the wide, elm-shaded mansions on Union Avenue, which Henry James called the most beautiful street in America, Arvin had modest expectations. Yaddo had begun receiving working guests only two years earlier. Its formidable director, Elizabeth Ames, a war widow from Minnesota, had invited Arvin to stay for two months, and although his suitcase contained the first four chapters of his book on Hawthorne, he had four more chapters in outline, more than he could hope to get written in that time. He anticipated a quiet room, interesting company, and an atmosphere of sedate contemplation—a temporary respite from student bluebooks and the oppressive heat of Northampton in summer.

What greeted him was a scene beyond his imagination: a community of a dozen and a half people like himself, young intellectuals and radicals, none of them near rich, with the run of what felt like—indeed, was—a private castle. As Malcolm Cowley, who was to pay his first brief visit two years later, would recall:

> The guests were artists, it is true, and most of them worked hard, but they led soft lives, almost as if they had been invited for the summer to a Newport "cottage" owned by robber barons. If they did not choose to appear for breakfast a tray was discreetly placed outside their doors. Luncheon was served in the huge dining room, with an array of crystal and silver. At four o'clock a table in the downstairs hall shone with fine china and the Trask silver, besides platters of confiseries prepared by the Bohemian cook.

Mrs. Ames had ably supervised the renovation of the barns, sheds, and carriage house into studios, and gas lamps throughout the buildings had recently been replaced with electric lights. She hired, John Cheever later wrote, "a hard-nosed butler, a first-rate chef, a housekeeper with a keyring, and a host of maids." But Yaddo's mission was to provide guests with a place apart, so that each felt as if the world within its walls existed solely for his or her use. Privacy—to be alone and create—was sacrosanct, with quiet hours between ten A.M. and four P.M. and then again after ten P.M., when visitors were forbidden to be on the grounds. All rules were strictly enforced by Mrs. Ames, who left stern handwritten notes on blue stationery for those who disturbed their fellow guests.

Had Arvin believed in a final reward, he might have thought this was it. Like Brooks, he'd held, with absolute conviction, that America's business civilization destroyed its artists. But at Yaddo the artist was treated as little less than a god. Surrounded by the sort of opulence that he and the other guests would normally have branded sybaritic, Arvin must have realized the irony, but was too decorous to mention it.

As at Smith, Arvin had little trouble attracting admirers. One night when he had been at Yaddo only a few weeks, a newly arrived, modest, twenty-three-year-old book and theater critic named Louis Kronenberger slipped and fell down the grand staircase in the baronial great hall, where guests mingled about, sipping after-dinner coffee. Arvin approached him and reached for his hand, easing his embarrassment, and the two soon began taking late-afternoon walks together. Though Arvin was just five years older, Kronenberger was struck by his "great maturity of mind." If Yaddo had a fault, it was an excess of humorless young aesthetes who hadn't yet found themselves, but Arvin "already seemed formed," Kronenberger later wrote. He was starting to grow bald, his schoolboy face made him look young, his gold-rimmed glasses gave him a studious appearance, yet something in his careful use of words proclaimed him a "born man-of-letters."

Arvin's exaggerated friendliness and highbrow usage—he rhymed *cantaloupe* with *soup* and called Kronenberger *Kronenbairger*—might seem irritating and unnatural, but Kronenberger, like Hicks, found him thrilling company. "To say that Newton never spoke a slipshod sentence sounds priggish in him and fatiguing to his listener," he wrote. "Actually it was inherent in him and fascinating to his listener." Mostly what impressed Kronenberger was the sheer reach of Arvin's learning, which he wielded sharply but without malice. "Decidedly scholarly, he yet struck you at once as not scholar, but critic, and a critic whose immersion in literature argued no dissociation from life . . . Politics, morals, intellectual movements, social atmospheres, cultural patterns, economic pressures all went into his thinking about literature itself."

Kronenberger had never met anyone so *imaginatively* cultivated, so remarkably well-read in so many related fields that his understanding of his subjects seemed virtually complete. Like Hicks, whom Arvin would soon introduce to Yaddo, he quickly became part of Arvin's fledgling network of literary friends, a group for whom Yaddo began to serve as a combination baroque club house, union hall, and home base.

Arvin dug into Hawthorne with all the pent-up fervor his new surroundings were meant to unleash. The softness of life in the mansion, which might have inclined the guests toward decadence and complacency, actually had the opposite effect, raising stores of discipline and energy many didn't know they had. Freed of the obligation to make money and every other encumbrance, including personal responsibilities—with nothing, that is, left in the way—they could devote themselves utterly to work, going hard for days and weeks at a time. Arvin drove himself, as he wrote of Hawthorne during a similarly productive siege, "like a dragon." He had a rare ability, once he knew what he wanted to say, to chart a book so completely in his head that one draft was usually enough. He seldom needed to rewrite, even to make minor corrections. Working each day at a medieval-looking desk in an elegant studio, overlooking the broad Mohawk Valley all the way to Vermont, he finished his manuscript in less than eight weeks.

It helped that he was now tracking Hawthorne's exodus from his dismal chamber out into the world—a journey Arvin only needed to look around to realize that he, too, had begun. At thirty-five, after years of self-banishment and solitude, Hawthorne left Salem to work as a measurer in the Boston Customs House, spending long hours weighing coal and salt on the wharves of a busy port. During the previous two years, following the publication of his first book, *Twice-Told Tales,* he'd hit a dead end. More important, he felt incomplete and longed for intimacy. "The conviction had for some time been growing upon him that what seemed the incurable emptiness of his life was due largely to his ignorance of so deep a human experience as the love between the sexes," Arvin wrote. Demonstrating what Arvin called a "new seriousness in his adjustment to reality," Hawthorne met a patient and cheerful young woman, became secretly engaged, and moved to the utopian community at Brook Farm. ("The duties of a customshouse official had not proved compatible with creative activity: perhaps the labors of a ploughman and a stable boy would turn out to be more propitious," Arvin noted with rare sarcasm.) Then he got married and spent three years in Concord, Massachusetts, taking care of the Emerson family's Old Manse, before returning to Salem to work in the customs house there.

In all of this Arvin detected a familiar artificial enthusiasm, but it worked. With a devoted wife to return to and a less taxing job than in Boston, Hawthorne came home at night and labored on a story, which had long haunted him, about an adulteress forced to wear an embroidered letter A on her bosom. The symbol obsessed him, as Arvin especially understood. "For how deep a wrong might it not be the expiation, and how terrible loneliness the cause!" he wrote.

The Scarlet Letter was an immediate triumph, selling out its first edition of two thousand copies in ten days. Hawthorne became internationally recognized as a writer almost overnight. "Suddenly," Arvin observed from his mansion aerie, "at what seemed the lowest ebb of his literary fortunes, he stepped out of the shadow and the stillness and found himself standing in the intense light of the fame he had quite given over expecting." It could not at that moment have been hard for Arvin to imagine himself standing in that same intense light after his own years of reclusion.

As Van Wyck Brooks had suggested, Arvin also was able to "do something" with the relationship between Hawthorne and Melville. Exhausted by his labors and sudden fame at the age of forty-six, Hawthorne in the spring of 1850 retreated with his growing family to a small red frame house overlooking the waters of Stockbridge Bowl and the granite slopes of Monument Mountain, in western Massachusetts. Melville, thirty-one years old and the author of eight books better known for sensational descriptions of cannibalism than for signs of literary genius, had recently moved his family from New York to nearby Pittsfield, to a large eighteenth-century farmhouse surrounded by pastures and hayfields, with a fine prospect of Mount Greylock, to the north. Living a dozen miles apart, Hawthorne began writing *The House of the Seven Gables* while Melville shaped out his "wonder book," *Moby-Dick*.

Meeting during an afternoon hike, each instantly fell under the other's thrall. "The divine magnet is on you, and my magnet responds," Melville wrote to Hawthorne. "Which is the biggest? A foolish question—they are *One.*" Such fervently sexual writing could not escape Arvin's attention, but it was with far more chaste and measured emotion that he wrote about what it may have signified. The suggestion of physical intimacy between men remained a forbidden subject, and Arvin, in his state of confusion, could hardly have been expected to raise it in his discussion of two respected, married nineteenth-century worthies. But Melville's letters to Hawthorne thrilled him, and he wrote compellingly of the men's mutual attraction. "Through all the press and bustle of his adventurous life, Melville had gone about locked up in a solitariness no whit less bleak and overcast than Hawthorne's own," he wrote. "His 'dismal chamber' had been the stinking, crowded murk of the forecastle on an unseaworthy whaler; but it had been, for a born poet and philosopher, no less a wilderness." As Arvin, perhaps alone among the critics reading and writing about two of America's darkest writers, saw, they were drawn together by an unrelenting loneliness that no one else, certainly not their wives, could slake.

Excited, Arvin wrote to Brooks in mid-August, two weeks before his departure from Yaddo, to tell him of his progress. By now, as Arvin remained only dimly aware, Brooks had descended to the depths of a guilty isolation even Hawthorne could not have matched. Between his inability to work to support his family and the torment over his brief extramarital affair, he felt he had "betrayed his manhood" and no longer deserved to live. Brooks had spent the previous fall and winter in an elegant private sanitarium outside London, where he shattered and swallowed the crystal of his watch, repeatedly tried to throw himself in front of automobiles, and fantasized compulsively that Parliament had passed a special law to bury him alive. On the boat home in May the ship's doctor ordered him locked in his stateroom for the entire voyage; forced to guard him, his wife, Eleanor, told a friend she felt her hair turn gray.

Arvin's letter reached Brooks at Monhegan Island, off the Maine coast, where, in desperation, Eleanor had sent him after Carl Jung, sending word from Zurich that a cure for Brooks's "chronic melancholia" would be difficult, if not impossible, declined to treat him. On Monhegan, bizarrely, he was under the care of the Reverend Gerald Stanley Lee, popularizer of the notion that if Jesus were in America, he would choose as his disciples "inspired millionaires." Fifteen years earlier, Lee, who lived in Northampton and was married to a former Smith English professor, had published a bestselling book called *Crowds*, in which he preached the "civic religion" of public relations and advertising. Two years later Brooks had singled out Lee's business evangelism for special scorn in his *America's Coming of Age*. Now, Lee tried to teach Brooks to "inhibit" his demons by balancing balls on his head and the back of his hands for two hours a day.

Frustrated and hostile toward Lee, and all but out of touch with reality—a friend would soon find him crawling about in the grass, pulling out weeds, fingering things, his dead gaze fixed on nothing—Brooks nonetheless managed to answer Arvin's letter; he wrote, "Congratulations and three cheers for the book." Three months later, returning the completed manuscript after reading it, Brooks offered his opinion. "I think you have written by far the best book on the subject. Better than Henry James'." With the exception of a brief note the following month, it was the last Arvin would hear from him for the next three years.

Brooks wasn't the only one cracking up. As the Jazz Age clattered to a bad end, the writers who had come to New York after the war and invented what Fitzgerald called "the metropolitan spirit," and who made writing synonymous with alcoholism, blasphemy, and fun, were paying the price for a decade-long binge. Edmund Wilson's manic-depressive episodes had driven him into a clinic in Clifton Springs, New York, near Rochester. Dorothy Parker repeatedly slashed her wrists and took overdoses of Veranol. In Fitzgerald's famous circle of Princeton friends, successful writers, and rich émigrés, a frightening number of talented, respected, even brilliant individuals were obsessed with what he called "the idea of the Big Out." One way or another, they were disappearing into America's "dark maw of violence."

"A classmate killed himself and his wife on Long Island, another tumbled 'accidentally' from a skyscraper in Philadelphia, another purposely from a skyscraper in New York," Fitzgerald wrote. "One was killed in a speak-easy in Chicago; another was beaten to death in a speak-easy in New York and crawled home to the Princeton Club to die; still another had his skull crushed by a maniac's axe in an insane asylum where he was confined."

Arvin recognized that he was probably fortunate never to have made it to New York, though he hoped to yet. Still, he'd missed the excitement, and thought he ought to venture into the wide-open, hard-living, ceaselessly modern decade before it closed. In May 1929, with *Hawthorne* scheduled for publication by Little, Brown in September, and after seven years of teaching at Smith, he wrote to Lilienthal that he'd arranged to spend thirteen weeks during the summer touring England and France. "I shrink from it more than I can tell you," he wrote, "so I *must* do it."

He sailed in mid-June from New York, stopping before his departure at the Algonquin, already starting to fade as many of the witty men and women who lunched there daily either left the city or were in swift decline or both. Spotting one of their members, Ring Lardner, whose sardonic stories Hemingway had copied in high school, Arvin was startled to see him in obvious misery and nervous pain, the tight skin stretched on his handsome skull, his fingers trembling to light a match. He "looked as solemn as a man would have to look who had seen so much fatuity and so much coarseness so closely as he has," Arvin reported to Lilienthal. Arvin's romantic notions of the voyage itself were likewise confounded. Standing day after day on the deck of the White Star *Homeric,* gazing out at the interminable distance—what Melville called, in the last line of *Moby-Dick,* the "great shroud of the sea"—he found the open ocean "very grand and very monotonous."

He was lonely, and despite his pleasure at feeling himself both alive and, at last, a real writer, was close to despair over his countrymen, "the crazy boatloads," as Fitzgerald called them, who, "spewed up by the boom," had turned the romance of seeing Europe into a mass clique of overstimulated Americans looking for something to do. In London, Arvin visited Dunhill Fields, Charterhouse, Smithfield Market, and St. Paul's Churchyard. He wandered in the crowds at the Tate and the National Gallery, standing alone before the gilded portraits and armor. Finding himself "a bad traveler," he wrote to Lilienthal of his "temptation to take a boat home." After twenty-five days in Paris, at the Hôtel d'Alsace, suffocating in the heat, he sailed back to America on the *Homeric* and arrived in Northampton in late September, before the start of school.

If home is the place you return to, then Arvin was home. He was not made to travel—he realized that—but the trip had served another purpose, one in which it had been more successful: defusing his prepublication anxiety. No writer can deny the breathtaking mixture of pride and dread that grips him at the appearance of his first book. Arvin had managed to preoccupy himself with a physical adventure, and thus was relatively calm about the arrival of *Hawthorne,* which he first saw on his return. It was a handsome volume, the cloth burgundy, with robin's-egg-blue type inside a small art deco border that made for an especially appealing spine, one that conveyed quality, dignity, and good taste. The dedication—a combination of genuine gratitude and prideful vengeance—read *"To* MY MOTHER *and* FATHER."

To Arvin's joy and relief, the book was well and widely reviewed, both as a critical study and a biography. The *New York Times* wrote, "Whether one agrees entirely with Mr. Arvin's thesis or not, it is impossible to read his book without having the pleasant experience of seeing new light (or, perhaps, light from an unexpected angle) thrown upon the works and character of Hawthorne. The assiduity and integrity of the critic are never in doubt." The *Herald Tribune* called it "a concise, accurate and gracefully written account of the familiar facts of Hawthorne's life, and an equally graceful analysis of his work," and the *Evening Post* said it was "of the highest critical distinction." "One of the most intelligent and well-written biographies that we have recently had in America," noted the *New York World.* It had taken longer than he'd hoped, but Arvin had done what he'd set out to do, which was to write an important literary biography animated by feeling and imagination. He was especially pleased that the reviews validated that approach.

Brooks had been right. He'd predicted that Arvin's real life as a writer would begin when he was "thirty or so." Arvin had just turned twenty-nine. Excited, he began to think of another project when, four days before the *World* review, Wall Street panicked and crashed, bringing the last of the roaring, tenuous, violently shuddering twenties down with it.

Chapter Three

AFTER THE STOCK market crash Arvin insisted to Hicks that they learn more about communism. Reforming the old order no longer seemed feasible or desirable. Business had no solutions to America's crisis. Nor did Washington. Even radicalism had failed. The country wasn't getting up from its troubles. "Why not communism?" Arvin urged, more as a point of moral exigency than a call to arms. Like a growing number of writers and intellectuals, he believed that the Crash signified a dividing line in American history. Those who had ruled before, the businessmen, were bankrupt. It was up to those with new ideas to put them forward. If the country needed a revolution, he argued, who else was there to lead it? With capitalism sinking, what other system remained to be tried?

Hicks wasn't sure he wanted to be involved in political work, for he'd come to feel—due mainly to Arvin's influence—that scholarship should be the center of his life. He wanted to teach and write about American literature, and the communists he had met and read hadn't impressed him with their intelligence or integrity. Arvin persisted. Hicks felt guilty about the idle and hungry men he was seeing on the street. Arvin convinced him that they couldn't stand by and watch the country collapse. Gradually, they moved toward studying, discussing, and, inevitably, writing about communist thought.

The success of *Hawthorne* was making Arvin's career, raising his standing both in the world of letters and at Smith. Moving beyond Brooks's di-minishing shadow, he now had a promising reputation, newfound confi-dence—his own gravity. He was at the center of a group of young instructors, Hicks and a few others, who cared passionately about the same things he did and were eager to hear what he thought they should do. He set himself the goal of a deeper and richer social life.

One of Arvin's new circle interested him more than the others. Howard Doughty was tall and dark, with dashing good looks and a deep Brahmin voice echoing bloodlines traced back to Cotton Mather. Hicks thought he had a romantic resemblance to early portraits of Hawthorne. After gradu-ating from Harvard in 1926, Doughty had spent a year in Paris, then arrived at Smith as a first-year English instructor. He was difficult to know, but Arvin, emboldened by his sense of belonging, drew him out. Doughty often visited the Hickses' duplex, where, though the group on the whole was se-rious, there was gin and gaiety and a sense of excitement at being at the vanguard of new ideas, and where Arvin, despite his shyness, for the first time experienced what it was to be popular. Those who gathered there, al-most all of them under thirty, enswirled by great forces, suddenly fashion-able as radicalism came into vogue, were intoxicated with a sudden sense of "being somewhere near the top of the world," Hicks would write. Arvin was their bright light.

Hicks left Smith in the fall of 1930 to return to Harvard for a year of graduate work, assured by President Neilson that it would be up to the En-glish Department to decide whether to reappoint him. Arvin, who was now an assistant professor, confidently indicated throughout the year that Hicks's colleagues considered him an excellent teacher and wanted to re-hire him. Then Neilson's position shifted. He began hearing from troubled alumnae that there were too many radicals on the faculty. Some had been greatly offended by the public statements of Harry Elmer Barnes, a histo-rian and outspoken member of the Hampshire County Progressive Club. Neilson, who hadn't forgotten Hicks's role in the Sacco-Vanzetti matter, was "not inclined to invite further difficulties," according to Hicks. He told Hicks there was no opening in the department, and if his colleagues at-tempted to rehire him, he, Neilson, would veto the appointment "on fi-nancial grounds." When faculty members, including Arvin, questioned him, Neilson expressed his opinion that Smith had reached the "saturation point" of how many faculty radicals it could safely employ.

Arvin continued to move leftward after Hicks found a job at Rensselaer Polytechnic Institute, in Troy, New York, a conservative engineering school. He began a Marxist study group at Smith, and when he went to New York to see his publisher or the newspapers and magazines he wrote for, he visited the office of *New Masses,* a communist publication. He told Hicks, who also formed a study group, that they needed more contact with the revolutionary movement, and he promptly organized two conferences in Northampton for local progressives to meet members of the Communist Party. But there was little rapport between intellectuals and party members, as both sides were discovering, and Arvin left the meetings feeling that, while he could support the Party, it was too doctrinaire and anti-intellectual for him to work with closely.

Privately, Arvin longed for intimacy and targeted Howard Doughty, who, like Arvin, maintained a public façade of being heterosexual. Both were terrified of being found out, but they began that fall to have a secret affair, which forced each for the first time to confront Smith's unspoken, paradoxical view of homosexuality. Women professors who were publicly linked or even lived together in so-called Boston marriages were well within the college's acceptance of discreet but intense female friendships. What they did in private was not discussed by Neilson and the trustees. Arvin and Doughty had no such protective cover, and were deeply reticent about expressing their feelings, even—indeed, especially—to each other. For Arvin, who had recently decried "whatever shuts up the spirit in a dungeon," the guilt of his feelings for Doughty and the pain of denying them became unbearable, and the men soon broke off the affair. Each became severely depressed, aching for what he couldn't have, but was unable to discuss it with the other, much less anyone else.

Throughout what would be the most dismal winter and spring of the Depression, Arvin felt he'd reached a deep divide. Politically, there seemed to be no half-measures. Banks were locking out depositors, striking coal miners had been shot to death by police, half of Detroit's nearly 500,000 auto workers were idle and its smokestacks cold. Ragged, hungry veterans were wandering off desolate farms to sleep in doorways, under newspapers and scraps of cardboard, and to line up for the dole. When thousands of them converged on Washington, demanding war bonuses, President Herbert Hoover sent orders to General Douglas MacArthur, his army chief of staff, to clear them from the capital; MacArthur responded by routing the weary men with tanks with hooded machine guns, four cavalry units, and a column of infantry with fixed bayonets and tear gas. The long-standing grievances of the twenties were suddenly exploding into open warfare. Even the apolitical Fitzgerald wrote, "To bring on the revolution, it may be necessary to work inside the communist party."

Arvin, believing that capitalism was doomed to failure and collapse (and faced with his own unacceptable longings), concluded that only communism offered a real future. He agreed with Dos Passos that, given the country's dire straits, the Socialist Party, which most intellectuals preferred because it refuted class warfare and proletarian "dictatorship," was "an easy sop to troubled consciences—near-beer." When Hicks reminded him that the communists they'd encountered had been "a pretty unpleasant bunch, single-minded and loud-mouthed and not to be depended on in the ordinary affairs of life," Arvin responded with a long, inspired declaration:

> It is a bad world in which we live, and so even the revolutionary movement is anything but what (poetically and even philosophically speaking) it "ought" to be: God knows, I realize this, as you do, and God knows it makes my heart sick at times: from one angle it seems nothing but grime and stink and sweat and obscene noises and the language of the beasts. But surely this is what *history* is. It is not just made by gentlemen and scholars . . . Lenin must have been (from a conceivable point of view) a dreadful man; so must John Brown, and Cromwell, and Stenka Razin, and Mahomet, and all the others who have destroyed and built up. So will our contemporaries in the American movement be . . . I believe we can spare ourselves a great deal of pain and disappointment and even worse (treachery to ourselves) if we discipline ourselves to accept proletarian and revolutionary leaders and even theorists for what they are and must be: grim fighters in about the most dreadful and desperate struggle (perhaps) in all history—not reasonable

and "critically minded" and forbearing and infinitely far-seeing men. My fundamental conviction about the whole thing, at this stage, is that everything gives way before the terrible social conflict itself: that the power of imperialism must be fought at every turn at every moment with any weapon and without quarter: that the consciousness of the proletariat—its sense of power and anger— must be built up by every device: and that meanwhile, the kinds of questions we are interested in must take their places where they belong, out of the thickest dust and along the rim of the arena. Let's salvage as much as we can of the rather abstract things we care for, but let's realize that there are far more basic and primitive things that have to be taken care of first (as long as men are starving and exploited), and do absolutely nothing, at any moment, to impede the work of the men who are fighting what is really our battle *for us.* Obviously you believe this too.

It was a compelling statement of conscience, one that could perhaps have been written only by someone with Arvin's faith in ideas and wide-eyed inexperience. In 1928, he had voted for Norman Thomas, a socialist, for president. Now, within two months, he would publicly support the Communist Party candidate, William Z. Foster, as would Hicks, Doughty, Dos Passos, Edmund Wilson, Sherwood Anderson, Lincoln Steffens, Theodore Dreiser, and more than a dozen other writers. Meantime, he finished teaching his courses, prepared a list of prospective contributors to a Marxist symposium on American culture, flirted with writing a biography of Whitman, and prepared to return to Yaddo, where he and several other radical young critics, including Crowley and Kronenberger, were becoming influential.

Hicks, who loved rustic living and whose wife, Dottie, hated Troy, had bought a run-down farmhouse on forty acres in the rolling country fifteen miles east of the city, toward Vermont, in the small town of Grafton. Unable to restrain his excitement at becoming a householder, he wrote to Arvin immediately of his plans, hoping that Arvin would buy the house with them or help them with the mortgage.

Arvin replied that he was thrilled and wanted to help, but couldn't, at the moment, spare much money. "I think," he wrote unexpectedly, "it's conceivable that I might want to get married."

A generation earlier Mary Garrison might have been a "swell," one of those wealthy, fashionable, well-connected, fun-loving Smith girls who ruled student life, tolerating but never befriending the pale, worn, morbidly sensitive "digs," who, dreaming of careers, disdained athletics and studied because they liked to. Born in 1909, the middle child of a staid, puritanical, well-to-do family from West Hartford, Connecticut, she grew up on the same street as Katharine Hepburn, and, like Hepburn, she strutted and was fiery. Her father was an executive of Travelers Insurance Company, and she was his pet, which strained the relations of both with her mother. Volatile and emotional, she was also verbal and bright—high strung—and those around her feared upsetting her.

As soon as she got away from her parents, Mary rebelled. A picturesque blonde, she was tall and robust—a Valkyrie—and from the beginning of her freshman year, in 1927, she dove into the world of parties and sports and bathtub gin. She swam on the all-college team as a senior, standing in the back row for the team picture with the other tall girls, a youthful figure shining with health. Not a beauty, she was still striking, with a full face, bobbed hair, long limbs, and sumptuous breasts. Facing graduation, she was determined not to return home. Her parents' world, unshaken by the Depression, appalled her. She thought she would like to teach children, but teaching was a low-status option for women of her class.

Arvin had met her that semester, when she was in one of his classes, and he was impressed with her personality and verve, so unlike his own character and that of the purposeful young men and women with whom he mingled. He liked shaping young minds and probably thought he could shape hers. He had seen how marriage had been a tonic for Hawthorne and, after the frightfulness with Doughty, was desperate to find a "normal" life. Quickly, he came to believe that Mary, who was flattered by the attention he gave her, might enable him to do so.

After graduation, Mary stayed in Northampton, working at a private day school as an assistant. Though the school was only a few blocks from his apartment and the college, Arvin was more comfortable writing about his feelings than speaking about them, and he wrote to her of both his affection and his concerns. "I'm terribly aware of the tender string on which our being together as passionate friends inevitably lives," he confessed on May 15, shortly after his letter to Hicks. The difference in their ages, nine years, troubled him. Would they be able to get along and understand each other? Could they tolerate each other's friends? Deeper were Arvin's concerns about himself. He worried that if he told Mary the truth about his sexual desires, she would turn against him, break down as if it were her own shame, and perhaps denounce him to the college. Arvin simply could not come out and confess his affliction. Painfully, he resolved to raise the issue indirectly, in the hope that she would understand without their discussing it.

He gave her an edition of Whitman's *Leaves of Grass* and urged her to read the "Calamus" poems, odes of comradeship then in vogue among progressives. The poems had become fashionable not for their homoeroticism, which most readers only dimly perceived, but as anticapitalist broadsides on the annealing power of love between men. Arvin, tortuously vague, told Mary to read one poem in particular, "When I Heard at the Close of the Day." He wrote, "It *suggests* something that means something to me." The poem, an ecstatic celebration of friendship, ends with the lines: "For the one I love most lay sleeping by me under the same cover/in the cool night . . . /And his arm lay lightly around my breast—and that night I was happy."

Perhaps because no student wants to admit ignorance to a teacher, Mary responded with equal tentativeness. She couldn't conceive that Arvin wasn't heterosexual, because nothing in her experience or his behavior had prepared her for such a thought. And she was awed by his brilliance, his ability to recite by heart whole sections of the *Canterbury Tales* in class, which kept her from asking questions he might construe as childish. Letting him know how much the poems also meant to her, she demurred from making comments that might offend him or cause him to think less of her. In fact, she never read them.

Arvin exulted in Mary's apparent forbearance. "Darling Child," he wrote ecstatically on May 31, Whitman's birthday, "thank God for you—

thank God for you—thank God for you—and thank *you* for your sweet note and your miraculous inexplicable acceptance of everything, even of the things I thought I should never have the courage to speak of—such as my almost unconquerable inhibitions. I was sorry to strike the discordant note of melodrama, but, if I was to 'come clean' at all, it had to be that way, and now it is over once and for all." Promising her that "as time goes on, we can talk as freely as you wish," he assured her that she was right in "taking such things as you do." Reticence and discretion were virtues that Arvin was hardly alone in believing comprised the bedrock of a sound marriage.

Within a week they were engaged. Mary returned to West Hartford to tell her parents, who relievedly gave their blessing, and to arrange the newspaper announcements. Arvin traveled to Yaddo, excitedly telling "everything important" to Elizabeth Ames, who invited the young couple to have their wedding there, in August. Breathlessly, Arvin wrote Mary daily love letters in which he sounded every inch the humble, enraptured swain. "I am lost in wonderment, for the millionth time," he wrote. "I know how far I am from deserving my happiness—how beautifully blind you are in seeing my limitations so little as you seem to do." Or else he acted the romantic hero. After Mary wrote complaining of menstrual cramps—"cruel paroxysms," Arvin called them—he responded, "It will be long before I accept the inevitableness of the thing without a struggle," adding jauntily, "Disturbed as I was to hear of the circumstances, I couldn't help, like an old ass, perhaps, being a little relieved to hear of the general fact," implying that they may already have had sex.

After years of solitude, Arvin felt he was finally "coming into port." Whatever his misgivings, he wanted to reassure Mary that she needn't have any herself. Capably, he took care of the wedding arrangements—finding a justice of the peace, securing lodging in Saratoga for Mary's family, advising on a ring—and seemed to take pleasure anticipating the moment when they finally would be together. "This will be the last letter I can send you, sweetheart, before you arrive in my waiting arms again," he wrote on July 27. "I am getting extremely impatient with this mode of communication. We shall have another week of it before we are wholly through—and that, I am sure, will be about my limit." Starting most letters with either "Beloved Child" or "Precious Child," he treated her much the way his father treated his mother, as a benevolent, somewhat distant, provider and protector. He could chide her tenderly—"*Vanity Fair* forsooth!" he wrote after Mary told him what she'd been reading. "Heave it out at Mr. Chaplin's cow, and get down your Lenin, young lady. What decade are you living in?"—but, having put her on a pedestal, he couldn't but patronize her.

The wedding at Elizabeth Ames's two-story Tudor cottage, Pine Garde, on the far side of Yaddo's tennis court, was small and sedate, though the weekend itself was tumultuous. August was racing season in Saratoga Springs, and Arvin had placed Mary's family in the Rip Van Dam, a noisy hotel in the thick of the tourist brawl on Broadway. Mary's closest friends attended, as did the Hickses, Doughty, and a few other Yaddo artists. Lilienthal sent his and his wife's regrets. He and Helen were living in Madison, Wisconsin, because he had left his private law practice to regulate the state's power companies, and they couldn't get away. After the wedding, Arvin and Mary spent the weekend recovering in Glens Falls and at the former Trask estate on Triuna Island on Lake George, feeling spent but, as Arvin wrote happily, "beyond separation at last."

Back in Northampton in September, they moved into a clean, airy apartment in a four-story brick "block" just off campus. Despite the Depression, it was a favorable time for a young couple to set up housekeeping. Landlords, desperate for tenants, had begun culling the wedding announcements in the *Gazette,* and had sent Arvin invitations throughout the summer to inspect their vacancies. He had received letters from furniture stores as far away as Manchester, Connecticut, offering low prices, big discounts, and alluring terms. ("We should count it a privilege to show you through our store and then if you are interested get right down to figures.") Smith, unable to raise faculty salaries, had managed not to lay anyone off. Arvin bought a packing trunk in Springfield for $42.50—"probably the last one I shall buy before the revolution," he wrote to Mary—a sofa, chairs, standing lamps, a bedroom set, kitchenware, and other items as he and Mary went about setting up their first home. Arvin, hoping to rescue her from drudgery, hired a cleaning woman to come in twice a week.

Despite his efforts at being a good husband, though, it was soon clear that they were not enough. Arvin was busy—teaching, churning out articles, continuing his Spanish instruction, and campaigning for Foster and at least two communist "fronts," the National Committee for the Defense of Political Prisoners and the American Committee for the World Congress Against War. Now that they were married, he depended on Mary for cheerful support, but he hadn't the ability or the inclination to satisfy *her* need for closeness. Sensing from the beginning that she was unhappy, he apologized, but he didn't know how to help her. In November, the first election in which Mary could participate, they both voted for Foster—the only two in Northampton—and the subversiveness of the act thrilled her. But she wanted more from Arvin than he could give. By Christmas, she was exhausted, her period was late, and she was "nervous" and depressed. Arvin packed her off to her parents' for a period of "rest," writing solicitously, "I hope, my dear child, that you won't be too worried about that darned old menstrual flow: all the tearing around . . . may have slowed it up; and even at the worst, we can face it if you don't 'come round.' "

The following day he wrote to her again: "I realize how good I ought (and must) be to you in order to make you happy and keep you by me. I wish that I could be a god and a saint and a knight and a good companion for your sake." If Arvin was to fail as a husband, it would not be for want of trying.

In mid-1935, when Arvin and Mary had been married almost three years, he received a Guggenheim Fellowship to work on his biography of Whitman. Following the first American Writers' Congress, in April, his enthusiasm for literary communism was at its height. The congress had been called by the rejuvenated *New Masses,* and Hicks, the magazine's new literary editor, had presided. Hicks was now a card-carrying—open—member of the Communist Party, a rising figure on the literary left, and the congress was a Party attempt to enlist intellectuals. Arvin himself had recently published essays on "Literature and Social Change" and "The Writer as Partisan," and his pursuit of Whitman was mainly political. Always in search of his literary ancestry, he urgently wanted to determine whether Whitman had been a socialist.

Mary returned to Hartford to work as a typist while Arvin spent two months at Yaddo and then returned to Northampton in August to prepare for an extended research trip. Living apart had become a necessity and a test for them, as it was for other young academic couples trying to make ends meet. But living together, they'd discovered, was worse. The strain of being in the same room, sharing a bed, was unnerving. Arvin, always hypochondriacal, obsessed over Mary's least frailties as if they were his own. At the same time, having daily contact with her was, as he'd once written to Lilienthal in another context, a torment, like holding his hand in the fire "for an intolerable length of time." Mary was often in ill health, hurt, sad, disappointed, not herself, or was suffering violent menstrual cramps, which led to her being prescribed "gland treatments," that is, hormones. With her natural gregariousness smothered by Arvin's need for solitude and quiet, she was chronically tired yet agitated, and often cried. She took Amytal to sleep. Each had imagined they could change the other, and perhaps themselves, and both found out they couldn't do either and that they were trapped.

They began drinking, and quarreling, more, and though Arvin's relief whenever Mary got her period suggests that they were intimate, it can't have been comforting for either of them. They had reached a stage in their relationship where they couldn't communicate without Mary feeling hurt by Arvin's distance and disapproval, and Arvin, in turn, becoming cross and dismissive, then adopting a tone of long-suffering contrition in his letters to her.

After two months apart, and with their anniversary coming up in two weeks, Arvin arranged to spend the first weekend in August with Mary and her family in Hartford. Then, pleading overwork, he abruptly begged off. After sounding distant on the phone, he typically asked for forgiveness. He wrote:

> My feeling was that it was a mistake for us to try to spend the week-end together so long as I was as completely out of the running as I was, and I wanted to express this if possible without hurting your feelings. But I was anything but sure I could do this, and I don't suppose I did. I apologize as humbly as possible and hope you will make what allowances you can. I also really thought it

wouldn't be a very good idea for you all to come up yesterday, but I despaired of saying *this* without being misunderstood. However, since you all felt that too, it turned out all right. It is obviously a great mistake to count on me for anything.

All Arvin wanted was to work. But marriage was a nightmare for him, and he responded by making it a horror for Mary, who couldn't bear his querulousness or believe him when he expressed sympathy or remorse or wrote in his letters that he loved her. Not only were they utterly wrong for each other; real intimacy with *anyone* was more than Arvin could achieve. Like Hawthorne in his solitude, he was locked miles deep in guilt-filled isolation. After forgetting their anniversary, he wrote the next morning, coldly, chillingly:

Darling Child:

It looks as if I am certainly becoming the thoughtless, selfish, and unfeeling husband: at least yesterday's performance must have had that effect on you . . . I *would* go and take a trip that put the whole idea out of my mind, until it was too late to do anything but respond lamely. It was terribly sweet of you to think of telegraphing me, and I was much affected by your telegram; I hope you can forgive my apparent (and in only one sense real) heedlessness. I am looking forward to seeing the gift you speak of, which I'm sure will be extremely nice . . . Three years ago today was the day we spent so beautifully at Triuna!

In early October, Arvin left Northampton for a month-long trip through Camden, Philadelphia, Washington, D.C., and New York, while Mary remained in Hartford to work. By now they were making separate plans, and Arvin's letters consisted mostly of inquiries about her health and state of mind, discussions of upcoming visits, facts about work and money matters, and news of friends. In Philadelphia he stayed with Howard Doughty and his new wife, Binks, to whom Arvin, who'd known her and her family since he was in college, may have introduced him. The visit was warm but disappointing; Binks had tonsillitis, "which meant that Howard and I had to stay in and take care of her and we couldn't have much real talk or gaiety," he wrote, in a way that now seems a private code that Mary was not meant to understand.

From there he traveled by train to Washington, checking in at the Dodge Hotel, which, he wrote, was "pretty cheap." He saw Hicks once for dinner and read often in the newspapers about Lilienthal. A fast-rising star of the New Deal, Lilienthal had been appointed to the Tennessee Valley Authority, the federal government's attempt to revive one of the most depressed regions of the country by competing with what Lilienthal called the "remote-controlled" power trusts. The TVA was under relentless attack on Wall Street as state socialism, and Lilienthal was President Franklin Roosevelt's man on the board, dining with the President and frequently taking on hostile committees in Congress. Though he and Arvin remained close, seeing each other when they could, and though each admired the other's accomplishments, the men now lived and worked on formally opposing sides, not an unusual Washington friendship.

Arvin's research was successful, and he was eager to begin writing. After several days in New York, he stopped overnight with Brooks to draw up final plans. He had decided to rent a room for the winter in Westport, a short walk from Brooks's house, to consolidate his research and start the early chapters, rather than to join Mary at home, and he was anxious to do only what little he had to in Northampton. He told Mary that he would stop in Hartford along the way but couldn't stay overnight, since it was "barely possible that I might spend a night in any room I might find, get my trunk up to it, unpack, etc., and then move on for a day or two."

Whether Arvin was inextricably absorbed in planning his book or was simply avoiding her, it was now clear that he was happier when they were apart. Mary hoped he would at least come for Thanksgiving at her parents' house, but Arvin was in such an intense state that when he told her he couldn't and Mary got upset, he burst out angrily in a letter:

> I cannot, cannot, cannot go on having time raped like this, and I
> just hope you can make it clear to your father and mother *why* I

can't come . . . It is just something that an individual has to take entirely on his own shoulders, and then enter upon a long, grim, unyielding fight with the rest of Mankind to defend . . . *no one*, literally no one in the world, has any idea why a writer should want uninterrupted solitude and leisure, and no other person will ever really cooperate with him to get it. However, *you* at least know what the problem is, and that is a great support. I hope you will try to make it clear, whenever the subject comes up, that I am to all intents and purposes a dead man, and cannot do *anything*.

Now that he had got to the point of launching his book on Whitman, with the rare luxury of a year away from Smith, he sought to strip himself of every encumbrance. He asked Cowley at *The New Republic*, for which he wrote regular book reviews, for a three-month sabbatical, even though, as he wrote to Mary, "It'll mean ten dollars or so less every month, and who knows how much we might regret that." She, meanwhile, moved to New York to seek a better job and was living at the Hotel Barclay on East Forty-eighth Street. Though Arvin worried about her working too much and living alone in the city, he encouraged her. "I am glad you decided not to take the $18 a week job and to wait for something better; you certainly are worth a hell of a lot more than that." While they needed Mary's income so that he could write his book, Arvin took pains to support her and cheer her up.

Arvin faced a critical decision about his book. As he wrote, since "the next inevitable step in human history is the establishment and construction of a socialist order," was Whitman a "socialist poet" or, as he himself had said, socialistic only "in my meanings"? To Arvin and other leftist critics, the distinction was crucial, far more important than Whitman's standing as a poet. Either Whitman was a *petit bourgeois* individualist—"the most complete and thoroughgoing anti-Socialist in all literature," as Floyd Dell called him—or a staunch and visionary foe of industrialized society and monopoly capitalism. Because he was a significant national voice and major cultural asset, America's most emblematic poet, it would be a coup to claim him for one's side in the struggle over the nation's future.

Arvin labored to get started, but his almost daily contact with Brooks daunted and distracted him. Brooks, remarkably, had survived what he called his "season in hell" and had returned to productivity after a year in a Westchester sanitarium and, more important, receiving financial aid from his wife's family. A few months after the Wall Street Crash, with Brooks trying to starve himself, and Eleanor having no independent income, her cousin, Secretary of State Henry Stimson, established a $100,000 trust to ensure her support. Relieved of ever again needing a job, Brooks was suddenly free to write what he wished. He returned to Westport fragile but filled with ideas, and for the past five years had toiled on the first part of a monumental history of American literature, *The Flowering of New England,* which was now all but completed and which Brooks believed was his finest work.

During Brooks's illness, the times had passed him by, and he'd depended largely on Arvin to catch him up. The process had been difficult for both of them. Brooks, an idealistic socialist, had inspired the literary left, but it had moved on, and he disapproved of its new direction. Arvin, for his part, doubted they were still allies. He criticized Brooks publicly, particularly his *Life of Emerson,* which Arvin faulted in *The New Republic* for failing to expose Emerson's class bias. Though Brooks was dismayed by Arvin's backhanded compliment that the book was "the only [one] on its subject which will survive the final collapse of Emersonianism," he avoided a split. He joined the League of American Writers, apparently unaware that it was communist-led, and helped Arvin to win his Guggenheim. Arvin also overlooked their differences, but it was harder. The "scientific" nature of Marxism forbade excusing one's ideological enemies, especially those with trust funds.

As Arvin got settled in Westport, he was stricken with uncertainty and doubt. He wasn't at all sure that Brooks, who believed that "communist thinking is closed to a very large area of human feeling," wasn't right. He still didn't know how to reconcile Whitman's life, poetry, and politics, which seemed almost impossible to unify in one man. Meanwhile, he was shaken physically and emotionally. He had a cold, his bowels hurt, he was chronically tired, and he had no one besides the Brookses to care for him, and he feared imposing on them. He felt himself sinking, alone. Craving extreme solitude to write, Arvin was finding that such isolation from the social world was bearable only when there was someone else in his life.

Inevitably, perhaps, he turned to Mary, writing on December 3:

> I have less physical drive and much less mental clarity and *grip* than I could wish . . . Collecting "materials," taking notes, reading, etc., can be done even under such circumstances, but one needs some real physical and mental rest in order to write anything but bilge, and just now that is about what I'd be writing . . . I should not turn to you and worry you in this way if I knew how to avoid it or just what else to do. But you are inevitably concerned and involved. I'd give worlds if I knew you could be spared all this, and do want very vehemently to assure you that nothing desperate is at stake.

Throughout December, he pushed himself to put words on paper, feeling more and more inadequate even as he began to locate a broader conception for his book. He was arriving at the un-Marxian idea that Whitman's poems might not be fully explained by the class-bound politics of their author, a Jacksonian Democrat who exalted "the grand body of white workingmen," as Whitman called the mechanics and farmers of the middle class, yet who supported the Mexican War because Mexicans were an "ignorant, prejudiced and perfectly faithless people . . . a nation of bravos"; a poet-journalist who could write, magnificently, "Whoever degrades another degrades me," but who kept his distance from abolitionism and considered Negroes "invariably—almost without exception—a superstitious, ignorant and thievish race."

> Without setting up any mystical dualism between "the man" and "the poet" [Arvin wrote], we have always to remember how far the creative artist is from being entirely absorbed and limited by the profane individual of biography. Goethe the privy counselor will never explain the whole of *Faust* . . . and Whitman the editor or government clerk is something less than the author of *Leaves of Grass*: the two are not mechanically identical. What the salaried citizen may think on the topmost layer of his mind is often, and fa-

miliarly, at war with what he may see or feel in his moments of deepest excitement and truest insight.

Here was Arvin's struggle—the struggle between the "salaried citizen" and the inner self—and once he finally put it into words, his dark caul seemed to lift. His health improved, and he began churning out new pages with relative ease. He also rediscovered his affection for Mary, who, he now realized, by tolerating his moods, taking lowly typing jobs, moving alone to New York, and encouraging him, had helped him to reach a point where he could see the rest of the book's architecture unfold. Though he still addressed her as a child, a new tone of humility and appreciation was apparent in his letters:

It is very nice indeed [he wrote on January 2, 1936] to feel you care so much about the book "and all," and I can very honestly reassure you about it now. VW said the first chapter was splendid, and even interrupted me once to say something was "very good." I take this at a discount, for he is too generous to do anything else, and I have only to listen to a few pages of his manuscript to realize that I shall never speak Attic like a real Greek. But this doesn't trouble me at all: I realize how necessary it is (and desirable) that all kinds of *more* or *less* good books should be written, and that when no one else appears to be doing a certain job it should be done as well as possible by the available person . . . You gave me a lot of encouragement by seeming to like the first chapter so well when I read it to you, I think you are a more *candid* critic than almost anyone else I did read it to, and hence I am much more impressed by what you say.

As with *Hawthorne,* once Arvin knew what he wanted to say, the writing came easily, and he felt a jolt of confidence that made him far less thin-skinned and anxious. He quickly moved ahead, writing three chapters in four months, and by March he thought he would finish in June, an aim he'd long given up. His feelings toward Mary improved, although he continued to avoid seeing her, writing on several occasions that they were better off saving the money on train fares and hotels. But now he longed for companionship. Confessing "I do need you," he urged her to visit him for a full weekend in Westport, instead of his traveling to New York, as planned. "I do feel it is an awful lot to ask," he wrote. "But there is no one else I can really turn to—or for one moment want to turn to except you; and maybe you will not feel such an errand of mercy is wholly purposeless."

It was not, as Arvin affirmed in his next letter. "Sweetest Child," he wrote, "your being here yest. and Sat. was a real life saver for me, and I feel as different from what I felt Sat. a.m. as Stalin and Trotsky. Straight goods." Arvin often tried to bolster Mary's spirits with smarmy consolation, but this time spent with her after "ten dank days of solitude, eye trouble, etc." was a tonic, and he wanted her to believe that he loved her and hoped that she loved him. He continued, playfully, "So you see I am not stringing you along—not just handing you a piece of Taffy, as they used to say when I was a little girl in the 'Ah Wilderness' era. If your stay here was half as helpful to you, I should feel very cheerful indeed."

What caused such an abrupt turnaround is not clear, but it seemed heartfelt and true, and was soon reflected in Arvin's writing on Whitman. He was approaching the "Calamus" section, the most intense and complicated material in the book, and as he puzzled through it, Arvin found new pieces of himself. As when he first wrote about Hawthorne's emergence from his "dismal chamber," he minutely examined Whitman's experience through his own and discovered new meanings in both.

Whitman had added the "Calamus" poems to the second edition of *Leaves of Grass,* in 1860, writing in an introduction that their "special meaning . . . mainly resides in their Political significance." As Arvin understood, Whitman had come to recognize that individualism, which he celebrated so ringingly in his first edition, isolates the common man. Like Hawthorne, he believed the adjustment of the individual to society was "the big problem—the only problem: the sum of them all." Whitman proposed to correct it. "He had resolved," Arvin observed, "to be the 'poet of comrades' as well as of selfhood, and in the 'Calamus' poems he had given bold utterance to that 'manly attachment,' that 'intense and loving comradeship,' that 'adhesive love,' that 'beautiful and sane affection of man for man,' which he maintained to be as strong and normal an emotion in men as love between the sexes."

Arvin had in a sense done the same in his own writings, celebrating the urge toward a deeper social life among men. But of course neither of them could ever wholly mean, or accept, "comradeship" at face value. "What Whitman half-consciously meant by manly attachment," Arvin wrote, "was not simply a normal brotherly feeling among men but homosexual love." It is what he had tried unsuccessfully to explain to Mary when he gave her the poems years earlier.

Arvin's understanding of the relationship between Whitman's sexuality and ideas tested him as a critic as nothing had done before. Whitman was under attack, most recently by the poet Mark Van Doren, as having no serious political meaning, because his poems of solidarity were not an outgrowth of socialist principle but, as Arvin put it, "the unwitting expression of his own abnormal sexuality." Arvin surely realized that he could be subjected to the same charge, even though his homosexuality was a secret, well covered by his marriage and further camouflaged by a manly communism. "No society," Van Doren argued, "can be made out of [Whitman]. We could not be like him if we would. He has revealed himself to us, and that is all." The more Arvin read into the "Calamus" poems, he knew, the more he risked similar exposure. And being discredited politically would be the least of his disgrace.

With his usual care and precision, Arvin posed the problem more broadly. "Does all this mean . . . that Whitman's whole prophecy as a democratic poet—and especially the poet of 'universal democratic comradeship'—is invalidated by having its psychological basis in a sexual aberration?" he asked. No, he declared, writing with a fervor that, compared with that in *Hawthorne,* seems constrained but no less deeply felt:

It is hardly customary, and it would certainly be uncritical, to dispose of the ideas in *The Republic* because there is a homosexual strain in Plato, and homosexuality is only one of the eccentricities or pathologies that may give a particular bias to a writer's work. The sense of impotence, the feeling of inferiority, an abnormal horror of the physiological, the delusion of persecution—these are others; and the history of literature is eloquent of what splendid fruits may be grown in such bitter and unlikely soil. *Not in its obscure and private origins but its general and public bearing is the test of a great creative conception, and from this point of view what really interests us in Whitman is not that he was homosexual, but that, unlike the vast majority of inverts, even of those creatively gifted, he chose to translate and sublimate his strange, anomalous emotional experience into a political, a constructive, a democratic program.* [Italics added.]

Arvin could not have spoken more stirringly had he been writing about himself, which in many ways he was. On the first level, he was reinforcing his conclusions about Whitman, who indeed was a socialist poet because of his ecstatically fraternal spirit and rejoicing in the average citizen, not because of any explicit political beliefs. At the same time, he was justifying and legitimating his own writing, also a product of "eccentricities and pathologies," and defending his political role. He, too, had chosen to "translate and sublimate his strange, anomalous emotional experience" into a positive and democratic world view.

But the lines carried a larger, more personal meaning, too. What Whitman had done in "Calamus," most remarkably, was to celebrate *himself.* Instead of withdrawing, shame-faced, because he loved other men, he had broadcast his truest, most forbidden feelings to the world. What homosexual in Arvin's experience could regard such an impulse as anything but fatal? How thrilled and frightened he must have been to write these lines, for they permitted him for the first time to argue *for* his homosexuality, which, while still suppressed, filled with self-disgust, and publicly unadmitted, was after all no different from the "Good Grey's." "There is, so to say, a harmless, wholesome, sane 'homosexuality' that pervades normal humanity as the mostly powerless bacilli of tuberculosis appear in the healthiest of lungs," Arvin declared. Even if he felt that in himself homosexuality was a sickness, he glimpsed through Whitman the possibility of a benign, healthy strain of it in others.

About Mary, Arvin was freshly torn. He still wanted fiercely to have a normal marriage and dared not accept that he was incapable of one; he was a good and generous provider and would not give up. But he and Mary couldn't afford to live apart indefinitely. Their sole option seemed to be to return to Northampton and try again to live under one roof. By April, with his work going smoothly, he felt revived, almost joyous. He characteristically resigned himself to reuniting with Mary, then tried to put the best face on his mixed feelings by lavishly proclaiming his love and begging her not to worry about the future. He wrote how desperately he missed her even when he seemed relieved to be apart.

Little did he understand that Mary might be feeling conflict as well. Now living in the Latham Hotel, on East Twenty-eighth Street, near the flower district, she had become enthralled by the city's charms. She dreaded returning to small-town life, just as Arvin had at her age. She also realized that she'd been naive, lunging foolishly into a hopeless relationship with an emotionally and sexually unsatisfactory older man because she was flattered by his attention, seduced by the danger of his politics and force of intellect, and desperate not to return to West Hartford. By now she knew the marriage had been an errant act of rebellion, a mistake. She was desperately unhappy, but she couldn't afford to live on her own or to express her real feelings. Inside, however, the titillation of marrying her radical professor had long faded to boredom, dismay, and disillusion.

Arvin's expressed scorn during much of the past year left her hurt and confused. As they prepared to reunite, Mary felt oppressed by Arvin's ceaseless mothering; she wrote to him finally not to trouble himself about her anymore, that she was "nothing to worry about." The remark, typically, alarmed Arvin, who worried that she might be contemplating suicide. He tried to mollify her: "I beg you not to say such things . . . that sounds too distressingly desperate—even wild—and no one who ever saw you would know what you meant by saying it. Please set down all my violent talk to a bad state of the jitters, and believe that I am rapidly getting rested and refreshed up here. You may not 'know' me when you see me."

Arvin returned to Northampton in mid-June, too late to find a summer sublet. The only possibility was to house-sit for friends of his whom Mary disliked. In the end, they took the house because it was rent-free, but not before Arvin sought to reassure her once again that he was eager to have her back and desired only her happiness. "Darling Lamb," he wrote to her at her parents' house, where she had stopped for two weeks on her way back to Smith:

> I think of you constantly and *hate* our being apart, and am miserable when I think you may not be in good spirits. *Try* to be for my sake and do come quickly on Wed.
>
> Beaucoup Amour,
N.
>
> P.S. *Please* buy those sport-shoes!

The suspension of such basic conflicts couldn't last. By January 1937, seven months later, Arvin was again sending Mary confusing messages about his desire to be with her. He wrote:

> I hardly know what to say about your coming home for the weekend—though on the hull [sic] I think I'm in favor of it, if you feel you can manage to do that much driving. It would be a long time to have to wait for you if I didn't see you until Monday night or Tuesday: I really miss you too much for that. On the other hand, after all, I do get along puffickly [sic] well in every material way, and as a matter of fact, if it seemed to be a really wiser plan, I'd be strongly in favor of your seeing it through to the end. (Reconcile those two views if you can!)

Mary no longer wished to try. Once again, living with Arvin had become a dulling strain, a trial. He was always reading, writing, and insisting on silence, instructing her to tell friends who telephoned that he was meditating and couldn't be disturbed. "I never even knocked on his door," she later said. "If I wanted to say something, I put a note under it." Where Arvin was withdrawn and meticulous, Mary was voluptuous and starved. "She could make ten meals of Newton," recalled a friend who met them during this period. More and more, she grew weary as he said he loved her but acted as if he didn't.

She enjoyed his status at Smith—he had just been elected vice-president of the teachers' union, with the expectation he would lead it in the fall—but felt stifled by her own, as a young member of the Faculty Wives' Club, which met for afternoon teas. She had grown up with a cook and a maid, but she and Arvin moved every year, with only a housekeeper. They were drinking heavily, a fifth of whiskey a day. Nights that Mary started out gracious, sporting, and alive often spiraled into surliness, depression, night fear, and insomnia—for both of them.

In June 1938, Mary, apparently disconsolate and needing rest, left to spend a month with friends in Provincetown, on the tip of Cape Cod. Arvin was doing final revisions on *Whitman,* and though no "irrevocable decision has to be made," he wrote to her, their immediate future was uncertain. Before she left, they apparently discussed several options, including the possibility of her entering a sanitarium; then they decided that a summer at the shore might be more soothing. Provincetown, a windswept Portuguese fishing village, was also a bohemian refuge, a place where artists and playwrights escaped the whirlpool of Greenwich Village, though they reconstituted something very much like it amid the dunes and surf. Shrinking from saying anything that might further agitate her, Arvin begged her in one sentence to count on him for whatever she needed; in the next, he encouraged her to stay away as long as necessary. He urged her to have fun, relax, and "see how we all feel when you come back."

Each now craved not only separation but a separate life. Mary spent her days swimming and sunbathing, her nights in a whirl of parties and drinking. Arvin worked and read, until he was sated, and met colleagues for quiet meals out. Once, in mid-July, when Mary was scheduled to return to Northampton for a brief visit, he became distraught at the possibility of her overlapping with Granville and Dottie Hicks, who also were visiting and whom she apparently disliked. In a state of almost permanent contrition, he wrote Mary a frantic ten-page letter dissuading her from coming before the Hickses left, so that the four of them wouldn't have to lunch together. Their correspondence flagged. Mary let days go by without writing; Arvin, finally reassured that she was all right, responded with a torrent of penny postcards.

In September they agreed to a separation. Mary, in Provincetown until the end of the month, arranged to move to Cambridge; Arvin found himself an apartment for $26 a month in a converted three-story house near the college, across from the public library. He was so relieved to be living alone at last that he tried to convince Mary that she should feel the same. "I wish I could impart to you," he wrote, "some of my feeling that we can make things come our way if we decide we must and are going to, and that in the long run we'll both achieve really good lives for ourselves and be the very best and fondest of friends . . . I do hope you are getting over that feeling of being painfully uprooted: in one sense (an impractical one, I know) you really aren't."

But whatever room remained for her in his life was slight in comparison to his exhilaration at setting up his "den," the first home in six years he could call his own. "I have acquired a broom, a wet-mop, a garbage can, a little tin bread-box, some dust cloths, a pair of scissors (our old ones having disappeared), and some furniture polish . . . ," he wrote, barely containing his glee. "I know I am soon going to feel very much *chez moi*. I have your picture up on my dresser already."

They were apart when *Whitman* was published by Macmillan, in November 1938, to mostly enthusiastic reviews. *The New Yorker* called it "a careful, well-written examination, by one of the most responsible of contemporary literary critics." Lincoln Kirstein wrote in *The Nation*, "Mr. Arvin's mind is so clear, his attitude so admirable, his analysis so large and sober, that one hesitates to cavil at even a single statement." "Newton Arvin's biography of Whitman," *Time* wrote, "belongs with the best of the books about his poetry."

A few critics dissented. "A book which to any but confirmed Left Wingers will be more curious than convincing," said the *Boston Transcript*, a conservative paper. "We find . . . ," Wilson Follett observed in the *Times*, "many passing reminders of the actual Whitman as he spoke and acted. We find a great deal of astute, careful, sharply definitive writing that suggests an elaborate academic exercise *in vacuo,* a glorified Ph.D. thesis. And beyond these, I am afraid, not much."

In all, Arvin was sanguine, having achieved most of what he had attempted and more. He had written better than the "more or less good book" he'd humbly told Mary was his goal, a book that deepened his understanding of America, advanced his credibility and career, transcended the communist ideology that spawned it, and furthered his and Brooks's goal of reclaiming a "usable past." And he had addressed the explosive subject of Whitman's homosexuality, even at the cost of revealing perhaps more of his own tragic sense than he wanted to or knew. What he hadn't done—what perhaps no biography can, or should, do for its author—was fully absorb Whitman's hale fraternalism and make it his own.

After his initial relief over his and Mary's separation, Arvin descended into depression and self-disdain—"seediness," he called it. Comfortable as he was alone, he blamed himself for the collapse of his marriage and his isolation. He suffered, he believed, from "affectational impotence"—"a great and poignant need of love combined with an incapacity, at the last moment, either to possess or be possessed." True, Mary was wrong for him—too wild and vital and young—and of the wrong sex. But the larger issue was his pained aversion to intimacy. He recoiled from loving and from being loved, which, taken away, left little worth living for.

For Mary, being separated wasn't so much a solution to their problems as a grim exile. She had no place to go as the Depression ground on. At twenty-nine, without skills, she had spent almost a third of her marriage living in hotels or moving among friends until, periodically, she dumped herself, dispirited and out of sorts, on her family. Yet she was still married, still Mrs. Newton Arvin, without independent means. Throughout the fall and winter, Mary grew increasingly gloomy about her future. Her moods, alternately depressed and ignited by alcohol, paralyzed her, and she was frantic and unable to sleep.

Again the subject of a sanitarium was raised, and this time, desperate, she agreed. Arvin arranged in mid-March for her to be admitted to the New York Medical Center Westchester Division, a private psychiatric hospital in White Plains, New York. Mary was staying with her parents at the time, yet when she asked Arvin whether she could visit for a few days before entering the facility, he tried to dissuade her and, typically, offered a tortured explanation:

Darling Child:
I had never had any idea that, in general, you weren't *very* welcome to be here, or that, from my point of view, you had "no home." I felt only, in a stupid and confused way, that it might not be really good for you to be here this last week while I was trying rather tensely to get through last classes, graduate students, etc. I have got myself rather fatigued and nervous . . . and I couldn't be sure that it wouldn't have a bad effect on you. But I imagine that I have been very stupid about it, and that you would have been much better off here than anywhere else. I really hadn't realized that you yourself felt that you could be here in Northampton, and yet of course I knew that it was not a good idea for you to be in Hartford *for any length of time.* I thought it would be a very few days and that you were going to be preoccupied with getting clothes, etc.

If their relationship could get no worse, it was hard to see how it might improve. Arvin belatedly offered to help Mary do "whatever makes you easiest and happiest." If she wanted to come to Northampton before taking the train to White Plains, he wrote, "I will do what I can to show you a good time." Suggesting "at least there are *some* people here you enjoy being with," he proposed, perhaps, "a party or two." But the damage was done. Mary felt she had been turned away from her marriage for the last time.

She stayed at the hospital for more than three months, from mid-April on, receiving little psychiatric help but sufficient respite and sleeping pills to regain her bearings and return to a functioning life. Arvin continued to write solicitous letters, expressing hope that she was "in control" and urging her to have an "interesting and happy time," but her progress was slow. She was still there, deciding where to go and what to do next, when Arvin left in late July for Yaddo, which more than any person or place had become his refuge from life's exhausting turbulence.

It was at Yaddo that Arvin learned, a month later, of the Nonaggression Pact between the Soviet Union and Germany. Most of the guests huddled in shock and dismay around the one large radio upstairs in the mansion as the world outside suddenly turned more dangerous and confusing. For writers on the left, European fascism, not collapsing capitalism, now presented the gravest threat to humanity. Hicks, his faith in Russia shattered, decided to renounce his Party membership, but not before driving to Yaddo from Grafton to consult with Arvin. They agreed that from a communist point of view it was better for Germany to go to war with England and France than with Russia. But as Arvin pointed out, such logic would excuse England's capitulation at Munich.

Arvin was seriously troubled by Stalin's cynical embrace of Hitler, but his crisis of faith paled next to that of Hicks, now one of the best-known communists in America, since he had been hired a year earlier as a counselor of American history at Harvard, an incident that made national headlines. But the pact, and Hitler's invasion of Poland a month later, were ominous forebodings. Arvin believed that the world was headed for a catastrophic war.

Where would it all end? Part of the answer came later that fall from Mary, who wrote that she wanted a divorce. Arvin welcomed the idea, but divorces, especially in Massachusetts, were tawdry, public affairs, and he feared what each of them might have to say in court. He was now a public person concealing a shameful secret, and his troubled young wife was furious with him. Though he sympathized with Mary and thought she was doing the best thing for both of them, Arvin suddenly turned sharply adversarial in his correspondence.

He wrote to her on December 20, using the salutation "Dear Mary," thus signifying her at last by using her name. Since it was "virtually impossible" for him to get a divorce in Northampton except on grounds of desertion, and then only after three years, he urged *her* to seek the divorce "if this is at all feasible or practical." Furthermore, he wrote, they should obtain a legal separation "as soon as possible, if only in order that you may feel secure and in a well-defined position."

He also criticized vague statements that had been made about him, and "repeated" to Mary, that may have involved his homosexuality. "I should be charged . . . directly and to my face," he fumed. "I would then be prepared to reply that they are grossly and flagrantly untrue." Except perhaps with Doughty and certain friends at Yaddo, Arvin is unlikely to have had an active homosexual life during this time. He was not one to arouse suspicion. But his comments in *Whitman,* and his preference for bachelorhood over being married to an attractive young woman with large physical needs, would have raised questions about his manliness. Arvin implored Mary to "wonder about the motives of people" who repeated "malice" and "malignancy."

Mary filed for divorce in Florida after moving, in January 1940, to a hotel in Fort Lauderdale to establish residence there. She stayed for several months, taking a job as a waitress. Arvin sent her monthly checks, but he was also paying both of their lawyers, and Mary needed the extra income. She wrote that she planned to move to New York as soon as the divorce decree was final.

Continuing to have the same problems and failing to resolve them in the same ways, they wrote to each other only when necessary. When Mary complained that Arvin's letters were cold and hostile, he typically tried to convince her otherwise. "I imagine if you could know that I am really very tired all the time," he wrote on February 29, "you would feel less badly about it . . . But you yourself might be less troubled and more cheerful about things if you could think of my letters as dull and uninspired rather than as unfriendly." Only when the divorce was imminent, in late April, did Arvin stop trying to prove himself while appealing to Mary's sympathy. Enclosing a check for May, he began to tie up and square accounts. "I will make out a list of things if you continue to feel that you cannot trust me to send back whatever is yours," he wrote. It was the last of his letters that Mary Garrison would save.

Chapter Four

WHEN ARVIN TURNED thirteen, he'd been given a diary as a birthday gift. Lilienthal's family had just left Valparaiso, and Arvin pined to express his thoughts and feelings as freely as he had with his friend Dave. He wrote faithfully each day in his small leather daybook: about lawn socials and his paper route, about reading John Fox, H. B. Wright, Booth Tarkington, and Longfellow; about the opening of a Woolworth's and his sending away for book catalogues; about his dread of going into high school, his interest in the "Mexican trouble," his ambition to become "an advertising manager for a great manufacturing concern," and his support for the socialist program, which, he wrote, "listens pretty good to me." He wrote to give shape to his life and because it was painful for him to leave anything in an inchoate state and because he craved affirmation. Especially the last. "I feel so lonesome," he wrote in one of his first entries, "for an intimate friend."

In 1940, he began another diary, for the same reasons. Without Mary, he again was irremediably alone, with books and friendship substituting only so much for his "great and poignant need of love." Not that journal writing could take the place of intimacy, but it was an outlet; for a literary man alone and possessed of an insatiable need to write things down, the only outward record beyond books, articles, and letters of what one has done, witnessed, experienced, believed, felt—been. Arvin jotted something down each day, often only a couple of lines. He withheld from confessing his sins or any strenuous self-reflection. Later he would marvel at his reticence, but it was a time when much was left unsaid, even in secret.

He made two new friends at Smith upon whom he increasingly relied. Daniel Aaron was a dashing young Americanist who, after getting his doctorate at Harvard, stayed on as a counselor in American civilization, overlapping with Granville Hicks. He went to Smith because, "more than any other factor . . . Newton was there." Aaron considered Arvin "a highly significant figure," a paragon of meticulous, cross-disciplinary scholarship. Twelve years Arvin's junior, he was lanky and athletic, with long, diffident features, a straight shock of auburn hair, and, though he was a Jew from Los Angeles and Chicago, a breezy, incongruous WASP air. Married, an active leftist, he raced around campus on his bicycle with a squash racquet under one arm, puffing a pipe.

Arvin's other important new friend was a twenty-nine-year-old German émigré poet named Oskar Seidlin. Seidlin, half-Jewish and a member in his youth of revolutionary student groups, was a refugee from Nazi Germany, one of several who had found sanctuary at Smith during the 1930s. He had received his Ph.D. from the University of Basel, had learned English in a WPA training program, and he taught all his classes in German. He lived in an apartment in Arvin's building.

In February, a week after Arvin was made a full professor, and while Mary was living in Fort Lauderdale, he invited Seidlin to his apartment to listen to an NBC radio program of classical music, and the two slept together for the first time. Three days later Arvin gave Oskar a copy of *Whitman*, reprising, perhaps intentionally, his courtship of Mary, and Seidlin reciprocated with a book of his poems in German, *Mein Bilderbuch*. The gift moved Arvin almost to tears. Ten days later, on March 9, Seidlin slept over. As Arvin noted guardedly the next day in his journal, "Oskar here for breakfast all morning."

For Oskar, who was anxious, romantic, and still struggling with his English, Arvin must have been a stimulating partner but a taxing one. Still reeling from the divorce, he was also preoccupied by the widening war in Europe. On April 9, Germany invaded Denmark and Norway, occupying Copenhagen and Oslo. "Stupefying performance very evidently planned in detail for months ahead," Arvin reported in his journal. Like many displaced fellow travelers, he was scrabbling for a political foothold, and finding none. After attending a Socialist Party meeting in Northampton with Aaron's wife, Janet, at which the critic Richard Rovere spoke, he wrote in his journal, "A pretty gloomy experience." Worse, he was too troubled after teaching his classes to do anything at night but brood and drink. "Will I ever have a series of decent working evenings again?" he wrote plaintively two days later, on April 23.

A month later, on getting word that he no longer was married, he wrote two spare lines: "Found a card from Mary that indicated that the divorce decree was handed down on the 11th or thereabouts. Learned it, however, virtually without emotion."

Feeling less and less efficient, Arvin was staggered by depression. "The sense of stupefaction, as if from really physical shock," he wrote in mid-June, "—psychological air raids." Aaron and Seidlin, in their own ways, distracted him and tried to pull him up, but without success.

As always, when he was distressed, Arvin's health declined. He developed ailments and syndromes, followed by frustrating doctors' visits and questionable treatments. A case of sinusitis in mid-June put him in the hospital for a week, delaying his visit to Yaddo. A week later, complaining of fatigue, he visited a physician in Saratoga Springs who gave him testosterone shots, but the injections tired him out. Although a metabolism test showed nothing, he took Nembutal to sleep. Throughout August and September, Arvin sagged in the heat as he and Oskar took evening walks along Paradise, Smith's lovely millpond, which separated the campus from Northampton State Hospital, the sprawling hilltop psychiatric hospital that Smith girls called "Dippy Hall." He dragged himself through, but within a gathering gloom.

By October 1, a week after the beginning of school, he developed an alarming skin rash and all but stopped working, the surest sign yet that he was losing control of his life. "A rotten day," he wrote, "owing to too much Seconal last night, to overcome the noise below. Stayed here for lunch. Letter from Mary, then a telephone session with FSG [Frank Garrison, Mary's father] at his office. Exhaustion in consequence. Oskar and Dan to the rescue."

Arvin sank rapidly after that, reporting his decline in his journal:

Oct. 7: A beautiful day outwardly, but terrible inwardly. Fatigue, apprehension and tenseness. Spent the afternoon in Oskar's room. Dan here between five and six, very considerate. In the evening had an X-Ray treatment at Dr. Cooney. In spite of everything, read 100 pages of Henry Adams' stories.

Oct. 13: A bad night, owing to my loathsome affliction. Down to Cooney's office at 4:30 to see him . . . The rest of the day idle, followed by a worse night.

Oct. 14: A bad day again, after a trying night.

Oct. 27: Dr. Hobbs here in the morning. Agreed to let me have some morphine for the night.

Arvin's morass, like the widening war, was a snakepit of issues, causes, and effects. But what obsessed him—the "pain of the pain," as he would describe his inmost agony during a later crisis—was his homosexuality. At the age of forty, he was confronting the full reality of it for the first time, and was overwhelmed with shame. No longer could he deny that he was a man whose only sexual desires were for other men, one of "nature's mistakes," a legal and moral outcast. Within a year, millions of American men and women would come together in the greatest agglomeration in the nation's history, the World War II armed forces, and many of them would make a similar discovery. But Arvin's awareness, unlike theirs, was dawning in isolation, in a small puritanical town. From the time he had realized as a child the "insuperable chasm" between him and "normal" boys, he'd suffered his self-knowledge like a fever. He had tried to control it by marrying Mary, as if being a dutiful husband could mask or suppress any wayward urge. But now, with Oskar, it burst out, burning up his nerves, blinding his vision, erupting on his skin.

Arvin verged on constant panic. It fell to Aaron, who was taking him to many of his doctor's visits and filling in for him in some of his classes, to try to stop his slide. Aaron knew about Arvin's homosexuality, though it was not a subject they discussed. And while Arvin tried to disguise his depression because he feared the effect on his friends, Aaron had seen enough to know that Arvin was losing his grip. On October 29, after three weeks during which Arvin seemed to be teetering on the edge of a collapse, Aaron

drove him to Springfield, the nearest midsize city, to meet with a psychiatrist, who in turn referred Arvin to a specialist in Boston who had experience in treating homosexuals. Encouraged, Aaron took Arvin home and
helped him pack. The next morning, Oskar drove Arvin three hours across
the state to see Dr. Ives Hendrick, in a converted townhouse on Beacon
Street.

Hendrick, forty-two, was one of the city's first psychoanalysts, a future
president of the American Psychiatric Association. After graduating from
Yale and Yale Medical School, he'd trained at the Boston Psychopathic
Hospital and the Berlin Psychoanalytic Institute, then moved to the Back
Bay in 1930 to teach at Harvard Medical School and launch a private practice. His book, *Facts and Theories of Psychoanalysis,* was a widely used
primer on the works of Freud, whose own views on homosexuality were in-
consistent. Freud believed homosexuality was biological and that homosexuals couldn't be converted to heterosexuals. He also said it was caused
by sibling jealousy and other "early dynamic issues." Three years earlier
he'd written, "Homosexuality is assuredly no advantage, but it is nothing to
be ashamed of, no vice, no degradation, and cannot be classified as an illness."

After examining Arvin briefly, Hendrick committed him to McLean
Hospital, a wooded asylum in a town near Cambridge and a "clinical re-
source" of Harvard Medical School. McLean was where the cream of
Boston manhood collapsed from "exhaustion," prominent Massachusetts
families put away members who no longer could cope, and Harvard psychiatrists trained. Oskar drove Arvin to McLean, where he was installed in
a comfortable room. That evening he watched movies—"a curious experience"—with the other inmates. After an unremarkable night's sleep, he
met with Hendrick in the morning and went "on the couch" for the first
time—twenty years after telling Lilienthal he was "obsessed, literally," with
the desire to be psychoanalyzed.

What seems urgent and glamorous at the age of twenty may seem fatuous and unhelpful at forty. Arvin's analysis was a notable failure. Hendrick
believed homosexuality could be cured in cases where the patient had had
previous heterosexual interest and hadn't adopted the psychological traits
and habits of the other sex. Arvin appears to have slept with Mary, based

on the manly half-jokes in his letters. He wasn't effeminate. But there is little evidence that he desired women sexually, as he did men. Thus, his "psychoneurotic difficulties" were unlikely to be lessened by abstinence or normal sexual practices.

Arvin at first was buoyed by the sessions. Now that his sexual proclivities were slightly more out in the open—now that he had a diagnosis—he was cheered by the novelty of discussing and even making light of his situation. "I'm not at all sure that I am not a Grade-A faker," he wrote to Aaron. "And if it is true that I can probably be paroled in two weeks, no large bones will have been broken. Some may have been set . . ." He went on: "I think the stay here will be full of interest: certainly for the moment it seems very appreciably pleasanter than the Real World, and *naturally* there are a lot of nice guys here. Does it sound fatuous to say, they *would* be?"

Gradually, however, his optimism faded. On hearing the election returns on the radio in early November, he rejoiced briefly in Roosevelt's victory over the isolationist utility baron Wendell Wilkie, which made everything "brighter on one level," he wrote in his journal. But as the sessions with Hendrick continued, his hope for a cure grew dim. At one point, perhaps in frustration, Hendrick questioned Arvin's "queer pupillary reactions" and ordered a spinal tap. Apparently, little more could be done for him at McLean than in Northampton or Saratoga. Twelve days later Arvin met with Hendrick for "the last and futile time." On his discharge back to an unchanged world, he lugged his suitcases to Boston's South Station, took a train to Springfield, and switched to another train to Northampton; Oskar picked him up at the station and took him home. That night they went to see Sergei Eisenstein's Mexican movies at Smith.

Arvin couldn't bear the thought of standing at a blackboard and facing his students. Winter was descending, he felt fragile, and the bare trees and dying light compounded his gloom. He felt more trapped in Northampton than at any time since before his marriage, which, if nothing else, had made small-town life easier to bear by fostering certain illusions: stability, permanence, and a sense of home.

Agonizing over his options, he resolved to leave Smith, at least for a

time. There was no question of Arvin's academic stature. With two well-received books, countless essays and reviews, a Guggenheim, and a full professorship, he ranked near the top of his field, which he and others had
transformed from an academic backwater into a significant adjunct to most
college English departments, a discipline in which young people like
Daniel Aaron were now receiving Ph.D.'s. In a word, he was "distinguished"
if not "highly distinguished," and was likely to have his pick of any major
professorship if he were willing to campaign for it. Arvin disliked academia
generally and its careerism in particular. And he was too shy and uncomfortable to promote himself, especially after being hospitalized and admitting to himself, at least, that his "loathsome affliction" was probably
permanent and would follow him wherever he went. Still, as winter deepened, with biting cold and snow swooping down from the Yankee hills, he
completed his plans to get away.

In early January he discussed with Nielsen's successor, Herbert Davis,
another British-born, Harvard-trained literature scholar, the feasibility of
his taking a sabbatical. He put together an application for a fellowship at
Yale for the fall and took the train to Connecticut to visit Brooks, who encouraged him to make the move. He also continued to see Oskar, who
brought him sandwiches on the heavy days when he couldn't get out of
bed, and who increasingly blamed himself for Arvin's distress.

On an afternoon near the end of the month, they took a long walk and
discussed the painful subject of Arvin's "parallel lives." Again approaching
a low ebb, Arvin apparently realized how much he needed Oskar's closeness, and how little he could allow himself to have it. Even more than with
Mary, he suffered with the thought that he could neither love nor be loved.
Their discussion amounted to a break-up, although, as with Doughty and
others, the vagaries of the relationship meant that it merely passed to a
more undefined phase. Arvin, again feeling himself a failure at love,
plunged further into a private grief.

On February 6 he and Oskar braved the cold to attend a speech by
Eleanor Roosevelt at John M. Greene Hall. More than twenty-two hundred
students, teachers, and local Democrats packed the auditorium as the first
lady, wearing an afternoon dress and a corsage of orchids sent to her by
Coolidge's widow, Grace, stirringly addressed the twin evils of poverty and

starvation. She decried alike the conditions in Nazi concentration camps and in West Virginia, where there were no doctors and unemployed miners were dying of disease. Saying "Democracy must be worth defending," she urged students to support organized labor and the local Smith Alumnae Club's refugee scholarship fund.

Arvin slept poorly that night, owing to a "racket" coming from the hallway and an adjoining apartment, and in the morning he exploded at Oskar, who recoiled from his unreasonableness. Arvin was too frantic and upset to be calmed. He exploded again, muttering and weeping inconsolably. A doctor from the college infirmary arrived and sedated him. Then Aaron came. After a short consultation with the doctor, Aaron drove Arvin out West Street and up Hospital Hill, the town's sledding hill, and onto the grounds of the state hospital. In Arvin's condition, the physician and his friends now agreed, there seemed no alternative but to have him committed.

The campus was massive, many times the size of Smith's, with sweeping vistas in all directions. Unlike Smith, it was clustered not around "cottages" but around two huge, fortress-like structures. Aaron slowly followed the curving road that took them through snowbound meadows, where in the spring inmates played softball, and up to the main building, a gargantuan four-story brick edifice spanning the top of the hill.

He stopped the car at the main portico. The building was imposing, stretching almost a fifth of a mile from end to end, with wings upon wings buttressed by towers and with hundreds of windows caged in steel. Dwarfing Northampton's largest factory, it was a town in itself. Maple floors creaked and echoed as Aaron and Arvin entered through a cavernous rotunda capped by a two-story cupola, where grand staircases led invisibly past a marble fountain to the wards; women to the left, men to the right. As the formal entry hall of the former Northampton Lunatic Asylum, this was the core of the building, completed in 1855 and an outgrowth of the same reformist impulses and industrialized culture that had nurtured Hawthorne, Melville, and the transcendentalists, as well as early planned industrial cities like Lawrence and Lowell.

Arvin would have known the history of the place. In the early 1800s, those in Massachusetts who were deemed idiots, insane, and "furiously mad," and who weren't imprisoned or in almshouses, were generally kept home and "confined in cages, closets, cellars, stalls, pens . . . chained, naked, beaten with rods and lashed into obedience," according to Dorothea Dix, whose survey of the living conditions of the mentally ill led to the building of the state's first mental hospitals. Northampton, the third of these, was designed to provide moral and physical uplift by offering patients decent housing and food, manual labor, amusements such as bowling, games, and plays, clean air, and bucolic views. Now, with more than two thousand patients and dozens of worn buildings spread across more than five hundred acres, it was overcrowded, understaffed, and all but self-sustaining, a world more deeply isolated from life in Northampton than Smith was. Patients raised nearly all their own food; made, mended, and washed their clothes; made their own shoes; and cleaned and maintained the wards, all under the supervision of workers who mostly lived on the grounds in dormitories. There was a chapel with a pipe organ and an auditorium with a balcony lit by elegant fan windows. Arvin, heavily sedated, arrived at the infirmary and fell into oblivion, probably before he knew where he was.

He awoke the next morning "behind locked, unanswering doors," he wrote. Unlike McLean, this was "hard, bitter, unmasked reality, at the least and the worst." Arvin understood that he had failed to hold himself together and therefore was confined, for his own good, in a state mental asylum. His fellow inmates were "psychotic sufferers." Mrs. Nielsen visited in the late morning, and Aaron came and spoke with the physician. Arvin "thanked God" for the visits, he wrote. The next day Oskar came by with a friend and took Arvin for a drive, saving, he reported, "my poor reason."

On the third day, after demonstrating that he would be no trouble, he was released to Lower One, the least restricted of the wards. As it had expanded horizontally, the main building also had become hierarchical. The most disturbed patients lived in distant wings, in barred dormitories farthest from the rotunda—"back wards" typical of state asylums around the country, where horrific abuse and neglect were now first coming to light. The worst was Lower Four, the "bullpen," where the most violent and dangerous patients were kept tied to slatted beds or locked naked in seclusion rooms with nothing but a mattress covered with hard canvas, because when they were given blankets and clothes, their guards reported, they ate them. Less troubled patients who acted up were taken to the basement for "hydrotherapy"; they were submerged on canvas slings into tubs of warm flowing water for about three hours. Those who remained agitated were kept packed in wet sheets, spitting and screaming, sometimes around the clock for a month or more, unwrapped only so that they could be "repacked."

Arvin saw none of this. He shared a double room with an elderly ex-gambler named Jack O'Brien, whose breathing troubles kept Arvin up at night. He had use of the hospital library and was free to take day trips. Patients in Lower One were treated more like parolees than like inmates.

People in Northampton and at Smith generally feared the state hospital. Mothers whisked children indoors when its sirens sounded, terrified that someone had escaped. The work farm atmosphere—the image of men and women in coarse clothes toiling in the fields—had become part of the local landscape, tolerated for the good it did. By his fourth day, surprisingly, Arvin warmed to his new environment. He was not mistreated; he took walks in the afternoon where he could look out and see the whole Connecticut Valley, all the way to Amherst or, facing west, the rolling Berkshire foothills; he ate meals in the cafeteria that were fresh and plentiful. He even managed to get some reading done and find amiable companions who stirred his democratic impulses. "What strange and fine, loveable people some of my fellow inmates are," he wrote in his journal. On the fifth night, the staff gave him Amytol for sleep, enough to overpower even his roommate's snores.

Arvin remained in the asylum for eight days, becoming stable enough to go home, temporarily, but not to work. He brooded over what to do with himself, then perked up on February 19 when he received what he oddly termed "a very favorable offer" from the same private sanitarium in White Plains where Mary had been treated two years earlier. He welcomed the hospital's letter as if it were an invitation to accept a coveted fellowship, and three days later, after telling President Davis that he was taking off the rest of the semester, took a train to New York in a driving snowstorm. He stayed overnight at the Biltmore, boarding a train the following morning for White Plains.

Modeled on a country estate, the sanitarium was the antithesis of the state asylum; more like a serene, privileged club than an institution. On his first day—"a pleasant sunny day"—Arvin wrote letters and read the *Times* during the morning, before and after a walk; took a nap in the afternoon; and read a little of Carl Sandburg's poetry in a book lent to him by another patient, Dwight Morrow, Jr. He joined Morrow for supper in the dining room, and the two became instant friends, despite differences that, only a short time before, would have led Arvin to reject him as a bitter class enemy. Morrow's father had been a close associate of J. P. Morgan. As president of Coolidge's class at Amherst, he had supervised the positioning of Coolidge as a national hero after the Boston police strike, a favor for which Coolidge repaid him by appointing him ambassador to Mexico. Morrow's mother, Betty, had recently served as Smith's acting president, and his brother-in-law was Charles Lindbergh, whose anti-Semitism and isolationism Arvin reviled. Morrow's sister, the novelist Anne Morrow Lindbergh, was a Smith alumna whose recent writings sought to lay a basis for American neutrality in the war. Still, as Arvin had learned at the state hospital, mental asylums were great equalizers. Young Morrow had attended Amherst and Harvard, and Arvin enjoyed spending time with him.

During the next three and a half months, Arvin strove to be a model patient, which meant taming his outbursts while learning to play games and sports and mastering simple occupational therapies. He tried Ping-Pong, feebly; learned billiards, rummy, basketry, printing, metalworking, golf, and baseball. He found, encouragingly, that he could bowl, eventually scoring 173: "Three strikes in succession," he wrote in his journal. He showed pride in his accomplishments, tallying them, pathetically if not ironically, in his daybook: "March 14. Finished the basket today with great sense of achievement." Some of his satisfaction seems genuine, as when he managed to dance with two "lady" patients: "Not so formidable or as fatiguing as I expected it to be." He drew the line, however, at group singing in the auditorium, "a dubious charm for me."

Slowly his depression lifted and his temper quieted down. He appears to have spent no more time on the couch, although he did see psychiatrists, chiefly after episodes when his sleeplessness returned and he became distraught during the night. He wrote vigorous, hopeful letters and received more visitors, including Brooks, who came down from Westport three times and whose "kindness and fellow-feeling" gave Arvin special encouragement. Brooks, after all, had undergone far worse, for far longer, and had come back to produce *The Flowering of New England*, which, four years earlier, had won a Pulitzer Prize. Brooks didn't consider himself cured; years after his recovery, he would write, "There remained in my stomach as it were a hard ball of panic." Arvin recognized his goal not as being cured but as simply surviving. Surviving and working.

On May 23, he reported in his journal that Brooks had persuaded him not to go back to Smith in the fall but, instead, to work full time on his writing. Arvin stayed in White Plains a few more days, and, over the next month, circulated among the few places he felt safest—his apartment, Yaddo, the Hickses' house in Grafton—trying to decide what to do. On June 20, two days before the news that the Nazis had invaded the Soviet Union, he took a long walk along Paradise with Herbert Davis to discuss the matter. The heat was beastly, and Arvin panted for air under the branches. Afterward, they had a beer on the lawn of the president's house, overlooking the valley. Heat shimmers radiated from the fields. He told Davis he couldn't possibly teach the coming semester.

Ten days later Arvin left Northampton for Yaddo, the only place where, in the tense, uncertain summer of 1941, he felt that he could remain without fear of cracking up.

The "large season," as summers at Yaddo were called, had grown, and life in the mansion bustled. The novelist Katherine Anne Porter had been in residence since the previous year, the acknowledged queen of the colony. In June she had been joined by Eudora Welty and Carson McCullers, both young Southern writers enjoying precocious success, visiting for the first time and vying for Porter's attentions. The political squabbles of the 1930s, when Stalinists and Trotskyites refused to eat together in the baronial dining room, gave way to more personal complications.

McCullers, twenty-four years old, was New York's newest literary darling after the publication, the previous year, of *The Heart Is a Lonely Hunter*, although she looked more like a gangly sixteen-year-old boy, wearing men's jackets and trousers, straight bangs, and the half-smiling expression of a drowsy child. She was married to her teenage sweetheart but was mostly attracted to women, and at Yaddo she'd become infatuated with the chic, slim-hipped Porter, who lived in Katrina Trask's bedroom, an enormous boudoir with Moorish gingerbread over the alcoves and a bay of seventeen mullioned windows. One night she pounded on Porter's bedroom door, urging, "Please, Katherine Anne, let me come in and talk with you— I do love you so very much," then lay down across the threshold. By the time Arvin arrived, on July 1, Porter and Welty had commandeered a small table at one end of the dining room while McCullers and a group of four or five others seized another. The "Table of the Sensitives," one heterosexual guest called the latter.

Guests who had known Arvin for years were startled to see him choose to eat at that table. In 1939, he had been elected a trustee of the Yaddo Corporation, and he was visiting now not as a guest but as a "director in residence," a position of some esteem, as most directors didn't attend the colony as artists. He appeared, despite his recent hospitalizations, as formal and fastidious as ever, a mild, balding, middle-aged professor who, as one friend from the period would recall, "wore dark suits to breakfast, sat like a furled umbrella, and buttered his toast to the edges." He looked like a banker in an artist's world. But Arvin was fascinated by the conversation, as when the composer Colin McPhee talked openly about the Balinese boy whom he loved. And he was drawn instantly to McCullers, who told anyone who'd listen about her affair with the beautiful Swiss journalist and photographer Annemarie Clarac-Schwarzenbach.

Arvin and McCullers became urgent great friends, a colony staple but also the only kind of friendship in which the charming, needy McCullers seemed able to engage. They had similar molluscan work habits, holing up after breakfast and not appearing until the drinking hour, so they remained worn-looking and pale "when everybody else was brown as chocolate," McCullers wrote. Most nights after supper they rode into town in the Yaddo station wagon and headed directly to the sedate bar of the Worden Hotel, where they huddled and drank and talked until late about books, writers, the other guests, and, especially, their sexual lives. Arvin told her about Oskar, who she said reminded her of Annemarie. McCullers confided in him about her crushes on other women. A year earlier, impetuously, she had called on Greta Garbo, whose beautifully masculine femininity she idolized and who rebuffed her. McCullers was undaunted. "Newton," she announced, declaring her bisexuality, "I was born a man."

Though McCullers could be bold and lively, it was clear that she also was lonely, estranged, anxious about producing a second book worthy of the hyperbole that had greeted her first, and deeply, frightfully sad. Arvin, still partly submerged himself, consoled her and took her under his wing. Toward the end of the summer he invited McCullers along on a car trip to Quebec with the Hickses and their teenage daughter, hoping the change of scene would brighten her outlook. The week-long trip—"one sustained conversation with moving scenery," Arvin called it—marked a turning point for them both.

A few miles from Yaddo, Arvin told Hicks to stop the heavily loaded car at a liquor store. He and McCullers went in and returned with several gallon jugs of sherry and four bottles of brandy and whiskey, which they wedged around their feet as they sat, shoulder to shoulder, in the cramped rear seat. For two days, Arvin lectured her as they sipped their drinks. "But Carson," he announced, "that isn't Montaigne—it's La Rochefoucauld." And "But I really don't believe Yaddo could be called baroque, Carson." Loquaciously, he urged Hicks, who was about to turn forty and was still directionless two years after his break with the Communist Party, to settle on a career either as a critic or a novelist but not try to do both. "After forty they don't forgive you anything," Arvin advised.

In Quebec, Arvin signed in himself and McCullers at their hotel as Mr. and Mrs. Newton Arvin. But the next morning, he asked for a separate room. Hicks didn't know whether they parted because Arvin "was an insomniac and Carson had not had a good night's sleep, or if they had had some kind of sexual experience when one had perhaps pushed the other further than he wanted to go," but afterward McCullers adopted Arvin's habit of wearing eyeshades to bed. Clearly, Arvin and McCullers were influencing each other in ways that no one else had done. Arvin's spirits lifted markedly in McCullers's worshipful, sexually nonthreatening company, as when she told him he was her most precious friend and the most comforting man she knew. He, in turn, urged her to end her marriage in order not to face the same desperate, alienating dissatisfaction he had undergone. By the time the Hickses dropped them together in Northampton for a few days, McCullers had resolved to return to New York to seek a divorce, while Arvin, more confident than he'd been in a year, decided to return to Yaddo for the "small season" before he resumed teaching during the second semester. The Yaddo mansion, which required a ton of anthracite a day to heat, would be shuttered for the winter, but he could spend the fall as a guest in one of the smaller houses, resting and reading for his next book, a study of Melville. Yale, he decided, could wait.

Arvin wrote to Aaron from Yaddo about his change of plans—and of attitude. "I ride a good deal on the new bike, which is perhaps too heavy for a weakie like me, but I enjoy it enormously; and I do more or less work out of doors, on good days. I'm reading some Proust—and Balzac's *Peau de Chagrin* (have you tackled that?)—and intend to have a go at some Dostoevsky very soon . . . our days are very quiet ones." To Aaron's news that the college was looking for a new librarian, Arvin, who'd long lamented the gaps in Smith's collections, wrote exultantly, "I don't know when I've heard anything that toned me up so much. It reconciles me to coming back to Northampton for life more than almost anything (except, say, the prospect of finding an alluring mistress there or a profoundly quiet apartment) could do."

With his depression and anxiety largely under control, Arvin spent a pleasant fall at Yaddo, temporarily secure despite the changes wrought by the wrenching events of the past two years. He seemed tolerably resigned to the reality of being, in middle age, not only single but homosexual, and planning to return "for life" to a job in a small college town he had spent most of the past two decades trying to escape. He even felt strong enough to confront his new political foes. Since the Hitler-Stalin pact and the decline of Marxist criticism, the so-called New Critics had been on the rise. These were mostly academic intellectuals—Southerners, mainly—who rejected the use of history and psychology in criticism, favoring instead the more "scientific" notion that a text ought to be judged purely on its own merits, not on the author's intent or the context in which it was created. The New Critics fetishized form and thus were militantly apolitical, or so they claimed, leading Brooks to comment that they doubted the progress of everything save their own criticism. Arvin considered them puritanical and antidemocratic—reactionaries. "Their day is sunny just now," he wrote to Aaron, "but it will be brief, you may be sure. They are simply not in touch with the nature of things."

Around Thanksgiving, two weeks before Japan bombed Pearl Harbor, he wrote cheerfully to Aaron that he would be returning to "Hamp" the following Monday and urged him to stop by late in the day. "I am feeling fit as a fiddle, or rather I am and do (without exception) whenever I have a good night's sleep: when I don't," he added, "I feel like Mencken's suicidal flatfoot (who, as you may remember, tried to hang, drown, shoot and poison himself all in the same swoop)."

Early 1942 was an anxious, uncertain time. Leningrad had been under siege for more than six months. German U-boats along the Eastern seaboard were sinking oil tankers "so close that a chorus girl in a Miami penthouse could see men die in flaming oil," Eric Sevareid wrote. The Associated Press reported that Germany had two dirigibles outfitted to hover offshore while bombers released from their holds "loosed destruction on our cities." In Northampton, the former district attorney Edward L. O'Brien was put in charge of civilian defense, coordinating blackouts and air-raid warnings and marshaling "volunteer, unpaid protective units." During blackouts, Smith students joined local wardens patroling hushed streets under eerie, black-velvet skies.

Oskar, although not a citizen, was inducted in the Army and sent to Wyoming for basic training. Arvin, ostensibly bereft, was probably relieved to see him go. He was looking forward to "settling down" to Melville, a task for which, as always, he needed extreme freedom and isolation. At Yaddo that summer he had overlapped with McCullers only for a few days, and was named chief "fire warden" of the colony, informing the guests "of the necessary measures Yaddo would take in case the Luftwaffe happened to be in the vicinity of Saratoga," according to Alfred Kazin, a first-time visitor.

Living in the thin-walled tenement on West Street proved no easier than it had before his collapse. Arvin still had nights when he couldn't sleep, and his weariness and gloom made working there almost impossible. A spiritual pall descended on him. Wallowing, he missed Oskar's soothing presence but couldn't allow himself to find comfort with anyone else. "Every capacity for tenderness is present," he wrote to Doughty, "except the one power of penetrating or being penetrated with the last intimacy." In this, as in many of his letters to Doughty, the double meanings of certain words suggest that his impotence may have become more than merely "affectational."

During the fall, Arvin was buoyed by the presence at Smith of Edmund Wilson, for whom he had campaigned as a visiting lecturer. When Wilson, whose criticism Arvin admired nearly as much as Brooks's but whom he didn't know personally, sent him an admiring note of thanks, Arvin responded with pained modesty, as if his career, inadequate as it had been, was long over. " 'Work' seems pretty much in the preterit tense to me, after just twenty years of schoolmastering," he wrote, "but that doesn't keep me from being genuinely pleased by what you say of what I used to write."

Arvin rejoiced at having regular contact with a literary intelligence as ravenous as his own. Wilson drove over each week from Wellfleet, on Cape Cod, to give a public lecture, a two-hour seminar, and a three-hour course on James Joyce, which he crammed with a preliminary study of Virgil, Dante, Shakespeare, Pushkin, and the history of the novel. Like Arvin, he was too formal and reticent a lecturer to be a good teacher, and, as Aaron recalled, had no idea—and little interest in—how to teach students. Like Arvin, too, he was less than collegial toward others whose work he didn't respect, and some of them felt his sting. Kazin, also at Smith that year, remembered Wilson, who was five feet six inches and weighed almost two hundred pounds, for "a certain seediness . . . the lack of small talk, the grumpy conversation on every topic he came to." Kazin wrote, "With his round bald head and that hoarse, heavily breathing voice box coming out of the red face of an overfed hunting squire, Wilson looked apoplectic, stiff, out of breath." But Arvin and Wilson became close friends, sharing similar politics and literary tastes and an active disdain for the classroom. After twelve weeks of commuting, Wilson wrote, in exhaustion, "I've decided the whole thing, for a writer, is unnatural, embarrassing, disgusting, and that I might better do journalism, after all, when I have to make money."

For Arvin, who had tried journalism and failed, the problem of how to remain a writer within the constraints of teaching for a living became ever more onerous. The college now shared its campus with the Naval Reserve Midshipmen's School. Sitting in his office, in a two-story Victorian cottage overlooking Paradise Pond, Arvin was jarred by the marching footsteps of Waves going to their classes. He was getting nowhere with Melville and was tumbling deeper into lassitude, unsure that he would ever write again. He craved solitude, a place of his own as tranquil and sacred as an abbey.

Near the war's end, he thought he found one. In September 1944 he moved to the quiet third-floor walk-up at 45 Prospect Street; it would become his first, and last, adult home. The house was severe and brooding, yet for Arvin it was perfect. Though it was two doors down from Smith's private day school, Gill Hall, it was literally above the noise, even during school hours. It had been built around 1870 by James Russell Trumbull, owner and editor of the *Gazette*, giving it a sturdy literary provenance. Arvin's four attic rooms, narrow bath, galley kitchen, and screened-in back porch, which offered a commanding view of the town, the fertile Connecticut Valley, and a strand of emerald-colored hills—the Holyoke Range—were laid out almost exactly along the axes of a compass, providing a sheltered lookout in all directions.

Arvin arranged it to suit himself. His furniture was middling—bentwood chairs in the living room, a solid wood dining table and four straight-backed chairs in the middle room, a gateleg table for a desk, a couple of heavy chests for his wardrobe. Arvin never learned to cook—he took most of his meals at the faculty club or inexpensive restaurants "downstreet"— so the kitchen, though barely big enough to turn around in, sufficed. The bathroom was tiny, with a small washbasin barely twenty-four inches high, and a narrow, fifty-four-inch tub, too small to soak in. Still, the apartment had important amenities for a man alone. For the first time Arvin had a spare room as a study with a daybed for out-of-town guests, ample shelves for his books, and more than enough closets: two in the bedroom, one containing a built-in chest in the study, one in the bathroom, and a long walk-in under the eave in the living room. The place was Arvin's attempt in middle age to settle down and have a real home. If he couldn't have a normal life, he felt, he could at least have the comfort and trappings of one.

Too soon, however, he had trouble. Inwardly he was so distressed that no mere change of domicile could salve him. Even in his new study, a peaceful, tree-shaded room with a view, across the street, of Northampton's most historic house, the eighteenth-century homestead of Jonathan Edwards's grandfather, Arvin couldn't find the energy to write. By January, facing another bleak winter alone, he all but gave up. Walking by Paradise, he stopped to watch a group of skaters on the pond. He then stumbled home, opened a bottle of liquor, put on a recording of John McCormack singing Hugo Wolf's musical setting of Ganymede—the Greek myth about a Trojan boy of great beauty who was carried away by Zeus to become cupbearer to the gods—and swallowed sixteen Nembutals. He was discovered the next morning by Aaron, who took him to the hospital, where his stomach was pumped.

With the end of the war that summer, Arvin was in a chronic state of depression. Although his place in twentieth-century American letters was secure, the war had reversed the country's political currents. Leftist writers like Arvin, who had dreamed of an American socialism, found themselves increasingly out of step and in retreat from the anticommunist New Critics on the right. All this compounded Arvin's gloom. He had failed at marriage, was in anguish about his homosexuality, was trapped at the edge of small-town life, and was becoming a political pariah. Worse, he had been unable to write all but a few short pieces.

Again it was Edmund Wilson who helped elevate him briefly. In April 1946, Arvin sent Wilson a volume of Hawthorne's short stories that he had introduced and edited for Knopf, along with a handwritten note complimenting him on his work at *The New Yorker,* where Wilson was on staff, and stating "how remarkable a piece of work" he regarded Wilson's lascivious new novel, *Memoirs of Hecate County,* which would soon be banned as obscene. "About some things in it," Arvin wrote flatteringly, "I have that rather rare feeling, 'How much I wish I had written them!' " Wilson had recently written an especially cruel review of McCullers's *The Member of the Wedding,* to which Arvin gently took exception, but the letter apparently was intended as a bouquet meant to inspire Wilson to review *his* book. It worked. Two months later, Wilson praised *Hawthorne's Short Stories* in his *New Yorker* column, singling out Arvin's twelve-page introduction as "absolutely a triumph of its kind . . . It is pleasant," he wrote, "to find a book of this sort in which the anthologizer is worthy of the anthologized."

Arvin was exultant. He had considered the introduction a test—to demonstrate to himself in the wake of his breakdown "the capacity to write five thousand continuous words and make sense of them." Given Wilson's enthusiastic review, he believed he may have recovered enough to resume full-scale efforts as a biographer. "There are not three people in the country whose good opinion would mean so much to me," he wrote to Wilson appreciatively. "I think I have at least two more books in me, and even if it takes ten years to write them, I am in very good heart for the undertaking." Feeling free at last of the "sloth, acedia and self-distrust" that had long plagued him, he resolved to spend the summer at Yaddo, immersed in Melville.

This was the semipublic Arvin, the hopeful Arvin of letters to friends whom he sought not to trouble with his depression. But, as always, there were private agonies. Even if he believed he could write again, which now as always meant more to him than all else, his fear and self-loathing were not easily let go. "Woke again just after five," he'd written recently in his journal. "Thoughts of death and self-destruction. 'Morning tears.'" As he prepared to leave for Yaddo, Arvin was less sure of himself than his letter to Wilson may have suggested. Typically, he sought comfort in the presence there of old loves like Doughty, and in Yaddo's protective shell, which for a few weeks allowed him to live as open an emotional and sexual life as he believed possible. "You know how much I love you," he wrote to Doughty, already in Saratoga. "It is a luxury only to allow oneself to *say* it from time to time. I am still, after all these years, incredulous that I should have come upon you. Is a completer mutual sympathy conceivable between fallible human beings? I should certainly not expect it."

Chapter Five

ARVIN TRAVELED BY train to Saratoga on June 12, 1946, one day after a freak tornado ripped through Northampton. As usual, he was frantic to get away and, especially, to avoid the tiresome end-of-term hoopla at Smith, which ran for five days and included the traditional last chapel service, two performances of the senior Rally Day show, an alumnae parade through town, a picnic, several luncheons, the ritual planting of ivy, the nighttime illumination of the campus with thousands of Japanese lanterns, a baccalaureate service, organ vespers, and, finally, graduation itself. Dr. C. E. Kenneth Mees, vice-president in charge of research at the Eastman Kodak Company, was scheduled to speak on "Philosophy and Atomic Energy."

Evacuating Northampton as early as possible had become an annual rite—one of the things that enabled Arvin to return and survive the year—but this year Yaddo beckoned with special urgency. Not only would he be with Doughty, but the mansion had been reopened for the first time since early during World War II, ensuring a large, lively season. All America was returning headlong to "peacetime normalcy." Yaddo's guests, after years of rationing and shortages, craved more than ever its *fin de siècle* grandeur. The visitor list looked especially salutary and strong: besides McCullers and Porter, the leftist journalist Agnes Smedley was already in residence, as was Leo Lerman, center of a New York cultural circle that included William Faulkner, Evelyn Waugh, and Marlene Dietrich. There were some promising younger writers (the novelist Marguerite Young; the poet and critic John Malcolm Brinnin), and Doughty had written excitedly in a letter about one in particular, the twenty-one-year-old short story writer Truman Capote.

"The child really has an uncanny talent—almost frightening," Doughty, who was forty-two and taught at Harvard, wrote on June 2. What Doughty did not mention was that he and Capote had slept together, and that Capote, whose literary accomplishments so far consisted of being fired as a messenger at *The New Yorker* and having a few well-received stories published in a women's fashion magazine, had all of Yaddo spinning, even the worldly Porter, whom Capote called "St. Katherine Anne P." Entranced by the sight of McCullers and Capote dancing together one night in the grand kitchen—McCullers, the taller of the two, jouncing mannishly while the towheaded, bottom-heavy Capote spun around her, inventing clever pirouettes—Porter had turned to Elizabeth Ames, who was half-deaf, and shouted, "From where did he come, dear?" to which Ames responded, "From *Harper's Bazaar.*"

Except perhaps for McCullers, who'd befriended him in New York the previous year and sponsored his visit to Yaddo so that he could work on his first novel, no one had ever seen anything like him: a Southerner, a *child*, flitting about like some exotic bird, yet riveting all attention and animating everyone around him. "He has a child's directness, a child's indifference to propriety," Brinnin wrote in his journal, "and so gets to the heart of matters with an audacity strangers find outrageous, then delightful. Yet nothing he says or does accounts for the magnet somewhere in his makeup that exerts itself like a force beyond logic: he's responsible for turning the summer into a dance of bees."

Arvin was smitten at once, despite his weariness and gloom. Ensconced in Katrina Trask's enormous boudoir, the most esteemed studio on the grounds, he was directly downstairs from Capote's Tower Room, once Lady Katrina's "secret hideaway." An all-white, light-flooded aerie filling the peak of the mansion's five-story central turret, the room was decorated with painted choir stalls, marble busts, and a comfortable brass bed, and was the most private one in the main house. Within two days, he and Capote began exchanging nightly visits. Doughty, so recently a Tower Room guest himself, abruptly returned to Cambridge, simplifying—and perhaps deliberately facilitating—their liaison.

"I can't down the desire to tell you, and only you," Arvin wrote to Doughty several days later, saying he had been hit by "this Thing that one can surely expect but once or twice in a lifetime." After so recently confessing his love for Doughty, Arvin's indiscretion may have seemed insensitive, even cruel, but he was consumed with feelings that just days earlier he had thought impossible, and Doughty understood. It was as if nearly a decade of anguished self-loathing, of fearing he would never write again and that he had no life, receded all at once into the dim past, and Arvin was suddenly alive, tasting every pleasure as if for the first time. "The weather was supernatural on Friday, and again on Sunday, and on Tuesday too," he continued, "and maybe sometime I can tell you what the cool blue air, and the green light, and a certain wash of moonlight falling into this room of mine as the twilight fused imperceptibly into it—what things of this sort did to my eyes and my command of speech and my senses, and my whole nature."

Capote, too, was swept up. Despite the extreme differences between them, he found Arvin "a charming person, cultivated in every way, with the most wonderfully subtle mind. He was like a lozenge that you could keep turning to the light, one way or another, and the most beautiful colors would come out."

Neither could have imagined the effect the other would have on him, or he on the other. Capote, who cared about writing as much as Arvin did, was dazzled by Arvin's learnedness, erudition, experience with language, and passion for books. Arvin, who so recently feared he was incapable of love and shamefully hid his homosexuality from the world, melted irresistibly in the glow of Capote's youthful salaciousness. The phenomenon was well known. Oscar Wilde had famously described it as "that deep physical affection that is as pure as it is perfect . . . [which] repeatedly exists between an elder and a younger man, when the elder man has intellect, and the younger man has all the joy, hope and glamour." At the time, Wilde was on trial for indecency, and would spend two years in a filthy London prison, ruined and disgraced, largely because of this statement, an impromptu reply to a prosecutor's question: "What is the 'Love that dare not speak its name'?" Yet Arvin and Capote were in the throes of just such an affection, blinded to any other reality that might make their feelings for each other unworkable.

The two were seldom apart. At Yaddo, they ate lunch and dinner together, walked into town to the movies, took long moonlit walks around the grounds, and launched a two-year love affair that encompassed the happiest, most productive period of Arvin's life. Arvin promptly read three of Capote's stories and pronounced them "lovely and frightening and pure and tender." As with McCullers, who, like Doughty, left the colony soon after Arvin's arrival, Arvin found in Capote's Southern gothicism a darkness and beauty as rich and poetic as Hawthorne's. Sitting in the mullioned window bay of his huge room, with a portable typewriter propped on his knees, he furiously typed love letters to his "Little T":

> But you know, dearest T.C., that if I ever really began a "letter" to you it could have no imaginable end—or even beginning—for it would just have to circle for ever and ever, like a great wheel, about the one central fact; and you know what that fact is, and there are either millions of ways of telling it or one way. I love you dearly, and if you wish, I will write that over and over again until this page is filled up, and many more pages, like a bad boy kept in after school, whose teacher (in some perverse way) wishes to make him happy instead of wretched. Only I am not a bad boy, and neither are you; we are very good indeed and we shall be better and better as time wears on—for we are at the source of good, and we are drinking the water of truth, and what we are making between us is purely beautiful. Is it possible to be better than that?

Arvin's shame about his sexuality, so troubling before, quickly dissolved in Capote's flamboyant presence. Returning to Northampton for the fall term, feeling flushed and revitalized, while Capote went back to New York, he even indulged in sexual joking, writing in a letter after one of their visits, "LOST probably in Manhattan, one peppermint stick, beautifully pink and white, wonderfully straight, deliciously sweet. About a hand's length. Of great intrinsic and also sentimental value to owner."

Arvin became during the summer and fall, in one sense, a new man—freer about his sexual desires, less ashamed, more open, happier than ever before—although his old fretful, cloistered self clung on. He was especially torn as he and Capote discussed the possibility of their living together. New York, where Capote still lived at home with his alcoholic mother and step-father on Park Avenue, was out, surely; Arvin had long since surrendered any hope of surviving the bustle of a teeming metropolis, and he shrank from the glittering social world for which Capote seemed inexorably headed. So, realistically, was Northampton, where Arvin lived under more or less strict protective cover as a faculty bachelor. It was unthinkable that a staid New England townsman, even a reluctant one like Arvin, would co-habit with someone as flagrantly *undisguised* as Capote, who raced through town on his visits trailing a signature long scarf. And yet Arvin knew that there was an even steeper impediment to their truly sharing a life: himself. "Precious," he wrote one Saturday after Capote, who was struggling un-successfully to get writing done at home, pressed to spend more time to-gether:

> It distresses me unspeakably that things should be such hell for you there in the city, and that you should be so far from well, in the midst of everything else. The impulse is almost overwhelming to call you on the phone or wire you, and insist on your coming back to Northampton and staying with me indefinitely. I have just barely enough courage to tell myself No—courage enough and perhaps cruelty enough. But, dearest Truman, I cannot conceal from myself that this might be a terrible disappointment for both of us, and if it were, might do something to our happiness that I cannot bear to have done. I have never felt such grief over my own limitations as I do this fall. But self-knowledge can be flouted only at deadly peril, and though I cannot explain it even to myself, still less to you (and therefore not at all to anyone else), I know too well what this primordial unanswerable hunger for a certain number of hours or days of solitude means, or is—I know too well to be will-ing to lie to you. Maybe if I had ever been analyzed, I would un-derstand it better, and perhaps, even, not feel it at all. But I *haven't*

been analyzed, and never will be now, and I must make out as best I can. It is as if something physical like blood were ebbing out of me—not always, but much of the time—when I am not alone; and the point comes when my identity begins to slip away from me, and I cease to be a whole person even for someone I love.

Whether Arvin had forgotten—or, more likely, was reluctant to tell his young lover about—his futile sessions at McLean with Dr. Hendrick, his confession bore an undeniable pathos and truthfulness. He simply was too solitary a figure to surrender himself to another person, no matter how beloved. *"It is as if something physical like blood were ebbing out of me . . ."* To Arvin, solitude was oxygen, virtually a life force. And as he had learned with Mary, the too-near presence of another human soul was certain slow death. As much as he loved Capote, as much as he had never felt more loved or complete, the ultimate intimacy of a shared life, he was sure, could only suffocate him. The same impulse to yank back his hand from passion's flame overwhelmed him now as it always had, even as he understood that he might never again so utterly love anyone.

Throughout the fall, Capote visited every other weekend, racing from the train station and up Arvin's stairs. He sat in the back of some of Arvin's classes, then continued back at Arvin's apartment the literary education he'd neglected by not having gone to college—Proust, Hawthorne, Melville, Whitman, James, dozens of major and lesser poets, Shakespeare. "It's beautiful here, the weather crystal," he wrote to a friend. "The mountains rimming the town are burning green and blue and there is a cold brown touch of Autumn everywhere. An enormous apple tree, very heavy with fruit, grows under the window; aside from burning leaves, is there anything more nostalgic than the odor of ripening October apples? I am working hard, and *thinking clearly,* and am so very happy here with Newton: he is so good to me, and for me." To Doughty, he wrote, "I love October so much and wish it could always be." But for Arvin, who eschewed nostalgia, their love had already evolved into something else, something more limited and self-preserving: "our beautiful, double solitude," he called it in a letter to Capote.

"You are . . . ," Arvin wrote, "a little wizard or magician or alchemist of some wonderful Gothic kind, my darling, and you have drawn a ring around me in the midst of which I stand helpless and benumbed and spell-stricken: only when you kiss me do I come to life. I love you!" The contradiction was that to resist falling utterly under Capote's spell, Arvin drew a second, tighter ring about himself.

In January 1947, America faced the first great political test of the postwar era, combining the country's two most volatile national security issues. The first was how to maintain primacy—and secrecy—over "the atom." The other, equally charged and foreboding, was how to combat the secret menace of domestic communism, now that international communism was America's global enemy. The country seemed ideologically rigid. Though the Communist Party was all but defunct, its strength among intellectuals during the Popular Front period of the late 1930s had left a political and cultural residue that aroused fear, hatred, and suspicion among fervent anticommunists. As the two issues merged for the first time, the man at the center of the dispute was Lilienthal, Arvin's oldest and still perhaps most trusted friend.

Lilienthal, who had been appointed by Roosevelt to chair the TVA and was reappointed by Harry Truman, emerged from the war, like the country itself, exhausted but bristling with ambition. By the war's end, the TVA had become the largest utility in America, and Lilienthal, its Jewish, Harvard-trained chairman, was associated with galloping socialism more than any other top New Dealer. He had learned about the power of the atom belatedly, along with the rest of the nation, when the first atomic bomb exploded over Hiroshima in August 1945. Then, less than a year later, Truman appointed him to head the new civilian controlled Atomic Energy Commission, formed by Congress both to usher in the new age of atomic power and to direct the country's nuclear arms buildup in its race with the Soviet Union. Though he doubted his qualifications for the job, Lilienthal, at the age of forty-six, believed the country faced a new and grave danger "unless the people are properly informed of the facts" about the atomic whirlwind ignited by the war's end.

The position he was to assume was potentially as important as any in Washington after the war, but Lilienthal was a highly controversial figure,

and Truman regarded his confirmation as a test of both the country's political will and his own. The military, which had been in charge of atomic research from the outset, was yielding control grimly and with grave
reluctance. Many considered Truman a weak leader, unequal to the Soviet
threat. There was fear that if Russia obtained our nuclear secrets, it would
use them to destroy us. Meanwhile, accusations were mounting that the
New Deal, in which Lilienthal had played such a prominent part, had been
riddled with communists. In an increasingly bipolar world, loyalty was fast
becoming the main—the only—watchword.

Amid ratcheting tensions, Lilienthal's confirmation hearings in Congress, which began on January 27, became instantly explosive, a national
sensation broadcast widely by the news services. One Republican senator
labeled the TVA "a hotbed of Communism" and implied that Lilienthal was
disloyal because he couldn't tell the committee the exact location of his
parents' birthplaces in Eastern Europe. Another, Robert Taft, called Lilienthal "a typical power-hungry bureaucrat" who was "soft on the subject of
Communism." Taft's coinage was new—ideological "softness" had never
before been a patriotic litmus test—and Lilienthal answered the charge,
and the strains of nativism and anti-Semitism underlying the questions
about his lineage, with an unrehearsed soliloquy that many would regard as
the most passionate and prophetic defense of liberal principles of the postwar era:

> I deeply believe in the capacity of democracy to surmount any tri-
> als that may lie ahead provided only that we practice it in our daily
> lives. And among the things we must practice is this: that while we
> seek fervently to ferret out the subversive and antidemocratic
> forces in the country, we do not at the same time, by hysteria, by
> resort to innuendo and sneers and other unfortunate tactics, be-
> smirch the very cause that we believe in, and cause a separation
> among our people . . . based on mere attacks, mere unsubstanti-
> ated attacks upon [individual] loyalty.

Arvin read admiringly about Lilienthal's response on page one of the *New
York Times*. But he was also immediately fearful. During Arvin's own years

as a Red, Lilienthal had repeatedly tried to dissuade him from his radical views. If Dave could be attacked as disloyal and "soft" ideologically, he wondered, where did that place him? Arvin's past as a leftist writer was all but behind him—he admired Truman and planned to support his re-election— but in the current climate, that didn't protect the individual from egregious attack.

Lilienthal became the chief guardian of the nation's nuclear secrets, including the detonation of Russia's first nuclear weapon and the development of the "super"—the first hydrogen bomb, which he had originally opposed—just as Arvin was weighing which of his closest friends to tell about his affair with Capote. During the coming months he and Lilienthal kept in touch, but as each had reached a point requiring heightened discretion, they exchanged little real news. Lilienthal, despite his belief in open government, worked under armed guard, amid admonitory signs like HAVE YOU LOCKED YOUR SAFE? He complained of not being able to tell Helen—nor did he want to burden her with—the terrible secrets he knew, and of needing a bodyguard even to go to the theater. Celebrated on the cover of *Time* magazine, he chafed at being famous for orchestrating vital activities he couldn't divulge. Arvin, meanwhile, semipublic about the affair at Yaddo and Smith, chose not to tell his oldest friend that he was finally, truly, in love, for fear of compromising them both.

As both understood, America had entered a period when it was best not to know too much about the private lives of others, lest one be required to answer questions about them later on.

That summer Arvin and Capote shared a cottage on Nantucket, where Arvin worked on his Melville biography while Capote struggled to finish *Other Voices, Other Rooms,* the novel he had been writing at Yaddo the previous summer. They worked in the morning, then split up most of the afternoon as Capote swam and sunbathed with friends while Arvin shut himself indoors, reading Pascal, Schopenhauer, Shakespeare, and Cervantes. They drank martinis or Manhattans before dinner and entertained friends, which Capote enjoyed but which Arvin found unnerving. Capote was now the best-known unpublished novelist in America, having been anointed by *Life* magazine, which led an article about up-and-coming writers with a full-page picture of him, even though the others—Jean Stafford, Gore Vidal, and Tom Heggen among them—had already produced their first books. The "dance of bees" had spread dizzyingly throughout publishing circles, where he was heralded as the most promising writer of his generation by people who still had heard only of the boyish appearance, squeaky voice, and outsized talent. Fearful of the limelight, uncomfortable with Capote's instant stardom and incessant frolicking, Arvin withdrew, moping and fretting about the toll their relationship was taking on his concentration. "I am uncontrollably eager to get back to Hamp this week," he wrote to a friend, in desperation, "and dig my way in at the office for a long, steady, uninterrupted spell of work on the [Melville] book, such as I can only do there at home, and must do, if the goblins are not to get me."

Strangers in each other's world, they tried awkwardly not to be—to develop a life outside the shell-like seclusion of Yaddo and Arvin's apartment. Capote introduced Arvin to gay New York, with troubling results. On a night in late November, he took Arvin to Harlem for an annual drag dance at the Celebrity Club, a mostly gay dance hall, where, in the midst of parading queens, they were caught in what they thought was a police raid. Though the officers were only checking for fire-code violations, Arvin groaned, "My reputation, my reputation," and went to hide, terrified, in a phone booth. Arvin's staid universe of important critics and professors proved equally hostile to Capote. Arvin squired him to dinners and lunches with Hicks, Brooks, Wilson, Harvard's F. O. Matthiessen, and Lionel and Diana Trilling, most of whom were less than impressed, if not downright chilly. "A not unpleasant little monster, like a fetus with a big head," Wilson called Capote. As Capote would lament, bitterly, "I must have looked like a male Lolita to those people. It must have been very hard for [Newton]."

Even Smith's liberal penumbra, which sheltered numerous Boston marriages among women professors and alumnae, seemed inhospitable. As Arvin showed off his "Little T," like some glittering prize, to a group of faculty friends, most were put off by the overt sexual connotation, so alien in the modest, proper, asexual Arvin they knew. Aaron would remember that when he first met Capote, Capote kissed him. "It was as if he had given me a blow to the face," he recalled. "I think he sensed that Newton was ashamed and ought not to be . . . and he wanted to get back at him a little bit." Madeleine Fisher, the young wife of Al Fisher, Arvin's closest ally on the faculty besides Aaron, would "baby-sit" Capote when Arvin had to teach or attend meetings, a task no one else wanted but that she welcomed. They danced and sang together and rode horses at the Smith stables. Once she took Capote downtown to McCallum's, Northampton's premiere department store, and Capote bought a pink woman's sweater—for himself—mortifying onlookers. Arvin later chuckled but must have been horrified, too.

In the end, they were happiest by themselves, alone, in Arvin's apartment. Even though New York or even Boston might have offered the promise of a more open companionship—Harvard's Matthiessen, for instance, lived with his lover, Russell Cheney, in a splendid apartment in Louisburg Square, on Beacon Hill—Arvin was now, as Aaron noted, "encysted" in Northampton and at Smith. And so he and Capote retreated to the safety of his rooms, quietly celebrating Christmas and New Year's alone there while Random House, Capote's publisher, began shipping *Other Voices, Other Rooms* to eager reviewers and stores. "Something of an Event, inevitably," Arvin wrote to Hicks, "and one hopes that the publishers and others have not Built it Up to a dangerous hubristic extent."

Arvin dreaded the book's publication in mid-January more perhaps than he let on. Largely autobiographical, it told the story of a Southern teenager who, after trying to become a normal heterosexual boy, accepts his destiny as a homosexual. "All those New York gents (and ladies) will destroy him if they can," Arvin wrote in his letter to Hicks, "destroy him as a writer, I mean." Capote, remarkably, had dedicated the novel to Arvin, who was both flattered and mortified and who had dedicated *his* first book—dutifully, respectfully—to his parents. Even more provocative was the jacket photo of Capote, lying seductively on his back on a divan, looking no more than thirteen years old and pouting sensually beneath tousled bangs and come-hither eyes. When Arvin first saw the picture, which Capote had carefully staged with a photographer, he wrote to him, "There is a look in those eyes I know oh, so well, and that I decidedly hope no other human being knows in the same way. Do assure me that you were thinking of Notwen Nivra when you assumed that look!" Arvin's light tone aside—

Notwen Nivra was mirror writing for Newton Arvin—he must have realized that Capote, by exposing himself so broadly, would also expose him.

More discomfiting still was the book's reception. As it became a best-seller, the object of many horrified reviews and the most discussed novel of the year, Capote's sultry eyes suddenly seemed to loom everywhere. Arvin recoiled from the publicity. He did not wish to share Capote with the world, nor, in truth, did he think the novel as good as some of its enthusiastic champions believed.

> I can well understand one's having reservations about Truman's book [he wrote to Hicks]. It's not as if I don't have any of my own. But somehow—and it's open to anyone to remark that I might be ever so slightly biased—I can't think it's terribly important to insist on the reservations just now. Whatever its limitations, the book is the work of a *writer*: the work of a boy born to be a poet and an artist, who touches with a kind of magic everything he draws near. Really, of how many young contemporary American writers can one possibly say that? And isn't it the crucial point? So many journeymen; so many *made* writers; so many hacks. And then here comes a book that, to be perhaps pretentiously Jamesian, is very evidently the right real thing. Shouldn't we simply, for the moment, thank our stars for that; and make our reservations in parentheses?

Throughout early 1948, as Capote became a lightning rod—a kind of homosexual Jackie Robinson—it was Arvin who succored him when he deserted New York, rushed with his suitcases from the train station, bounded up the twisting stairs, fell into Arvin's fatherly arms, tumbled into his bed. And it was Arvin, inevitably, who could not sustain the part of the helpmate, selflessly assuaging Capote's large public needs. After *Other Voices*, Arvin was as ambivalent toward Capote as a lover and friend as he was as a critic. Capote's openness had enabled him to accept and enjoy his homosexuality, almost without shame, for the first time. Capote's vivaciousness warmed and braced him. But ultimately Arvin was, as Capote put it, a "weekend caller," unable to maintain a full-time, intense, permanent relationship with anyone. Arvin was forty-seven, Capote twenty-four. Mc-

Cullers, who resented Capote's burst of fame as it supplanted her own and condemned his affair with Arvin, whom she still considered her dearest friend, hoped Arvin would end their romance. Arvin, feeling life ebbing from him, longed to have back his solitude and independence.

In May, Capote sailed to Europe. While he was gone, Arvin initiated an affair with a young New York writer and one of Capote's closest friends, Andrew Lyndon. Counting on Capote to return in September, as planned, he was disappointed to hear in early August that Capote was cutting his trip short and was eager to see him. In a letter to Doughty, Arvin complained, "Poor kid! I love him to death, but I'm terribly afraid this longish interval has proven to me beyond cavil how incapable I now am of getting my breath and filling my lungs in that rather intense and high-pitched atmosphere he so touchingly and lovably evokes around him." If Arvin had bedded Lyndon in order to provoke a break-up, he understood he was to have his chance sooner than he had expected. Putting off the unpleasantness, he delayed their reunion by accepting an invitation to visit Lilienthal on Martha's Vineyard.

Capote returned to Northampton bearing gifts and sensing Arvin's distance. Then, as always, he set out to discover what he had missed during his absence by carefully prying open Arvin's locked desk drawer and reading his journal. Capote had long since learned that Arvin, overcoming the reticence he had initially shown concerning his trysts with Oskar, documented those occasions when he slept with someone with the letter X, treating his sexual encounters as if they were not quite real until they were written down and pressed, like flowers, between the covers of a book. And so Capote discovered that Arvin had begun having sex with Lyndon the day after he left for Europe and continued doing so until the day before he returned. Unable to confront Arvin directly, because he had purloined the information, he eventually took it up with Lyndon, who protested that Capote seemed as eager to end the relationship as Arvin did. Capote, saving face, didn't deny the charge, though clearly it was Arvin, more than he, who wanted out.

They continued to see each other through the fall and early winter, remaining affectionate and sleeping together, though no longer with the same passion and intensity, much to Arvin's relief. Returning to his *Melville*,

Arvin again felt unencumbered enough to do his work, which was all, in the end, he wanted. By the time he learned, in early February 1949, that Capote had a new lover, a dancer named Jack Dunphy, and that they were planning to move in together, Arvin seemed to have overcome any sense of failure or regret. "Sad and also tender and without bitterness," he wrote in his journal. If he couldn't let Capote love him, Arvin was pleased to know that Capote at least would be loved by someone else.

For Arvin, the 1940s were ending much as the twenties and thirties had, in self-induced exile coupled with a yawning disillusionment. In 1929, he had returned, alone and miserable, from Europe, only to conclude after the stock market crash that America's commercial civilization was doomed. He had scrabbled leftward, skirting the general crack-up. In 1939, he was separated from Mary during the waning days of the Depression when the Hitler-Stalin pact sealed his disenchantment with communism. Again he hunkered down. Now, he had chosen to live life alone rather than to share it with Capote, amid an ideological backlash that, since Lilienthal's confrontation with Congress, had grown only fiercer. Like most secret homosexuals, Arvin was expert at adopting the protective coloration of the surrounding world. He made efforts to fit in with the new conservatism—rediscovering the Episcopalianism of his youth; writing fewer articles for *The New Republic* and *The Nation* and more for *Vogue* and *Harper's Bazaar*, which incidentally paid better.

The end of the forties coincidentally marked the end of *his* forties, and, as he had in the waning years of the previous two decades, Arvin struggled to finish a biography that, neatly if unintentionally, summed up his views on both America and his own life. Just as his *Hawthorne* was the product of a reclusive, sexually ambiguous young aesthete, a member of the Lost Generation who had renounced "the dark connection between secrecy and guilt" amid the collapse of perhaps the most philistine era in American history; and just as his *Whitman* reflected the constricted soul-searching of an unhappily married homosexual and communist sympathizer during the latter half of the Depression, when the nation unexpectedly revived, phoenix-like, out of its own ashes; his *Melville* represented the powerful but frustrating self-awareness of a middle-aged man who, having come to terms with himself during a period of fear, repression, and reaction, found himself and his country fatefully at odds.

Arvin had taken a year's sabbatical from Smith and finished the early chapters, covering Melville's youth and first successful writings about his South Seas adventures, while he and Capote were still seeing each other. He would eagerly read new sections aloud to Capote, as Capote had read aloud to him from *Other Voices*. Then, sometime around February, when he learned from Capote about Dunphy, he plunged into the book's massive, difficult midsection, a fifty-page chapter entitled, simply, "The Whale." Already he'd examined Melville's move to Pittsfield and relationship with Hawthorne, which, as he'd noted twenty years earlier, had helped ignite Melville's greatness as a novelist. As the older figure in a passionate and formative relationship between two male writers, Arvin had probed the "most fateful" of nineteenth-century American literary friendships with thinly veiled self-reference and considerable intimacy. Citing an essay in which Melville wrote, "It is that blackness in Hawthorne . . . that so fixes and fascinates me. Already I feel that [he] has dropped germinous seeds into my soul. He expands and deepens down, the more I contemplate him; and further and further shoots his strong New England roots in the hot soil of my Southern soul," Arvin went on to observe, "It is an astonishingly sexual image, but probably only such an image could adequately have expressed Melville's feeling, for the moment, of receptiveness and even passivity in the acceptance of impregnation by another mind."

Now, however, he began grappling with Melville's masterwork, and his inspiration grew, as Melville's had, primarily out of his powerful and lonely intellect.

It was a drastic, trying time. On February 11 the Washington Red hunts, fueled by the Alger Hiss case, suddenly struck within Arvin's circle. A page-one story in the *Times* cited a secret report, prepared by General Douglas MacArthur's intelligence staff, naming Agnes Smedley, who had written several books on Red China and was living at Yaddo, as a Russian agent. Within days, two FBI agents arrived at Yaddo to interview all of the guests and, in particular, Elizabeth Ames, whose secretary, it turned out, was an FBI informer. Though the War Department soon conceded that it had no evidence to support the charges against Smedley, the matter wasn't dropped. The poet Robert Lowell, at the time heavily influenced by the anticommunist New Critics, drinking violently, and verging on a nervous breakdown, was also a visitor at Yaddo that winter, and when the agents told him that the colony was "permeated with communists," Lowell urged a meeting of the board of directors and demanded that Ames be fired at once.

The accusations plunged Yaddo—and Arvin—into crisis. Lowell vowed to alert dozens of his literary friends if the board didn't renounce Ames, whom he called "a diseased organ, chronically poisoning the whole [Yaddo] system." In Saratoga and on Wall Street, the colony's supporters feared its reputation would be ruined and Yaddo destroyed. Yaddo became a "stricken battlefield," Cowley wrote, as Lowell began marshaling allies to fight the communist evil he said he had witnessed there firsthand.

"Down into the pit," Arvin wrote in his journal on February 19, after receiving an anguished telephone call from Ames. Realizing that any investigation into communist activity at Yaddo might quickly engulf Hicks, Cowley, himself, and the other leftist critics on the board, he frantically phoned Hicks, then sped by train for Hicks's farm, where he and Hicks huddled to formulate a response. The next day they drove to Troy to meet with Lowell and two other guests. Lowell's condition had deteriorated. A convert to Catholicism, he believed he was crusading "against the devil himself," and would soon suffer a psychotic break so forceful that it would take four Chicago policemen ten minutes to subdue him. Arvin was terrified. "Ghastly conversation," he wrote.

For two weeks, Arvin wallowed in despair, taking mostly to his bed. He wrote a letter of resignation to the Yaddo chairman, John Slade, but kept it until after the board acted on Ames. "Got my will, the bonds, etc. out of the safety deposit," he wrote ominously on February 28; two days later, "Still half alive today. Fire is very low." If a sympathetic liberal like Ames, a Quaker, could be caught up in such a horror, he worried, what would happen to him when the FBI delved into his past? Unlike Hicks, he had never joined the Party, finding it too dogmatic and himself too irreligious to conform to "party discipline." He and Hicks both were now active Democrats.

Neither defense would matter. Arvin understood that the focus of such hunts was on the shadows in one's past, and that, because of his political and sexual histories, he was doubly vulnerable.

Despite quicksand fears and black depressions, Arvin kept writing, managing a page one day, two the next. Developing pharyngitis, obsessing about his will, he seemed to verge on his second nervous collapse in a decade. But each day as he returned to his office overlooking Paradise and dug further into his chapter on *Moby-Dick,* his troubles receded, and he felt girded, renewed. "Wrote almost four pages in Chapter Six despite low spirits," he reported in his journal in mid-March. Doughty visited from Cambridge a week later, and after they'd spent most of the day talking about the Yaddo morass, Arvin even conducted a bit of sexual healing. "Howard rather *deprime* but X, rather brilliant, took care of that," he wrote.

By the time the Yaddo board met in New York on March 26 to review the charges against Ames—"The Day of Wrath," Arvin called it in his journal—the headlines had died down and so had Arvin's anxiety. There were three camps on the board. Certain directors, especially the group's lawyers and businessmen, accepted the charges against Ames as stated and believed she had to be purged; others, who were loyal to Ames, rejected the allegations out of hand; the third group, which included Arvin and Hicks, took a middle ground. "The communist issue was negligible," Hicks wrote, "but there had been serious laxness in the administration of Yaddo" in letting Smedley stay on as a permanent guest. After meeting for five hours in the boardroom of Spencer Trask and Company on Wall Street, the directors decided to keep Ames, censure Lowell, and adopt reforms aimed at making Yaddo more efficient and, in the process, less vulnerable to charges that it was dominated by radicals. Ames went to a nursing home to recover. "An ordeal for everyone," Arvin wrote.

Arvin's own ordeal had been subsumed in his writing. He soon completed the chapter on *Moby-Dick,* apotheosizing the kind of learned, passionately argued, ferociously *personal* criticism that Brooks had first inspired in him and that he'd spent the past three decades trying to perfect. Everything was there—the great gusts of Melville's genius, Arvin's exquisite parsing of the multilayered text, the erudite references to Melville's most obscure sources. There also was something prescient and modern in Arvin's recognition that the *Pequod*'s apocalyptic voyage might be the vengeance dream of a tormented, sexually injured, father-hating hero. Like Wilson and other literary critics of the era before deconstruction, Arvin was a master of discernment through descriptive fervor. He wrote, "Ahab is what our wildest, most egotistic, most purely destructive malevolence could wish to be, this old Quaker skipper from Nantucket; obsessed to the point of monomania with the will to destroy the hated thing, yet free from all mere smallness, 'a grand, ungodly, godlike man.' He is our hatred ennobled, as we would have it, up to heroism." The description richly encapsulated the fulminating spirit of the postwar period, as seen by a quietly aggrieved man who, approaching fifty, felt, after a perilous brush with exposure and blame, that he had no choice but to go on living and working in shadow.

With the book all but finished, Arvin took a few days off in May to visit Lilienthal in Washington. During his stay, he asked whether Lilienthal would object to his dedicating *Melville* to him. "I have thought about it from every possible angle," Arvin said. "I can't myself see any valid objection." Eyebrows might have risen at the mere suggestion, given the stormy political climate: a former fellow traveler, himself having recently been similarly honored by the glaringly homosexual Truman Capote, dedicating a scholarly biography to the man the *Times* would soon call "perhaps the most controversial figure in Washington since the end of the war," the keeper of the nation's most vital secrets, no less. But Lilienthal was both flattered and loyal. "I shall eat up the pleasure of it," he replied, "and mark off my unworthiness by saying, 'Us Valpo boys we stick together.'"

After the weekend, during which Lilienthal took time to join Arvin for a quick tour of the National Gallery, Lilienthal observed his oldest friend's exceptional enjoyment at roaming through the museum's marble halls. "For one who has as little emotional capacities, so far as anyone can tell outwardly, as Fred has," Lilienthal noted fondly in his journal, still using Arvin's boyhood name, "he gets an extraordinary satisfaction out of viewing pictures."

Chapter Six

AS THE FIFTIES dawned, Arvin's life was teaching him who he was. It was the life and death of another American literary critic of his generation, Francis Otto Matthiessen, that taught him who he wasn't.

They had first crossed paths twenty years earlier, when Edmund Wilson assigned Matthiessen to review Arvin's *Hawthorne* for *The New Republic*. Matthiessen had just been "called" to Harvard, at the age of twenty-seven, after two years as a Yale English instructor and was living, like many precocious anointees, mainly on promise. His first book, a biography of the nineteenth-century miniaturist of Maine farms and villages, Sarah Orne Jewett, had earned moderate reviews.

Wilson's pairing was a prescient one. The two young scholar-critics, neither of whom he'd met, had much essential in common. Like Arvin, who was two years older, Matty had been a bookish, solitary youth estranged from an absent father who came to New England from a small town in the Midwest to attend boarding school, then Yale, and was radicalized after World War I. A Rhodes scholar, he'd got his Ph.D. at Harvard, where he discovered Brooks's *America's Coming of Age*, which propelled him to become a critic. While sailing back from England in 1925, he'd met the naturalist painter Russell Cheney, twenty years his elder, and fallen secretly in love.

In his review, Matthiessen touted *Hawthorne* as a model of the revolution in criticism he hoped to lead at Harvard. "What [Arvin] has written goes right to the top of contemporary literary biography," he wrote, "and stands . . . as the rich many-sided type of criticism which we should have." Arvin, despite his disdain for academic distinctions, was flattered. Harvard, then as now, was the epicenter of American higher education, particularly the study of great books. Smith held a similar role among women's colleges but remained, like all other schools, in Harvard's shadow. During the next decade, as the two institutions led in pioneering the combined study of American history and culture, Arvin and Matthiessen became close rivals—publicly admiring though privately dismissive.

Matthiessen was invited by the publisher W. W. Norton, shortly after his *Hawthorne* review, to write an American literary history "from the new social and historical" angle. This, of course, was Arvin's territory; he and Matty were going over the same ground, driven more or less by the same politics and aesthetics, and, as homosexuals, veiled perspective and private demons. Short, square, mostly bald, with rimless glasses and a metallic voice, Matthiessen was no more physically impressive than Arvin. But he was a brash thinker and speaker—he'd been chosen class orator at Yale—and had a chip on his shoulder, and he set out to write a definitive study of the classical American literature of the mid-nineteenth century.

Arvin again beat him to publication, in the fall of 1938, with *Whitman,* which Matthiessen richly praised. Involved in many of the same Popular Front organizations as Arvin—he was elected vice-president, then president, of the Harvard Teachers' Union around the same time Arvin was chosen to lead the Smith chapter—he sympathized with Arvin's conception of Whitman as a socialist in his "meanings." He especially lauded Arvin's "final synthesis, which gives a more thorough grounding of the poet's thoughts in the matrix of his time than we have heretofore possessed for any American writer."

But Matthiessen, like Arvin, was beginning to suffer the strains of a dual life. Though he loved the older Cheney, and wrote to him every day when they were apart, he was tormented about losing him—Cheney, the scion of a Connecticut silk-manufacturing family, suffered from tuberculosis and asthma—and about the nature of their intimacy. Not too many years after Teddy Roosevelt's boisterous evocation of muscular Christianity,

Harvard still idealized manhood as the ultimate measure of character, and though there were homosexuals on campus, Matthiessen took pains to avoid them. His circle of friends and graduate students, a biographer recalls, "was more predominately heterosexual than was usual among Harvard literary groups, and he was unusually hostile to homosexual colleagues who mixed their academic and sexual relations." Among the latter group he counted Arvin, who, Matthiessen told friends, was too timid and unventuresome "to play with the big boys," according to Aaron.

Matthiessen became a hero to brilliant students like James Agee and Richard Wilbur, hurled himself into every faculty fight, and entertained a swirling circle of friends, hosting elegant dinner parties at his Pinckney Street apartment in Boston and summer lawn parties in Kittery, Maine, where he and Cheney retreated annually. But in the fall of 1938, just as he was reviewing Arvin's *Whitman,* he took a year-long sabbatical to finish his book, and his world dropped away. Frantic, unable to sleep, he entered a sanitarium, where he became "recurrently filled with the desire to kill myself" by jumping out the window. "I ran into a period of bad insomnia and frayed nerves," he wrote to Arvin from Kittery, "a wholly new experience for me, and one which I am now paying for, resentfully, by some enforced rest."

Matthiessen's *magnum opus*—1,006 pages of typescript; 300,000 words—was rejected as too dense and detailed by both Norton and Houghton Mifflin before Oxford University Press finally accepted it, with the provision that Matthiessen pay a third of the cost of publication. Yet when it was released, in the spring of 1941, under the title *American Renaissance,* the effect was galvanic. Arvin, still hospitalized in White Plains, didn't review it, but Kazin called it "indispensable," and most other critics agreed. Rigorously tracing the crosscurrents that united the writings of Emerson, Melville, Hawthorne, Whitman, and Thoreau not only to one another but also to the great literary outpourings that came before and after them, Matthiessen suddenly had outdone everyone else, including Brooks, in enshrining an American literary canon. He was credited with bringing, almost single-handedly, the scholarly field of American studies to fullness and with making Harvard its unrivaled center.

It was a distinction Arvin and Smith might well have claimed themselves. Arvin had preceded Matthiessen, inspiring his insights and multifaceted approach. And Smith was historically more committed to "skimming the cream" of its faculty for its program. As *Mademoiselle* would soon write, "Girls . . . can pedal from Pulitzer Prize–winning Oliver Larkin's beloved course in American art to critic and writer Alfred Kazin's twentieth-century American novel course, getting a provocative interpretation of history from Donald Sheehan, picking up their nineteenth-century literature from Newton Arvin, authority on Melville, Hawthorne, and Whitman—with finally a senior integrating course from Daniel Aaron." Still, as the study of American civilization mushroomed after World War II, it was Harvard, and especially Matthiessen, who dominated the field.

Arvin, stung by the reversal, retaliated with a scathing review of Matthiessen's next book, a study of Henry James, in *Partisan Review*. It consisted solely of sharply worded margin notes: "Quite impossible to follow F.O.M. here in the strangely wishful conviction that dogmatic theology can ever be reconciled with a revolutionary democratism."

Like Arvin, Matthiessen recoiled from the shocks of the postwar era. After Cheney died in Kittery, in 1945, he was alone and bereft. Unlike Arvin and many others, he remained an unflinching leftist—canvassing for the Progressive Party in 1948, lending his time and name to the labor movement. But he continued to feel suicidal. Stumbling home at night, he collapsed into bed, got a few hours of restless sleep, and then, in a pattern identical with Arvin's, awoke with a start somewhere between two and four A.M. to spend the remaining hours "lying there wishing I were dead."

As the government compiled scare lists, Matthiessen's name was on them. Publicly, he reaffirmed his progressive faith, but privately he was stricken, sensing that much worse was to come.

So did Arvin. "Unprecedented dissipation," Arvin wrote in his journal on February 18, 1950, a week after Republican senator Joseph McCarthy claimed to have the names of communists within the State Department who controlled U.S. foreign policy. McCarthy named no names—he had none—but that didn't stop the ensuing hysteria. The country had become so intolerant of Marxist ideas that one could be damned merely by innuendo. More, a Senate subcommittee had begun ferreting out suspected homosexuals and other "sex perverts" in government, firing them as security risks. Suddenly, political and sexual outcasts alike were being pursued, not for alleged crimes but for who they were. Two related witch-hunts, either of which could lead to Arvin or Matthiessen, gathered force.

Matthiessen, buffeted by years of depression yet unwilling or unable to defend himself, saw no way out. On Friday afternoon, March 31, he walked into the lobby of the Manger Hotel, across from Boston's North Station, and asked the assistant desk manager for "a nice airy room." After dining out that evening with friends, he returned to the hotel, meticulously arrayed the keys to his apartment, his Skull and Bones key, and a typewritten note, climbed out on the eleventh-floor ledge, and jumped.

Matthiessen's suicide staggered his friends and students. The most common explanation was that he was in despair over the political climate. "How much the state of the world has to do with my state of mind I do not know," he wrote in the last paragraph of his note. "But as a Christian and a socialist believing in international peace, I find myself terribly oppressed by the present tensions." For leftists, these were evil days, and Matthiessen instantly became a martyr, the first fatality of what would be known as the McCarthy era. "Professor Matthiessen is as surely a victim of the cold war and the Truman-Acheson foreign policy as those who face jail, blacklists and academic witch-hunts," the novelist Howard Fast wrote in a statement. "He, however, paid with his life . . . His death must not be in vain."

Arvin, "in the pit" for much of the past month, struggled with the news, which he found "shattering" but no surprise. Much about Matthiessen was too familiar for him to feel any real shock. The mystery wasn't that things were so bleak that Matthiessen killed himself, but how he'd gone about it, the violent leap in the middle of the night, which left him crushed and mangled yet still gasping for a few horrible moments on the pavement. Of all Arvin's fears, falling was the oldest and one of the most acute. One of his earliest memories was of his drawing a figure of a human being falling off the curved rim of the world and an elephant reaching its trunk out in an attempt to catch him. Alone in his rooms, Arvin could understand Matty's wanting to die, but not his need for hard, implacable punishment.

With his *Herman Melville* due out in early May, Arvin stood beside a glutted field. Only a year earlier, Somerset Maugham, in a preface to a new edition of *Moby-Dick*, complained wearily, "I have read Raymond Weaver's *Herman Melville, Mariner and Mystic*, Lewis Mumford's *Herman Melville*, Charles Robert Anderson's *Melville in the South Seas*, and Ellery Sedgwick's *Herman Melville: The Tragedy of a Mind*. I don't believe that I know much more about Herman Melville than I knew before." Since then, three more books—Howard P. Vincent's *The Trying-out of Moby-Dick*, Geoffrey Stone's *Melville*, and Richard Chase's *Herman Melville*—had also appeared. In an era unlike the one when Arvin was a young critic and most of Melville's novels were out of print, Melville had become something of a white whale himself, a godlike figure studied endlessly by symbol-hunters and mythmakers. The subject of countless articles, monographs, and dissertations, he was an academic industry.

Arvin's two-hundred-page critical biography had dazzled many of those who'd seen it in manuscript. "It's a beautiful book," Lionel Trilling wrote to him in February. "It would perhaps make my praise more convincing if I were able to come in at this point with some objections and reservations . . . but the fact is I don't have them." Young Irving Howe, writing from Princeton, ringingly agreed: "I think it's a magnificent job; really a crowning work; better than the previous two books, which God knows were good enough. I think you've beaten the 'new critics' at their own game of textual analysis and at the same time achieved a dramatic quality, a sense of the man that makes the book continually exciting . . . Really, Newton, *you've just gone and done it!*"

But these were friends, and as publication drew near, Arvin grew fretful and uneasy. He knew by now that the relief of finishing a book is often subsumed by a tide of self-doubt, about both one's value as a writer and the question of what to do next. In nonfiction, finishing is easy, starting is hard, so Arvin approached the end of the school year with more than his usual trepidation, for, unlike the past four years, he would have neither a big project nor Capote to engage him, nor would he be at Yaddo. Capote had visited him the weekend before Matthiessen's death, staying in bed nearly until two, sitting up to have some sherry with Arvin, and joining him for sex—twice, according to Arvin's journal. Then, on April 7, he and his lover Jack Dunphy boarded a Norwegian freighter for Italy, to resume their expatriate life in Sicily. Arvin, who found Capote a confining presence when he was in the heat of writing, was now faced with his absence at the moment he was likeliest to need comfort and support.

Arvin's spirit soared with the first reviews, which were little short of ecstatic. "Let's be blunt," H. P. Vincent wrote in *The Saturday Review of Literature*; "this is not just a first-rate book on the life and art of Melville; it is also a superb exercise of critical scholarship and an ornament to American Letters." Kazin, writing in the Sunday *Times Book Review*, introduced his article with this tribute: "Newton Arvin's short literary biography is the wisest and most balanced single piece of writing on Melville I have seen."

Never had Arvin's standing among his peers been higher, yet never had he felt so empty and alone, or so trapped in Northampton. "Struggled with dangerous thoughts and feelings. Torture. Left the light on all night," he wrote in his journal on July 20. As he did every summer, he took on extra writing, but postpublication anxiety unnerved him, despite the continuing accolades. A week later he wrote to Aaron that he was finishing an introduction to a collection of Henry Adams's letters and was feeling extravagantly low. "When it *is* done," he wrote, "I plan to collapse quite consciously and systematically, roll up my eyes till you can see only the whites of them, and breathe so little that a glass held before my mouth will hardly betray that I am living." Like most writers, he obsessed over every attention that was paid him, and anguished over each that wasn't. "Why did Edmund Wilson not review my book for *The New Yorker*," he wrote on August 4. "It would have made a greater difference to me than any other one thing of the kind." At the time, Arvin was reading galley proofs of Wilson's *Classics and Commercials*, which he would soon review favorably in the *Times*.

A few close friends in the English Department knew of Arvin's gloom and tried to comfort him. Aaron was summering with his wife and two young sons at Harwichport, on Cape Cod, but Al and Madeleine Fisher remained in town, and they saw him regularly, monitoring his instability and black moods. Al Fisher, strenuously heterosexual, was a Princeton-trained poet and scholar whose father was a Presbyterian minister. He was known at Smith for his stirring seminars on Shakespeare and Joyce, which he conducted in his living room, and for being a lively cook, raconteur, and, increasingly, connoisseur of Smith women. His first wife, M. F. K. Fisher, the food writer, believed Fisher was "frightened and repelled by the physical act of love," but that had apparently changed after their divorce. His second wife, the novelist Helen Eustis, had written *The Horizontal Man,* a *roman à clef* about the Smith English Department in which an Arvin-like character develops a female alter ego who murders a wildly heterosexual male colleague. Madeleine, whom Fisher began seeing while she was still a student of his, was lovely, vibrant, and free-spirited, and Arvin confided in her, as he did Fisher, about his sexual life.

Arvin also saw a lot of Elizabeth Drew. Born in Singapore, educated at Oxford, "Miss Drew" was a tall, slim-hipped, white-haired woman about Arvin's age who took staircases at a run and was celebrated as Smith's most energetic walker. A highly regarded scholar of T. S. Eliot and the author of a half-dozen major critical studies, acclaimed both here and in England, she had come to the United States during World War II to remove her son from danger after her husband, an Oxford don, left her for another woman. While she was teaching at Breadloaf, the Vermont writers' conference, she had attracted the attention of Aaron, who recruited her for Smith.

It was Drew who sensed most acutely Arvin's growing desolation. Arvin disliked burdening friends, but as his letter to Aaron indicated, he also was careful to signal them when he was nearing bottom. Matthiessen, on the night he killed himself, managed to take a lively part in dinner conversation, but could not, a colleague recalled, "permit himself the relief of depending feebly on others." Arvin was more self-allowing. As he sank lower, he let Drew know, in carefully chosen terms, how little energy he had left for living, a disclosure she promptly reported to Aaron in a letter on August 9.

"This will warn you of what is coming," Drew wrote. "Newt's in a very bad way & went to the President yesterday to ask if he might take a year's leave of absence, as he felt he couldn't go on." Drew admired Arvin's intelligence. But she also thought him selfish and histrionic, and was a veteran of tragedy herself: after she brought her son to the United States for safety, the boy was run over and killed by a car. She continued sharply:

I feel *very* doubtful of its doing him any good. Like most of us age-ing and lonely people, what he wants is to get away from *himself* & unfortunately you take yourself wherever you go! Moreover, I can't see Newt happy in the N.Y. literary crowd, with its drinking, gre-gariousness and personal squabbles, etc. Of course what he hopes for is—LOVE—but it has a way of not coming when you go out to seek it, & in any case with him will probably only lead to further heartache, I'm afraid. It is unlikely at his age, with his tempera-ment, to find someone with whom he can really make a life . . .

Poor man, I do feel sorry about it, as I know you will, in spite of knowing from experience that the Newts of this world get far more consolation than the plodding people like ourselves who feel we have to accept and go on to the best of our abilities.

Arvin was indeed in dire straits. He had visited Smith's new president, Benjamin Wright, at ten that morning to discuss taking a leave. He simply couldn't continue teaching, he told Wright, who voiced sympathy and con-cern. An hour later, he met with Fisher and Drew to inform them of his re-quest, and then had lunch with Drew as usual. After that he took a trolley to Look Park, in the upland Florence section of the city, hoping the change of air would do him good. The August sky was overcast, but the swimming pool was filled with shouting children, and it was cool in the pines. After returning home by four and taking a bath, Arvin put a new recording of a Mozart divertimento by Toscanini on the record player. But even Mozart, whom he loved, seemed only shrill and sad, a fellow sufferer who, as Arvin had noted a few days earlier in his journal, wrote to his wife in 1790, "If people could see into my heart, I should feel most ashamed. To me every-thing is cold, cold as ice . . . everything seems so empty."

Arvin poured himself a gin and tonic, and read some poems until six, when he switched on the radio. At 6:25, he again took sixteen Nembutals, washed them down with the last of his drink, and lay down. "Moments of absolute serenity," he later wrote, "—then nothing . . ."

Fisher found him around eleven-thirty. He phoned Arvin's doctor, Hugh Tatlock, plied him with coffee, and forced him to walk around until Tatlock arrived. Within minutes, an ambulance rushed him to Northampton's Cooley Dickinson Hospital, where his stomach was pumped and, fluttering in and out of consciousness, he was put in a private room. The next day Fisher and Drew drove him back to McLean, where Arvin seemed instantly buoyed by the change of scene. As Drew wrote that night to Aaron, "At the moment he is thinking himself a romantic figure in it all—or was yesterday, when Al drove him to the MacLean [sic] place. He was in very good spirits . . . though I don't think that is likely to last."

Writing to Aaron a week later, Arvin apologized for distressing his friends; as he and they both knew, his latest breakdown meant that his colleagues, in addition to caring for him, would have to teach his classes. On the other hand, he feared he hadn't the strength or will to desert Northampton, even though Wright had officially granted him a paid leave for the first semester, and he now was free to go. "The practical obstacles in the way of *moving* are almost too great for me to leap," he wrote to Aaron. "Another nine months in Northampton will hardly be easy spiritually, but then—who can ask for mere ease in such an era as this? I only mean that I seem to myself to have served at least a full term of life in *That Place*."

As Drew understood, Northampton was not the problem, nor was Arvin's nervous state. What he hoped to escape—his inner turmoil—was inescapable. But Drew seems to have been alone in sensing the fullness of Arvin's futility; most of his other friends reacted with sympathy and encouragement, which, albeit welcome, betrayed a lesser understanding of his needs. "That was a tough thing, you're getting pooped and worn down," Lilienthal wrote on September 9. "I myself know enough about the consequences of overwork and overtired nerves to regard it as something that yields to more sensible regime; but it is tough luck and I hope you are clear on top of it." Lilienthal, a veteran of several "smashups" himself, had been forced occasionally throughout his career to escape the pressures of Washington by taking extended periods of forced rest in Florida. That he could equate the violent pressures of what he called the "neutron-infested squirrel cage" to the stresses of teaching literature at Smith may have flattered Arvin but showed only a slight appreciation of his real troubles.

As winter approached, Arvin fell deeper into gloom. He had reached, as Drew observed, an insurmountable impasse. In order to produce the work he lived for, he had removed himself from the world. He was like a man sitting atop a flagpole. He could look out over everything, see it all, but only by himself, with no one to share the contents of his heart. His narrow perch on Prospect Street, once so bright when Capote was there with him, was now more like a bunker, a cold place. Meanwhile, the glowing reviews of his work continued to pour in. "Mr. Arvin's book is not only the best literary biography of the 1950s but one of the most valuable critical studies of the year and of the decade," Morton Zabel wrote in *The Nation* in December. Arvin found the notice in the public library the day before Christmas. "A great puff of wind for the sails," he wrote in his journal. But he soon felt himself either drifting desultorily or becalmed. Within days, the luffing subsided, and he was back by himself, in his rooms, hopelessly surveying the bleak horizons.

He forced himself to escape Northampton temporarily by accepting a post as visiting professor at Ohio State University, where he had friends and family nearby; predictably, however, the change did little good. Drew had warned in her second letter to Aaron that Arvin "may find he can't face making his break when it comes nearer, just as now he feels he can't face staying. I *hope* that doesn't happen, for it means he is dead as far as any real living is concerned." Once again, she was proved right. By February 1951, Arvin was sinking back into the pit. "The will to live burning low," he wrote in his journal on February 4. Four days later he complained, "Woke up at five. Intense depression. A tense day."

"Another irrationally anxious day," he wrote on February 9. And on February 18, "Miserable day. Repression, angst, etc." Feeling closed in, and teetering dangerously, Arvin brooded over how much longer he could last—until three days later, when he received a letter from Granville Hicks, a member of the literary jury, notifying him that he had won the new National Book Award for nonfiction. The news triggered an avalanche of congratulatory letters and calls that abruptly wrenched him back to the world of the living.

Arvin was jubilant. Taking the train from Ohio to New York for the awards dinner on March 5, 1951, he treated himself to a roomette. He arrived at Penn Station after eight A.M. and took a taxi to the Biltmore, where he checked into his room at about the same time the Rosenberg atomic-spy trial began in a federal courthouse downtown. After making several phone calls—to Capote's friend Andrew Lyndon; to Kronenberger, now drama critic for *Time*; to his publisher—he ate lunch and went to the Commodore Hotel around three-thirty. Besieged by photographers, radio men, newspapermen, and a bevy of well-wishers and friends, he gave a few interviews, then met privately with two of the other winners, Wallace Stevens and Brendan Gill. (William Faulkner, who won the fiction award, was in Hollywood and unable to attend.) After years of molelike activity, he was unsettled by the charged attention, but not, to his surprise, altogether unpleasantly. "Not as bad as I had feared," he wrote in his journal.

In his acceptance speech that night in the Commodore ballroom, Arvin honored Melville, "who spoke out for the 'august dignity' of the democratic man," and Emerson, about whom he planned to write his next book, "who cried out again and again, on behalf of the free spirit of man, and against the brutal power hungry and inhumane forces that would enslave our spirit." Given the McCarthyist tenor of the times, the speech could be read either as patriotic or subversive. Recognizing Arvin's cultural nationalism and status as a political and sexual outcast, it appears to have been both.

Capote hoped Arvin's success would at last enable him to leave Smith. He himself had just published his second novel, *The Grass Harp*, to favorable reviews, and was adapting it for Broadway. He had settled into a stable domestic life with Dunphy, with whom he lived several months each year in New York and the rest in Taormina, a picturesque hill town, near Mount Etna, which hosted a small expatriate colony that included André Gide, Eugene O'Neill, Jean Cocteau, and Orson Welles. Believing he could help Arvin thrive in a more open atmosphere, if only he could extricate him from Northampton, he was frustrated by his friend's determination to live in provincial obscurity.

On a night in November, at a black-tie party in the Manhattan East Side townhouse of the author John Gunther, Capote approached Lilienthal and his wife, Helen, neither of whom he'd met before, and urged their help. Lilienthal at first was shocked by the young man's florid appearance, thinking Capote "a very strange person . . . very short and dumpy in his body." Capote was wearing a dark corduroy suit and an embroidered Spanish vest, and his hands gestured oddly, like a dancer's. But Capote persisted. Arvin was "surrounded by mediocrity" at Smith, he complained in his oddly syrupy voice, "whereas he himself was a very remarkable person." He ought to be at Harvard or Yale but "won't lift a finger to do anything for himself," he told the couple. Lilienthal, who the previous year had stepped down as AEC chairman and was belatedly attempting to earn a fortune on Wall Street after thirty years of public service, pledged his assistance. But his contacts were in business and government, not academia, and there was little he could do, even after Arvin was inducted, in February 1952, into the American Academy of Arts and Letters, the most distinguished cultural society in the country.

In fact, the wreckage of Arvin's personal life was beginning to haunt his career, even as his literary standing grew. As Capote may have known, Harvard, in its search for a replacement for Matthiessen, had indeed approached Arvin about the possibility of his teaching in Cambridge for a year, and Dan Aaron, who would finish his own career there, believed the invitation signaled a permanent offer.

> He would have landed a job at Harvard if had shown any interest or if he could make people feel confident that he wouldn't break down [Aaron later said]. But his history dragged after him. It was like a man with a police record. There were all these accounts of his breakdowns and periods in mental institutions, and they became finally an incubus. Newton came to believe that that was his destiny; he couldn't leave. He was affixed, doomed to be in this circle, and though he loathed it, it was the only place he could come back to and feel at home in. He would have expired if he hadn't been able to come back there.

Arvin had finally achieved major success at a time when America was celebrating its elite as never before, but he was too ambivalent about his new status to exploit it. Part of his reluctance was political; he distrusted personal gain and academic careerism as toxic byproducts of the American business culture he'd spent his life opposing. Unlike Lilienthal and Capote, he had too much to hide to feel comfortable in the spotlight or in the sparkling salons where literary celebrities like Capote were drawing as much attention as movie stars. Yet, like them, he was attracted by success, so he learned to suffer through a double life in which fame and obscurity overlapped, where he could be seen and invisible, known and unknown, in the public eye and secretive, all at the same time.

That life had first haunted him five and a half years earlier, when *Life* sent a photographer to Yaddo to observe how the nation's writers and artists were faring in their return to peacetime normality. He and Capote had just met, and because of the mutual fascination of Capote and the camera, and Arvin's status on the board, the two of them were featured prominently in the magazine, including side-by-side pictures of Arvin, in a linen suit, making his bed, and Capote sitting at his typewriter in Lady Katrina's hideaway. For anyone who knew of their romance, the juxtaposition was tantalizing, as was another photo of Arvin, Hicks, and Ames lounging beneath portraits of the Trasks—three prominent leftists, including a former exemplary communist writer and a woman soon to be investigated for harboring Red spies, chatting beneath the placid visages of a Wall Street lion and his wife. Not for Arvin. He was mortified. As he wrote to Aaron:

> Thank God I have tenure at Smith, or the *Life* exposé—or libel—
> or burlesque—or whatever it should be called—might be the end
> of my useful and industrious career there . . . I won't bore you with
> the whole story, but it is the usual disgraceful one, and we can only
> say our beads, and beg to be spared a repetition for another decade
> at least.

On March 27, a month after Arvin's election to the American Academy, the Broadway production of *The Grass Harp* opened at the Martin Beck Theater. Capote had invited Arvin to the opening, but was too nervous afterward to remain backstage, so Arvin ushered him back to Lilienthal's Beekman Place townhouse, where Arvin was staying overnight, to wait for the reviews—a decision that later showed up as an "item" in Leonard Lyons's celebrity column in the *New York Post. The New Yorker,* raising its eyebrow at the oddity of a flamboyant young playwright crashing the wealthy home of the former keeper of the nation's atomic secrets, spoofed the item in its next issue. It imagined Capote arriving unannounced as

Lilienthal was about to start an after-dinner board game with three other guests—Harvard president James B. Conant; Roosevelt's top wartime science adviser, Dr. Vannevar Bush; and retired general Leslie R. Groves, director of the Manhattan Project—the ruling troika behind the A-bomb. What both the item and satire missed, of course, was Arvin, whose presence explained the unlikely pairing and who was happy not to be mentioned. And yet if the reporters missed the real connection, so did Lilienthal. Having seen Capote three times in the past several months, twice with Arvin, he still couldn't understand either Capote's strange genius or his hold on his oldest friend. "I gather," Lilienthal wrote in his journal, "Fred has had a good deal to do with encouraging and helping C. with his writing."

Having received an offer to teach at Harvard during the 1952–1953 term after all, Arvin prepared to leave Northampton. But, as Drew had predicted, as the date got closer he fell to brooding so heavily over his departure that he became paralyzed. He wasn't sure he could face the students. Several years earlier he had taught for a semester at all-male Wesleyan and had been seized by panic in the classroom. He feared the same thing would happen now. Reluctantly, he notified Harvard that he wouldn't be coming for the fall term, asked to be kept on for the spring, and, in October, traveled by train to Cincinnati, ostensibly to visit his sister, Ellen Zeigler, whose husband was a doctor. He stayed in Cincinnati for six weeks, and received up to a dozen electroshock treatments for his depression.

Like most experimental therapies, shocking the brain with electricity to induce convulsions had begun with a few primitive observations, plus a dearth of other remedies. Italian researchers in the 1930s, inspired by the work of a Budapest psychiatrist who claimed to be able to calm schizophrenics by putting them into convulsions with camphor, noticed that they could induce similar fits in dogs by jolting them with electricity. Their initial experiments were barbaric: they placed one electrode in the animal's mouth, the other in its anus, and half the dogs died of heart failure on the treatment table. Only when the researchers realized that the electrodes could be attached at the temples, and the voltage reduced to a therapeutic dose instead of a lethal one, was the therapy tried on humans.

Electroconvulsive therapy (ECT) failed to cure schizophrenia, but it did alleviate some of the disabling symptoms of psychotic illness, and American psychiatrists, in the 1940s, grudgingly accepted its use in keeping many suicidal patients from killing themselves. Van Wyck Brooks in his time had been prescribed tennis and ball-balancing, among other palliatives, to tame an overwhelming death wish. Arvin had already been treated unsuccessfully for his homosexuality, which the psychiatric community had reclassified earlier in the year as a disorder akin to rape and mutilation. Desperate, he hoped the new treatments would stop him from wanting to take his life, though that wasn't how the matter was discussed within his family. The Zeiglers' son, John, then in high school, would remember asking his mother what was wrong with Uncle Newton, and being told that Arvin was troubled by the country's political turmoil. As with Matthiessen, such an explanation for catastrophic depression was considered at the time both plausible and sufficient.

Arvin hoped at first that shock therapy might help him over time, but as the treatments dragged on, he began to worry. "My poor little memory is almost gone," he wrote to Aaron. "And the events of the last four or five months are bathed in a haze of vagueness & inexplicitness. [Still], I am told that this is a very normal consequence of these treatments, and that in the long run I will regain most of my very ordinary powers." He understood that his "crackups and breakdowns," as he called them, were interfering with the one thing that had always sustained him—his work—and he was mournful. "I believe this *contretemps* has been the major disappointment of my life," he continued. "Certainly I can remember *very few* things I ever wanted to do so intensely as teach in Cambridge this fall and winter."

Arvin's friends, trusting his doctors, tried to encourage him. Lilienthal sent money—a "loan," both insisted, to tide Arvin over until he got back on his feet—and awkwardly made light of Arvin's memory loss:

> I got a chuckle out of your remarks about the treatments slowing up your wits; boy, if they slowed you down to a fraction of their speed, you'd still be so far ahead of the rest of us, it wouldn't be funny . . . it would be nice to be in hailing distance of you, mentally, even if I know it is only temporary.

Returning to Northampton before Thanksgiving, Arvin was dazed but ready to resume what little life he could. Mostly, he felt battered and fatigued. He told Aaron, "I have to be very careful how I get launched on certain conversational topics lest they should prove to make too great demands on my powers of retention, explicitness, etc." As a youth, Arvin had teased himself about his meekness; when he turned sixteen, he wrote in his journal, "Got a haircut this morning and—ahem!—a shave! My chest is nearly $1\frac{1}{2}$ inches larger . . . It seems as if this were an epic in my life . . . Ah well, I might as well write a sonnet and get over this!" He'd entered his fifties feeling shaky, lonely, and blocked. Now, after two years of precipitous ups and downs, he was haunted and philosophical, still a forceful thinker and a graceful writer, but at times so apprehensive and befuddled that he seemed, to himself if not to others, much older.

On better days he knew that even if he couldn't change, he could survive, and that in itself was something to go on. His memory returned, and his equilibrium, and he began to see a future. But the urge to kill himself had not gone away, and Arvin doubted, more fatalistically than ever, that it soon would.

As names were named around the country, the Red hunts grew. In November, the House Committee on Un-American Activities, which had recently finished the Hollywood probe that led to the notorious studio blacklists, announced its next target: communist subversion on college campuses. The move had long been expected. The question of whether Reds should be allowed to teach had been debated at Smith as far back as the spring of 1949, when HUAC, responding to complaints about college curricula from the Sons of the American Revolution, requested that college presidents compile and submit to the committee lists of books and other readings used in their courses. Now, though Senator McCarthy himself called investigating colleges "an awfully unpleasant task," because of all the "screaming of interference with academic freedom," the committee pushed ahead with its work.

Its first—and most devastating—witness was Robert Gorham Davis, of the Smith English Department. A prolific, mercurial Boston Yankee, Davis, forty-four, had attended Harvard in the late 1920s and got his first teaching job at Rensselaer, where, after meeting Hicks, he began studying communism and first gained notice as a Marxist critic. He had returned to Harvard in the mid-thirties to teach and, as a secret Party member, held weekly meetings of the fifteen-man Harvard branch in his apartment. In time, he introduced Hicks to Aaron and Matthiessen, who were not members but who supported the group's work. Since 1943, Davis and his wife, Hope, had been part of Arvin's circle at Smith. Davis taught twentieth-century American fiction as an associate professor and contributed reviews, essays, and short stories to the *New York Times Book Review, Partisan Review, The New Republic, Collier's,* and *The New Yorker.* Like Arvin, he was correct, precise, a stickler for rules. No longer a Party member, he had leaned safely rightward in recent years. A gambler with a taste for horses, he was known to be generous with friends.

During his day-long testimony on February 25, 1953, Davis cooperated fully with the committee. He confirmed that he had been a member of a communist "cell" at Harvard in the late 1930s, and proceeded to name two dozen others who, he said, had been communists at Harvard and Smith. At Harvard, he identified, most prominently, Hicks and the historian Daniel Boorstin, later to be librarian of Congress. At Smith, he mentioned Dorothy Douglas, former wife of Democratic senator Paul Douglas of Illinois, who had taught economics for two decades before she retired amid controversy two years earlier. HUAC promptly used the names to widen its probe, calling Hicks, Boorstin, and the Harvard physicist Wendell Furry to Washington to testify.

Hicks, under questioning the next day, confirmed many of the Harvard names. Then, after telling the committee how he, too, had repudiated communism, he pleaded with its members to temper their conclusions.

The emphasis in all these investigating committees always falls on the fact of how much communism there is and never how little there is. It seems to me I have been sitting around here for two days in which it has been demonstrated that there were ten or twelve communists fourteen years ago at Harvard and that perhaps there is one still there . . . I would honestly think if you could just say to the public, "Look, that's all," instead of saying, "Look how much that is, isn't that terrible?" you might do a good deal to allay the fear that is sweeping over this country.

Arvin feared that he, too, might be hauled in, even though he hadn't been named and had never been a Party member, and that his homosexuality might be exposed and addressed. Though there was no indication that HUAC was interested in former fellow travelers, he had reason for alarm. Unlike Aaron, say, who had been in a Marxist study group with Davis and Hicks at Harvard but who ultimately had no fear of testifying because he didn't know enough to implicate others, Arvin worried that, as a homosexual, he could be "turned"—made a tool of the committee. In the 1950s it was easier to admit to being a communist than to admit to being a homosexual. Former communists like Davis might lose their jobs as teachers, but what happened to those exposed in the press as perverts? Arvin's dread of being found out meant he could be easily bullied, and he was tormented by his sense of vulnerability, of shame at the fact that he could be forced to betray others to protect his own secrets.

Arvin survived the HUAC hearings, bolstered by their failure to ignite a full-blown hysteria. As after the Red hunt at Yaddo, he was relieved to have been spared, and though he didn't expect his life to get better, he took comfort in believing that it was likely to get no worse. He had been welcomed at Harvard for the spring semester after all, and since arriving in January he had found a certain solace in living in a sublet on Story Street, reading extensively at Widener Library, teaching a conference course, and breathing an atmosphere different from Northampton's. He went to plays and movies with old friends, finding consolation, and sometimes great pleasure, in routine diversions. As he wrote to Aaron:

> The *staple* of life is certainly suffering, though surely not its real meaning, and we differ mainly in our capacity to endure it—or to be diverted from it. I myself never found it consoling to have this denied or minimized: it seems to me to give one *some* strength just to know that pain is normal, and disappointment the rule, and disquiet the standard—and that the things that have the other quality (work, friendship, the arts) are the wonderful, incredible

exception & mitigation. And I can tell you, from a certain fund of experience, that one can be taken down from the rack, closer to death than to life—and still have the most exquisite joys ahead of one.

⟸══⟹

When he visited other campuses, Arvin scouted for gifted young men whom he tried to lure to Smith, an appealing arrangement for all involved. Smith got talented young instructors, the young men landed good teaching jobs, and Arvin acquired handpicked youthful protégés to whom he was attracted and who he hoped would be attracted to him.

At Ohio State he had met a wide-eyed, though hardly naive, doctoral student named Wendell Stacy Johnson, who was hired by Smith the next year to teach Victorian literature. Among Smith's Ivy League–trained faculty, Johnson was an anomaly, having graduated from the University of Kansas City, a Midwestern commuter college near the bottom of the academic pecking order. But Johnson was six feet, two inches tall, open-faced, bright, poetic, flirtatious, charming, and twenty-five, and Arvin wasn't the only one smitten. Johnson's students adored him. So did W. H. Auden, who lectured at Smith while Arvin was at Harvard and who sublet Arvin's apartment. Like Auden, Johnson was outwardly homosexual, lascivious, and carefree. He gave Auden such thorough sexual satisfaction that Auden dedicated his poem "Plains" to him, rhapsodized about their affair in the passionate love song "The Willow-Wren and the Stare," and wrote him grateful letters: "Even your leathery old mother finds your brew of decency and scampishness more powerful than any martini."

Arvin appears not to have known about their affair when he returned to Northampton temporarily in late May, but he knew Wendell was a gad-about, and was immediately distressed and jealous to realize that his and Johnson's relationship had changed while he was in Cambridge. "Rather trying hour or so," he wrote dismally in his journal, "then X." Like Auden, Arvin understood that Wendell was flattered to have important older men fawn over him, but doubted the young man's sincerity in anything but what Auden called the "holy selfishness" of desire. Johnson, who was working on a study of Tennyson, knew what doors Arvin and Auden could open for him, as did they. And yet Arvin longed for his attention, his touch. Each time Arvin saw him during the next month, they drank and had sex, despite, Arvin wrote, "my inner terrors."

It was not just age and temperament that separated them, but Arvin's mortification at Wendell's openness. As with Capote, he feared being exposed, but he also sharply disapproved of "unmasculine" public behavior, which included fraternizing with other homosexuals. At the same time, he envied Wendell's freedom to be who he was and have what he wanted. In New York, homosexuals had begun to drop their disguises. Despite the dangers, young gay men were taking chances—being seen together, being known—that men of Arvin's generation, who had lived deeply in shadow, found destructive and terrifying. Of all Arvin's torments, this ambivalence—his tense, furtive desire for beautiful young men whom he knew he could never be like—now became the greatest. He felt he was debasing himself, but was powerless to stop it, and yet was at sea without intimate contact even when it brought him pain and humiliation.

On June 29, Wendell decamped for the summer, leaving Arvin alone in Northampton just two days after he returned for good, and plunging him once again into anguished solitude. "Intolerable day," he wrote in his journal on July 3. "A failure," was all he wrote the next day. The following morning, he couldn't get out of bed. "Whiskey," he wrote, and added, cryptically, "Attempted something else but failed." Whether "something else" was another weak suicide attempt, his friends recognized that Arvin was again about to fall apart. Two weeks later, Aaron and Fisher drove him to a Boston-area psychiatric hospital, Bournewood, where Arvin received more shock treatments. Again, they did little more than addle and confound him. Drinking more heavily than ever after he returned home, inconsolable, exhausted, his spirit and memory confused, he wrote desperately to Robert Davis, instructing him how to handle any such future collapses:

> I do not wish under any circumstances (if my wishes are at all to be considered) to be subjected to these [shock treatments] once more . . . their effect seems decidedly to be a deleterious one—on the will and on the memory and on the capacity to work. It may

well be that this means my being sent ultimately, or even sooner, to a state hospital; so let it be.

Arvin's relations with Wendell improved slightly in September and October as he struggled unevenly to regain his strength. He agonized over Wendell's weekends in New York, chastening himself in his journal for his "puerile resentment" and humbling himself with gratitude when Wendell returned, listening ambivalently to him recount the lusty details. Once, they had an intimate and soothing evening together in Arvin's apartment, just the two of them for drinks and supper. Seeing little future beyond such isolated moments of "reconciliation," Arvin considered breaking off the relationship, but felt too weak and dependent to try. He presented a brave face: "W leaves for another New York weekend, crazy boy," he wrote on November 3. But after another bad night of solitary drinking and insomnia, he was again haunted: "Obsessed with the problem of W and myself. Complete and hopeless failure of inner resources. Also of spirit. How long, Lord, how long?"

HUAC's main target had been Harvard, which guaranteed the hearings major press, but Robert Davis's testimony also thrust Smith center stage. As paranoia rose over communists in the schools, the college was forced to prove to the country, and especially to the prosperous business and professional men who proudly sent their daughters there to be educated, that it didn't harbor subversives. The administration and faculty agonized over the crisis. Davis, who had tenure, was kept on, as President Benjamin Wright, a former government professor at Harvard, lauded him for his brave honesty. Unlike the Hollywood studios, the college intended to stand behind its faculty, whether they named names or not. Still, the administration strove to have it both ways, saying it wouldn't require teachers to testify before government committees but hoping privately that they would.

Northampton was less sanguine. Its opinion makers, like most small-town New Englanders, were Eisenhower Republicans: flinty, sober, self-reliant, conservative, patriotic. The town had a distinguished history of rejecting witch-hunters like McCarthy. After Jonathan Edwards declared

that Northampton was damned because some children were caught titter-
ing over a midwives' handbook, he was exiled to Stockbridge, as deep into
the heathen wilderness as one could send a man at the time. Still, it preferred its anticommunism neat. After a group of professors, including
Aaron, released a statement questioning whether "we are not in greater
danger from demagogues in our midst than we are from conspirators" and
urging that "unless a teacher is guilty of treason or espionage, he should be
judged on the basis of his professional competence and his devotion to free
and honest inquiry," the Hampshire County clerk, Charles Kulikowski, said
it showed "Communistic and anti-American tendencies" and supported
certain "foreign ideologies." Davis had testified that communists at Harvard
and Smith observed a code not to indoctrinate their students: "We had a
lurking feeling that it wasn't quite good sportsmanship to try to influence
young people." The *Gazette* stridently disagreed, editorializing, "We should
have no communists in our government and no communists in our
schools."

Arvin absented himself from the debate, siding in principle with Aaron
while privately supporting Davis and Hicks. Then, in February 1954, he
himself became a target. Smith alumnae in the Hartford area received a
professionally printed appeal from a fellow graduate charging that Arvin
and four other senior professors at Smith "have been or are presently affil-
iated with many organizations cited as Communist or Communist-front . . .
by the Committee on Un-American Activities." The alumnae were urged to
withhold donations until Smith took action against the five. The letter, sent
to thirty-two hundred Smith graduates across the country, was signed,
"Committee for Discrimination in Giving, Aloise B. Heath, Secretary."

Allie Heath was the oldest sister of William F. Buckley, Jr., who three
years earlier had riled the academic world with his provocative first book,
God and Man at Yale, written while he was in graduate school. In it, he suggested that Yale alumni play a greater role in directing the course of education there, a repellant idea even to many conservatives. "Are these
perennial sophomores, who dress up in silly costumes and get drunk at re-
unions, who spend their thousands of dollars buying halfbacks and quar-
terbacks, and following the Big Blue Team—are they to be the nation's
mental mentors?" asked Bruce Barton, the anti–New Deal adman who,

thirty years earlier, had orchestrated Coolidge's attack on Red professors at women's colleges. But Heath, one of four Buckley girls to attend Smith, seized on her brother's proposal. Like McCarthy, she believed that tolerating communism was as vile as practicing it, and she sounded the alarm by leveling unsupported charges against the five professors, all of whom had tenure.

That evening, Arvin was summoned to Wright's house. "A nightmare, all of it," he wrote in his journal. The college intended to defend all five, as it had Davis. But it was only a matter of time before Heath's letter would appear in the press, and when it did, Wright believed, the outcome could be grave. Arvin's concerns, typically, were more personal. He had already been reeling after three years of depression and thoughts of death. The previous month—long winter weeks when the sky grew ashen and Arvin stayed in his apartment seeing almost no one—he'd been nearly incapacitated. "Complete ereinte [exhausted] by all this—and the pervading terror," he had written in his journal on January 20, more than a month before Heath's letter. "In the pit . . . with the pendulum. The less recorded the better," he wrote three days later.

How, in his condition, Arvin worried, could he endure a public persecution?

What was clear to others, if not to Arvin himself, was that underneath his weak exterior he possessed a steely resolve. In spite of himself, he had learned to survive his worst fears, and to suffer alone while none but his closest friends knew how close he was to the edge. "A quiet man with a violent mind," Brooks had once called him, "who would gladly have stood against a wall and faced a fusillade for his convictions." Aaron saw that indomitability in Arvin's handwriting; slashing and extroverted, it was fiery, "like Savanarola's." Arvin considered himself a coward. He was terrified. But he was often braver and more resilient than many of those he envied as "normal." Unlike Matthiessen, he had experienced nothing that depleted him so far as to make him succumb.

Arvin soldiered through the next two months. Wright attacked Heath for her "vague charges . . . insinuation, and . . . innuendoes." Donations and letters poured in from hundreds of alumnae in support of the professors and the college. Smith, conducting its own probe, contacted the U.S.

Attorney General's office, which confirmed that, although Arvin had been a member of numerous communist-linked organizations, there was "nothing of interest" in his file. Arvin, fearing revelations about his sexual history, was sharply relieved. Then the story broke in the press, and the state's anti-Red apparatus moved in. The Massachusetts Committee to Investigate Communism scheduled a hearing in Northampton on March 20 to hear the charges against the five professors. With two members, a woman state representative from Cambridge and a governor's appointee, the panel was hardly a miniature HUAC. Arvin was shaken nevertheless. He would be testifying under oath. He didn't know what they would ask him, or what he might say to save himself.

Eventually, he testified for twelve minutes and defended himself ably. He hadn't named names, possibly because he hadn't been asked to. Less horrible than he'd feared, the hearing taught him that he could withstand interrogation about his politics.

Despite his relief, though, Arvin's anxiety wasn't banished. "Ghastly day," he wrote two weeks later in his journal. "At night took two Nembutals and fell into oblivion." Two days later he couldn't get out of bed. He wrote only, "Whiskey."

In December, a discredited McCarthy was censured by the Senate, and active McCarthyism came to an end. Domestic communism was no longer viewed as the main threat to American decency and prosperity, even though the Cold War intensified and superpower contention between America and the Soviet Union enveloped the globe. Flush and at peace, America strode ahead, as it had during the 1920s, embracing everything new, fun, and modern: in science, art, music, consumerism, style, literature, and sex, though this last was predictably shadowed by a lingering puritanism. At Smith that spring, in warm weather, the girls started wearing Bermuda shorts to class, though college rules required them to cover up when they went downtown.

Arvin held on, staying out of hospitals and withdrawing further into his "dismal chamber under the eaves." On campus, he maintained a balanced presence, especially with younger colleagues and those serious students he accepted as advisees, who found him generally witty, accessible, opinionated, modest, and polite, however shy and nervous and, sometimes, cutting. A model of probity, he remained absolutely correct in dress and manner, his suits and shirts spotless and pressed, his shoes shined, as he tipped his hat to students and took pains to be liked by colleagues he despised. Underneath, however, he was unraveling. Unable to write or, he felt, love, he barricaded himself inside a private world of literature and drinking. He surrounded himself in his attic rooms with books and journals and pored over them until his eyes burned with fatigue. A deliveryman from Ryan's package store on Pleasant Street regularly hauled up to his rear landing a case of liquor—several bottles of top-shelf Scotch, Cutty Sark, J&B, or Dewar's; several more of port wine and sherry. Thus fortified, Arvin hunkered down in his lonely sanctuary, pleasanter than Hawthorne's to be sure, and sank into the decade's preferred mode of escape, a mode that the outwardly more manly and combative Matthiessen had tested but finally couldn't survive: invisible despair.

Chapter Seven

ARTHUR ELLSWORTH SUMMERFIELD had been one of America's top Chevrolet dealers, a man profitably attuned to middle-class hopes and values, when Dwight Eisenhower made him boss of the nation's postal system. A salesman's salesman, he'd first impressed Republican leaders in the late 1940s, when he marshaled General Motors dealers in Michigan to pay a dollar to the GOP for each car they sold. Such loyalty was rewarded. Summerfield, who had dropped out of school at the age of thirteen to take a job in a factory, and who got his start in business selling house lots after dark by the light of his car's headlights, was named Republican Party national chairman in 1949. In 1952, he delivered the Michigan delegation to Eisenhower, and then managed Ike's campaign in the general election. When Eisenhower needed $75,000 to buy a national television hookup for Richard Nixon's "Checkers" speech, Summerfield delivered the money.

As postmaster general, Summerfield, fifty-three, liked to boast that he ran "the world's biggest business." Besides his skill in raising funds, his other major job qualifications were a GM-inspired vision of a modern, efficient postal service, a strict Midwestern conservatism, and a core faith "that a dedicated salesman never stops selling." Stocky, silver-haired, and tenacious, Summerfield hired a press agent, bullied Congress by threatening "drastic" curbs in mail delivery if it didn't approve his spending requests, denounced communists and "union dictators," and loudly attacked the rise of "pornographic filth in the family mailbox." To Summerfield, the mail was "the very lifeblood of our person-to-person communications." Nothing so offended his sense of decency and patriotism as the poisoning of this lifeblood by "merchants of filth to warp and pervert young minds for profit"—racketeers and criminals who, under the guise of purveying "literature," had lately turned mail-order obscenity into big business.

In Washington, it pays to have good enemies. As the Red hunts drew to an end and McCarthy fell into disgrace, Summerfield's crusade against smut traffickers proved unassailable. Americans' anxieties about their children had spiked during the postwar period. Juvenile crime was up sharply, as was concern over a new sexual openness in movies, books, magazines, fashion, art, and music. Summerfield, finding a causal link between the two, targeted mail-order pornography as the main threat menacing American families, more treacherous than domestic communism, high taxes, or labor racketeers. Shrewdly, he picked for his foil a disreputable New York publisher named Samuel Roth, whose thirty-year cat-and-mouse campaign against federal censorship set the stage, in late 1954 and early 1955, for the first major tests in nearly a decade of the government's role in defining and combating obscenity.

Sam Roth represented everything Summerfield loathed. Born in a small town in Austria in 1894, he immigrated to America with his parents, was raised on the Lower East Side of New York City, wrote poetry as a child for Yiddish journals, went to Columbia University, where he published a campus magazine filled with excerpts of D. H. Lawrence and other radical authors, opened a bookstore in Greenwich Village after World War I, started another magazine in which he reprinted "lightly libidinous" French fiction, and eventually made a name for himself by reprinting mutilated chunks of *Ulysses* without Joyce's permission. He was prosecuted several times during the twenties and thirties for publishing literature deemed offensive by local courts, and went to prison twice; he also had a reputation for defying authorities and evading police. A tall bespectacled man with a courtly manner, Roth published scores of sexually explicit books and magazines under at least six different imprints, European "classics" but also collections of nude pictures, which he sold under sixty-two different company names. He boasted to a congressional committee investigating the causes of "juvenile delinquency" that he had mailed out ten million advertisements for his various publications, using mailing lists so indiscriminate that his circulars were sent to children and orphanages.

It was this last that incited Summerfield to action and that landed the issue of government censorship in federal court at a time when American interest in sexual images and ideas was starting to explode. By the midfifties, the Post Office had been investigating Roth for years, with postal inspectors in at least ten cities diligently answering his ads and ordering his publications. It also had been quietly confiscating literary classics under the so-called Comstock Act, which authorized the postmaster general to ban any book, pamphlet, picture, letter, or other material he found to be "obscene, lewd, lascivious or filthy." The law was named for Anthony Comstock, the portly, muttonchopped evangelical crusader and self-proclaimed "weeder in God's garden" who, during the boom years after the Civil War, persuaded Congress to give the Post Office custody of the nation's moral life.

Using the Comstock Act, Summerfield went hard after Roth. A postal inspector, responding to one of Roth's advertisements, ordered and received a copy of his *American Aphrodite,* a quarterly literary magazine containing Aubrey Beardsley's *Venus and Tannhauser,* which had been written in the mid-1890s and included an expletive-free description of Venus delicately masturbating her pet unicorn and lapping up his ejaculate—"her little apéritif," Beardsley called it. *Aphrodite* supplied the main evidence Summerfield needed to get a federal grand jury to indict Roth on twenty-six counts, and in early 1956 he was convicted. With his mail-order empire tottering, Roth announced that he would appeal to the Supreme Court, not on the constitutionality of the Comstock Act but on the government's definition of obscenity.

The High Court had long shied away from the issue of sex, having last weighed whether "indecent" material was protected under the First Amendment when it reviewed a New York State ban against Edmund Wilson's *Memoirs of Hecate County* in 1946. Wilson's salacious second novel—"probably the best damn thing I ever wrote," he said—had suddenly made him a best-selling author (and his first and only real money) when police raided four Manhattan bookstores and seized 130 copies of the book. Wilson's publisher fought the case up to the Supreme Court as Arvin, Dos Passos, Mencken, Trilling, and others defended Wilson's literary and moral credentials. But the Court failed to make a ruling. With Felix Frankfurter removing himself from the case because he and Wilson were friends, the other eight justices split four to four, a tie vote that let the ban stand without the Court's resolving whether it was legal. Critics disputed *Hecate's* power to arouse—Raymond Chandler accused Wilson of "having made fornication as dull as a railroad time table"—but Wilson was disgraced anyway. Meanwhile, the questions of what was obscenity and how far the government could go in protecting citizens from it remained unanswered when the Court agreed, in late 1956, to hear Roth's appeal.

By then, however, Summerfield was embroiled in a second, more direct test of his antismut campaign. The Post Office maintained a long list of proscribed books: classics like *Leaves of Grass* and *Uncle Tom's Cabin;* novels by Hemingway, John Steinbeck, and Norman Mailer; scientific and philosophical writings by Freud, Margaret Mead, and Simone de Beauvoir; even ancient Greek poetry—anything Summerfield and his censors found prurient or offensive. In August 1954, when Arvin was still recoiling from the Heath probe, a postal inspector in Los Angeles seized a rare, illustrated 1926 edition of *Lysistrata,* a 2,400-year-old antiwar comedy by Aristophanes. Noting that the text "contains numerous passages which are plainly obscene, lewd and lascivious in character and which are well calculated to deprave the morals," Summerfield ordered the volume destroyed.

Seven months later, in March 1955, the book's owner sought an injunction in Federal District Court in Washington—the first direct challenge of the Comstock Act in eighty years. Summerfield, whose political instincts so far had been sharp, was caught off guard by the outcry. "Mr. Summerfield, in private life an automobile dealer, banned a play that is on the shelves of virtually every public library in the country and in thousands of American homes," the United Press wrote. "This is no time for America to be breeding a community of common, steadfast dunces," *Collier's* editorialized.

Summerfield hadn't got where he was by fighting battles he couldn't win. Rather than invite a federal court challenge, he announced that he would voluntarily return the book to its owner, thus rendering the case moot. As he would soon write in his as-told-to book *U.S. Mail*, mail-order pornography was as noxious a threat to children as illegal drugs: "The filth racketeers have learned that, among youngsters, they can develop addicts to obscene literature and pictures who will be not much different from the narcotics addict. Their objective is to get the child hooked . . . They feed him an array of trash carefully geared to successive stages of perversion." Now that he controlled an apparatus that reached into every home and business in America, Summerfield refused to yield his Comstock Act powers to the Supreme Court, whose majority had been appointed by Roosevelt and Truman and represented, he said, "the laxness of the past."

"Dinner at the club alone," Arvin wrote in his journal on January 10, 1955. "But the proximity of W and four of his epicene companions was almost too much for easy digestion." Arvin was at a crossroads in his relationship with Wendell Johnson. He was put out by Wendell's unabashed affiliation with other male instructors, the "set of gay ones" who often sat together at the Faculty Club, chatting and laughing amiably and turning heads. Arvin had traveled a couple of times with Wendell to New York, tentatively making the rounds of gay bars and bookstores, awkwardly nursing a drink at a clubby "granny-catcher's" place on East Fifty-fifth Street, but Smith was not Manhattan. Discretion was paramount. Arvin was appalled by Wendell's heedlessness and insensitivity to the delicacy of Arvin's position if not his own.

He was plagued by the thought that Wendell was using him. Three days later, Wendell came up to his apartment for the first time in four months, a "difficult scene," Arvin wrote. He had applied for a Guggenheim Fellowship and was up for reappointment, and he wanted Arvin's help. Hurt and conflicted, Arvin was bitter and acted it. Then Wendell, in tears, told him, "I'm very fond of you," and Arvin succumbed. "I was close to tears myself," he wrote, "and terribly distressed. Misery after he left." If Arvin couldn't bear feeling that he had been treated as an expedient, or that he was dependent on his young friend's throwaway affections, he was tormented by the alternative: that Wendell would reject him and he'd be alone, possibly from then on. For the next six weeks, he plunged into a debilitating depression. "Unable to face the world," he wrote. "Tortured, except when wholly out, by insane thoughts of W." As before, Arvin's relationship with a lover didn't simply end. It survived, a painful, self-mortifying spiral of misery and reconciliation, as both men, for their own reasons, clung on. "W came up here for five minutes. X. We parted," he recorded on March 31. "Would to heaven I could restore and maintain without lapses a right relation between us."

Arvin went more often to church, asking forgiveness. On days when he felt well enough to face the world, he took Holy Communion at St. John's, the Episcopal church neighboring the campus. A crenelated heap of rock-face granite, St. John's was a distant cry from the tiny, gaunt parish church with stucco walls and cheap stained glass windows where Arvin's family worshipped back in Valparaiso. As a boy, he had thrown himself into the life of the church, glorying in his long cassock as a choirboy, acolyte, and crucifer. Not long after, he'd concluded that he was a hideous mistake and that God detested him: "So small a boy, and so great a sinner!" By the time he was in college and drawn to Bolshevism, he signed off his letters to Lilienthal with a jaunty "There ain't no hell!" though in truth he wasn't sure. His return to St. John's in the late 1940s had first been part of his search for political and sexual cover, but now he craved something else: absolution, strength, the will to change.

The rector, Father David Cochran, encouraged him to make a private confession. Cochran had counseled Arvin at his apartment during the darkest days of the Heath affair and considered him "a poor tormented soul." He was aware of Arvin's homosexuality, though they'd never discussed it. Moral theology condemned homosexual acts, but Cochran believed privately that homosexuality was "a natural human condition, though perhaps not God-given." Assuring Arvin that he faced neither eternal damnation nor exclusion from the church, he advised him that, by confessing his sins and taking the sacraments, he might find "a path to God."

Arvin resisted, preferring instead to kneel alone in prayer at the back of the sanctuary, even though such "general confession" elicited only "general absolution"—a blanket amnesty thought too weak to bring about a true rebirth. Arvin was serious about finding God, but he considered himself too wicked, and was too depressed and afraid, to risk telling Cochran about his hidden life. He might not believe in hell, but he believed in original sin. Even if Cochran absolved him, he suspected there was no place in God's good graces for a man who succumbed to pleasuring himself with other men.

In June 1955, Arvin attended a five-day retreat at Trinity College, in Hartford. Residing in a dormitory, he arose each morning in time for Communion at seven; attended twice-daily lectures on baptism, confirmation, marriage, and prayer; participated in seminars on "anxiety, negation, etc."; prayed during Vespers at Trinity Chapel; and sat with real interest through lectures by Cleanth Brooks, the most popular of the New Critics, on Christianity in Faulkner, Hemingway, Yeats, and Eliot. At first, he was unmoved. "Too many stories, too much slang," he wrote on Tuesday, the second day. But by Wednesday his spirits lifted. "A beautiful evening," he wrote. Even if he didn't agree with all he was being taught, Arvin found surcease from his suffering in the daily discipline of a well-practiced theology. His praying became deeper, and he enjoyed the other participants, particularly a Trinity undergraduate named Flemming, "an attractive boy."

He returned to Northampton full of resolve to forget Wendell, overcome his depression, and cut back on his drinking. For a month, his bad days grew rarer, but by August he tumbled "into the deeper waters again," drinking too much and suffering his "old foolish aching depression about W." He continued to drag himself out for seven-thirty Communion at St. John's, a block from his apartment, but dully, with little purpose, "only half there." The other half—the half that craved other men and was ashamed of it—remained distressingly unredeemed and unfulfilled. What Arvin longed for was reconciliation between the two, a humane, merciful acceptance of who he was. He kept trying. "Up early, much the worse for my dissipations," he wrote in his journal in mid-November, "but managed to get to church at 7:30 to ask forgiveness for my sins with, I hope, real contrition." One night when he lay awake wanting a Scotch, he drank some Ovaltine instead, and fell back to sleep until dawn. "This should be a model," he wrote.

The problem was temptation. Despite his horror at Wendell's insouciance and the newly self-conscious assertiveness of the "gay ones" at

COURTESY OF ED, BARBARA, AND CHARLES PIERCE

COURTESY OF THE PIERCES

1.

2.

COURTESY OF THE PIERCES

CHRIS HOUGH

4.

3.

ℬorn and raised in Valparaiso, Indiana (4), in the years before World War I, Arvin grew up feeling "uniquely misbegotten." He favored his mother, Jessie (2), a long-suffering housewife, while increasingly reviling his father, Frederic (1), a truculent farm-loan manager whom Arvin thought capable of "emotional cruelty." His grandfather John Hawkins (3), who aspired to teach singing but who drifted among menial jobs to support his family, embodied the poetic spirit that Arvin and other Lost Generation writers believed could only be crushed by life in a sterile Midwestern town.

"*I* am so lonesome for an intimate friend," Arvin wrote in his journal at age fourteen. Arriving at Harvard a few years later, he plunged into a world of books, Bolshevism, and free thinking and developed his first adult crush—on his roommate. After returning to Valparaiso for a semester to recover from eyestrain and anemia, he resolved to stay in the East and make his way as a critic of American literature, an uncharted field at the time.

1.

2.

3.

*T*hough he burned to move to New York City and do "literary work" at the height of the Jazz Age, Arvin (1), needing money first, took a teaching job at Smith College in Northampton, Massachusetts (3), home of President Calvin Coolidge (2, on the left). Believing it was his duty as a radical intellectual also to be a man of action, Arvin led the local campaign for Coolidge's third-party opponent, Wisconsin progressive "Fighting Bob" La Follette. "I think," he wrote, "it will possibly save me from the kindnesses of a lot of respectable (and very dull) people who rather enjoy a literary radical but gag at a political one."

1.

2.

*B*uoyed by the success of his first book, a biography of Nathaniel Hawthorne, Arvin nevertheless panicked about his homosexuality and married a former student, Mary Garrison (1), in 1932. Mary stayed home (2) while Arvin labored on a biography of Walt Whitman and worked for various Communist Party–front organizations. Trapped in a dry marriage, Arvin was alternately solicitous and cruel, and Mary eventually suffered a nervous breakdown before seeking a divorce.

1.

2.

3.

4.

*D*espite his fears and timidity, Arvin's circle of literary friends consisted largely of younger writers and critics whom he influenced profoundly. Granville Hicks (2), said Arvin, "knew what I only suspected, and believed with assurance what I scarcely dared express." Howard Doughty (3, on the right), with whom Arvin had an affair at Smith, modeled his career on Arvin's, becoming a critic and a communist fellow traveler. Carson McCullers (4) called Arvin "the most comforting person I know." Daniel Aaron (1) left Harvard to teach at Smith "because Newton was there."

1.

2.

3.

4.

𝒟uring the FDR years, critics and intellectuals assumed a watershed role in American politics and culture. Arvin, despite his deepening depressions, remained a key figure in their world. Tennessee Valley Authority chairman David Lilienthal (1), a boyhood friend who would soon become guardian of the nation's nuclear secrets as head of the Atomic Energy Commission, never stopped looking up to him; Edmund Wilson (2), whom Arvin recruited to teach at Smith, regarded only Arvin and Van Wyck Brooks (4), Arvin's mentor, as first-rate writers among the rising crop of Americanists. Alfred Kazin (3), who later won the first prize for criticism in Arvin's name although Arvin thought little of his work, extolled his biographies as "prime examples of a sense of history and a command of style."

1.

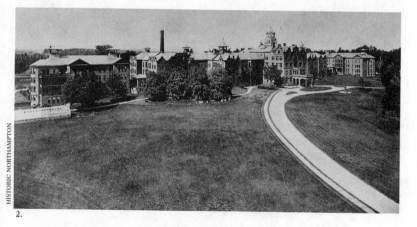

2.

*A*s America stood at the precipice of World War II, Arvin finally suffered a sharp collapse, taking him from the bucolic, ivy-covered world of Smith College (1) to the gargantuan state mental hospital next door (2), which Smith girls called "Dippy Hall." Reeling from the failure of his marriage, the retreat of domestic communism in the wake of the Hitler-Stalin pact, and the realization that his homosexuality—his "loathsome affliction," he called it—couldn't be cured, he took a yearlong leave from teaching and spent several more months recuperating in a private asylum in White Plains, New York.

1.

2.

3.

4.

ℜetreating after the war to the last safe place he knew—Yaddo (3), the distinguished writers' colony in Saratoga Springs, New York (1, left to right: Arvin, Elizabeth Ames, Granville Hicks)—Arvin met the young short-story writer Truman Capote (2, right) and fell instantly in love. So did Capote. The affair, which lasted two years and encompassed the happiest, most productive period of Arvin's life, was the most formative relationship either would ever have. "Newton was my Harvard," Capote would say. He dedicated his first novel to Arvin, who, upon seeing its famously salacious jacket photo (4), wrote: "There is a look in those eyes I know oh, so well, and that I decidedly hope no other human being knows in the same way."

Smith, Arvin was drawn to their open ways. Sex, he was learning, was no less powerful an urge at fifty-six than it had been at thirty-six, or at sixteen—powerful beyond reason, all the more for having been locked up, forbidden, denied. He had spent his life averting suspicion. He'd suffered through a dry marriage, closeted his deepest desires even from himself, acted "straighter than straight," fouled his psyche, was painfully well-mannered. He had too much to fear and to lose to experiment, as his younger colleagues did, with a gay "lifestyle." But he understood that was just what he wanted, more than ever. Much as he disdained Wendell and his companions for embracing their weakness, he was also jealous of them. He coveted their youth and beauty and freedom. He longed to be wanted by them.

In mid-winter 1956 Arvin inched, with violently mingled emotions, toward their circle. He met a young Mount Holyoke instructor whom he hoped to bring to Smith, and wrote frankly in his journal about having sex with him. "Paul came up and for the first time we got in bed together and made love. A beautiful, still, snowy night. Long talk after X, until after 2. Lovely." Ten days later he invited several young gay men, including Paul, Wendell, and Wendell's new lover, a sullen young man from a neighboring town named Buzz, up to his apartment for drinks—a first—and felt "childishly dejected" afterward when they didn't stay and go to dinner with him.

Then, too soon, came trouble. A visiting art instructor at Smith was caught by police having sex in a car with a boy who may have been a minor. There was no scandal—the man, fired on the spot, vanished from Northampton—but Arvin and others were appalled by his indiscretion. Another incident followed, equally disturbing. After a long and violent quarrel with Buzz, Wendell took refuge one night in Paul's apartment, in a quiet neighborhood near downtown. Buzz, drunk and frenzied, arrived and kept ringing Paul's bell until Paul called the police, who came and arrested Buzz. Assuming "that the melee must have some gay explanation," Arvin noted in his journal, another tenant reported the incident to Smith, which ended any hope of Paul's appointment. "A heavy blow for him of course," Arvin wrote. "And also to me. Life's timing of the incident, on the heels of [the earlier] arrest, could hardly have been more diabolical (—or perhaps more providential. Fond as I am of Paul, I know now he would have been a troublesome handful as a colleague)." Three weeks later, Paul came to Arvin's apartment to break off their affair, invoking a girlfriend in Cambridge. "Purely imaginary and intended as a deterrent to me," Arvin wrote.

Arvin's agitation heightened with his trips to New York, which he found "undeniably provocative." "Did some rather idle and wasteful cruising about," he wrote that June after a brief stay. Like other small-town travelers, he was mesmerized by the city's profane and glamorous underside, its dizzying social whirl of friends and friends of friends, all of whom seemed suddenly up on everything new and eager to hook one in. Greasing this new camaraderie were not only the all-male bars, each with a subspecialty—rough trade here, "fatties" there—but a thriving new industry in erotic pictures. Arvin was introduced to muscle magazines with names like *Tomorrow's Man*, *Vim*, and *Muscleboy*, which were openly displayed at newsstands. As was true with many homosexuals, the magazines were his first view of a wider gay culture, and he screwed up his courage to buy some and smuggle them back to Northampton. On another trip, seven months later, in March 1957, a friend invited him to view some "goodies"—"whatever on earth that may mean," he wrote to Doughty. After years of furtive intimacy with colleagues whose importance to him he was forced to deny on pain of losing everything, he was fascinated by the mere suggestion of something lascivious and carefree. "It all sounds quite mad and anti-Northamptonian, and perhaps it is fatuous of me to dash off this way," he added. "But I find it is terribly salutary to make these occasional excursions from the Cave of Prospect Street."

Others noticed a sudden rise in his vitality. "I don't recall you looking so well, so much yourself," Lilienthal wrote after seeing Arvin that August. Never the best judge of Arvin's inner life, Lilienthal this time had it right. Capote also would see it: "[Leo] Lerman was right. You do look ten years younger. Tell me what you use and I shall try the same." Clearly, Arvin's first tentative steps into the homosexual demimonde of the late 1950s agreed with him, despite his setbacks in Northampton. He still had more bad days than good, still struggled to get to Holy Communion and chided himself when he failed to. But he had raised his caul ever so slightly, and an airy October light pierced his autumnal gloom.

Back in his cave, Arvin tried to write. But Emerson, his next big subject, was proving as elusive for him as he had for Brooks, thirty years earlier. Part of the problem was Emerson himself, a chronic optimist. What he wrote seemed of little pertinence to a world living under the shadow of the Bomb. Arvin worried that Emerson had failed to plumb himself—or life's tragic nature—deeply enough for "[us to] ever again listen to [him] with the old reverential wisdom."

Mostly, however, it was Arvin's unmooring that roiled his concentration and kept him from writing. He had always been drawn more to eighteenth-century New England than to his own time and place. But after a lifetime devoted to peeling back history, he suddenly was consumed with the affairs of the present. His absorption with sex, bottled up after years of near abstinence, had become voracious. "He had a very driving, passionate, sexual nature," Aaron would later comment. "He used to say to me, 'You know, Dan, you'd think with old age sexual desires would subside. But they don't. They become more and more extreme, almost as if they were raging.' "

In the prevailing view of the time, Arvin had reached that reckoning, supposedly peculiar to the conspiratorial world of the homosexual, when debasement replaces mutuality, and desperation trumps precaution. In fact, he was the commonest of sufferers: an aging single man looking for a young lover to rekindle his spirits.

He thought he found one in Ned Spofford, Smith's new twenty-six-year-old classicist. Arvin's eye for talented young instructors fell upon the pleasing Amherst alumnus when they met over dinner at the faculty club a week before Christmas 1957. "A pretty serious youth," he wrote in his journal, "but very likeable."

Arvin wasn't the only one at Smith drawn to Spofford. Ned wasn't handsome, but he was lively and impish, a gifted pianist whose long, delicate fingers suggested the noble bone structure of an Anglican ancestry. His nose was severe, like Emerson's, and his feet so elegantly tapered that an Italian sculptor once asked to model them. His thinning black hair was cropped close to a widow's peak, and he wore scholarly horn-rim glasses. Casually rumpled in loose-fitting khakis, sneakers, and a crewneck sweater, he was the kind of charming, poetic young bachelor who, at Smith, shy students and unmarried women faculty lingered over longingly but never were able to possess.

Unlike most of the faculty, Ned had native roots. His grandparents had lived in Northampton, and he grew up in Lee, an hour away. His father, Roscoe, a large, gruff man with chin wattles, worked for his mother's brother as treasurer of a sand-and-gravel company, and Ned and his two sisters were raised in a stolid house that backed on the Housatonic River. When Ned was a child, the river flooded in spring. In the town's Catholic church, St. Mary's, the priest told the Irish immigrants who worked in Lee's paper mills and the Italian-Americans who cut marble out of its nubbly hills to offer up their suffering to God. In the white-spired Congregational church where Ned's family worshipped, the minister thundered that the floods were punishment for the sins of the town.

What attracted Arvin at once was Ned's open-faced seductiveness. He *made* people like him. Despite being an unathletic overachiever and member of Lee's Protestant minority, in high school he had been voted Brightest Boy, Most Studious Boy, Most Polite Boy, Model Boy Student, Class Orator, Class Musician, Class Actor, Did Most for Class, Teacher's Pet, and Most Likely to Succeed in a class of fifty-three students. On the night he graduated, he drove his father's Cadillac over to New York State with a few other boys to go drinking, and after that, he and one of them came back and masturbated each other. "It was delightful," he would later say, "wonderful. I didn't have the slightest sense that this was sinful."

Amherst was the only college Ned considered, yet when he arrived, in September 1950, he felt lost and unprepared. The school prized muscular Christianity, but Ned was neither muscular nor much of a Christian. More than 90 percent of students belonged to fraternities, and those who didn't—so-called independents—either were less well-off, lacked social distinction, or both. Ned was an independent. He suspected there were other homosexuals on campus, but their sexuality was thoroughly submerged. His classmates boasted of going to Greenwich Village on weekends, getting drunk, and beating up "queers" on MacDougal Street.

As in Lee, he triumphed in the classroom and became a favorite of the celebrated English and writing professor Theodore Baird, one of the dom-

inant figures on the faculty. Baird was formidable, virtuous, and conservative, and most students feared him. Ned, working hard, won Baird over. On
graduating near the top of his class, he was awarded a fellowship in English
at Cornell, largely due to Baird's sponsorship. He had been teaching two
sections of freshman English and studying Greek in Ithaca when Helen
Bacon, chair of the Smith Classics Department, spotted him in the spring
of 1957 and offered him a job teaching Latin.

Arvin courted Ned cautiously, for fear that he might reveal himself too
soon and frighten him off. First they met a few times for dinner. "Much talk
with him about Virgil, Ovid, Dante, etc. These poems are realities to him,
not just subjects," Arvin recorded. A shared love of poetry provided fitting
cover for deeper relations between a full professor and an instructor less
than half his age, and when Ned soon had Arvin back for lunch at the Faculty Club with the young poet Sylvia Plath and Plath's husband, Ted
Hughes, Arvin was delighted, even though he took an instant dislike to
Hughes. Arvin and Wendell Johnson had become reconciled. Arvin, who
had recently bought an 8-mm movie projector and learned how to operate
it, invited Wendell up to look at "two or three of the pretty silly reels I
have"—black-and-white movies of two youths wearing briefs tumbling over
each other. With Ned, however, he was reserved, professorial, and chaste.
After having dinner with him in early February, the third time in a month,
he wrote demurely in his journal, "He grows in grace with every meeting."

Arvin took pains to conceal his depression from Ned. Despite the energiz-
ing effects of his new social life, he still had ghastly days when he wanted
to kill himself. Ned, flattered by Arvin's attention, apparently saw none of
his blackness, although others did.

Plath, an alumna who had returned as an instructor, was making extra
money by grading papers for Arvin. She wrote in her journal, in early
March, "I . . . see Arvin: dry, fingering his keyring compulsively in class,
bright hard eyes, red-rimmed, turned cruel, lecherous, hypnotic, and holding me caught like the gnome Loerke held." The "acrid repulsion" she
sensed between Arvin and Hughes may have tainted her perception. Arvin
himself worried that he was too "dull and jaded" to be attractive.

But Ned was won over by Arvin's gentility, the current of animation in his talk, and by Arvin's obvious fondness for him. One night when he was leaving, Arvin said to him, "I don't think I've ever been so happy, not even with Truman." How, Ned later wondered, could he have known that Arvin was blanketed with despair?

Arvin's suffering wasn't all that Ned didn't see. Approaching his fifty-eighth birthday, he had begun taking the bus to Springfield to cruise. A regional transportation hub with ample amenities for travelers, the city had long attracted sexual adventurers from up and down the Connecticut Valley. Arvin's fear of discovery was partly allayed by Springfield's reputation for safety; the police evidently were paid well to be elsewhere, leaving several homosexual bars to operate freely. There was the Sportsman's Lounge, where the clientele was mostly professional and where Wendell and his friends liked to drink. Most famous was Blake's, renowned for its Saturday night dances—three hundred men in jackets and ties throbbing to jukebox music. Neither was to Arvin's taste. He preferred the Arch, at the north end of Main Street, a big smoky lounge with a circular bar that accommodated all types—educated men like himself, but also workingmen and young Negroes and married men and boys from nearby Westover Air Force base and students from the University of Massachusetts, which had outgrown its origins as an agricultural school and was attracting thousands of youths from around the state.

In early May 1958, near the end of the semester, Arvin and Ned went out for dinner, and then Arvin brought him to his apartment and ran off a couple of his movies. He was hardly the first suitor to contrive such a come-on, but Ned was notably unmoved. Pornography didn't interest him, he said. Arvin didn't press him. Several weeks later, after lunching together downtown, they returned to Arvin's apartment. This time they read to each other from a book by the Roman elegiac poet Propertius. "Very affecting to me to go through this beautiful poem with him aloud alternately, and then translating it more or less together," Arvin recorded in his diary. The next day Ned came back and they read more verses, then some poems by Auden. After weeks of indecision about whether to push further, Arvin's pleasure now yielded to torment. "Very happy for an hour or so," he wrote, "then tension overwhelmed me. Should I or should I not?"

Arvin adored Ned's "lovely vivacity." But he also detected an underlying disinterest, "mingled boredom and defiance," which may have re-minded him of Wendell and which, as he agonized over whether to act on his desires, reignited his age-old doubts. "Low day," he wrote a week later. "Will to live at low ebb . . . Death wishes."

He and Ned talked vaguely about renting a car and taking a trip through New England, until Ned told him he couldn't afford to pay half the cost and refused to allow Arvin to pay his way for him. Another member of the English Department, however, an assistant professor named Sylvan Schendler, invited them to drive with him in mid-July to Montreal, where he would be leaving by ship for Europe. The plan called for Arvin and Ned to spend a few days together in the city before driving Schendler's Volvo back to Northampton.

Arvin was encouraged as they checked in at their hotel; Schendler took his own room, but Ned, to save money, decided to sleep on a cot in Arvin's. That evening, Ned grew tense as he and Arvin had drinks in the cocktail lounge. "I was obtuse," he would recall. "I was also naive." Though experi-enced sexually, Ned hadn't realized what others had seen from the begin-ning: that Arvin wanted him. When he understood, he became troubled and confused. "What Newton wanted, what was optimal for him, would have been very strange for me. I couldn't have maintained that kind of re-lationship." Later, as Ned lay on the cot, Arvin made an awkward pass at him. Ned rejected the advances until Arvin, miffed, returned to his bed, pulled up the cover, and said, "OK, go to sleep," though he himself was un-able to shut his eyes. Facing each other at dawn, both were mortified. "A complete misunderstanding," Arvin wrote in his journal. Ned later ex-plained, "It just disturbed me very much. It seemed to me so completely out of the question. It had to do with his age. I felt no physical attraction to Newton."

If Arvin's worst fears were now realized—that those he desired could never desire him—it was also true that he and Ned had discovered the real nature of their attachment. Fond of each other, close in most ways, they nonetheless desired two things—love and sex—that no one individual could give them. A friend once told Ned, "You have a large antechamber, but it's very hard to get beyond it." Like Arvin's, his inmost chamber re-mained locked.

But Ned's rebuff also drew them into a new type of intimacy, powerful for each of them, as sexual co-adventurers. Ned lacked Arvin's interest in pictures, but he too had a driving sexual nature, and Arvin took pleasure in introducing him to his newfound world. Under Arvin's tutelage, Ned began hitchhiking and asking friends for rides to Springfield so that he could cruise. He was enthralled by the power and freedom, especially when his partner was a married man who professed no conflict or confusion but plainly wanted Ned in control. Since it was necessary for newcomers to be schooled in matters of taste, discretion, and safety, Arvin became Ned's teacher, Ned his student—an erotic relationship in itself.

By the end of summer, they were closer than ever but sexually independent, like brothers, each pursuing pleasure in his own way and sharing his discoveries. For Arvin, as ever, that meant not just being active but writing about it, both in his journal and in letters to certain friends. Extolling his new life to Capote, who was traveling in Greece while awaiting publication of *Breakfast at Tiffany's,* Arvin told him about Ned, his new interest in pictures and films, and his "Springfield pleasures." Capote, trumping him, reported back about the richness of gay life in Athens. "You can't walk a block without being accosted ten times: no exaggeration. There is a bookshop right in Constitution Square that specializes in photographs and literature of a particular nature. I bought quite a satchelful, and will pass it on to you."

On a night in late August, before school started, Arvin was home alone when he received a phone call from a recent acquaintance, a church organist. Arvin was leaving by bus the next day for Yaddo, but the acquaintance said he was at Rahar's, a popular tavern across from the Northampton bus station, and asked whether he could bring up two boys from the university. Arvin begged off politely, but a few hours later the musician arrived with the students, who, despite being "clearly the hetero type," Arvin noted, stayed for several beers and gin and tonics. The boys took off their shirts for athletic contests—push-ups, chinnings, tugs of war—while they all talked and laughed and Arvin played records. Both were in their mid-twenties and had been in the service; one was married. At around three A.M., they all agreed that, given how much they'd drunk, the youths shouldn't attempt to drive home. Arvin suggested that they all sleep in the living room so as not to disturb his downstairs neighbor, whose bedroom was under his. After drawing the draperies closed, he made up some bedding, and they settled on sleeping arrangements.

Because Arvin didn't know his new friend well enough to trust his judgment in such matters, he feared that the evening might backfire. The boys could make noise, insult them, beat them up, steal from them, blackmail them, go to the police. One careless slip could cost a man everything. Only the pain of being alone and the thrill of a rare opportunity made the risk of violence or exposure worthwhile. As it happened, Arvin was delighted to find the students, Sandy and Steve, "cooperative." He wrote excitedly the next day to Doughty in French, his preferred code for writing about "mes exploits amoureux," "Ils étaient tous les deux parfaitement 'passifs' (excusez-moi) mais parfaitement disposés à se laisser être admirés, touchés, maniés, etc., etc. [They were perfectly passive but perfectly disposed to let us admire, touch, handle them, etc., etc.]." Continuing in English, he wrote:

> Sandy was entirely matter of fact, loquacious, kidding, and amusing about our attentions, rejecting tributes to his beauty, dimensions, etc. with pretended incredulity, skepticism and the like; but he really was extraordinary. They were both as nice as they could be, and I actually took to Steve somewhat more, perhaps because he seemed to be more strongly affected, even excited, somewhat more affectionate in gesture, etc.
>
> After perhaps an hour of this, [. . .] and Sandy withdrew to the bed in the bedroom, and I believe fell asleep rather soon; I remained with Steve, who seemed willing to go on and on, and we did go on for a half an hour or so; finally we did drop off, but when I woke in the morning, Steve, still sleeping or half-sleeping, wanted, or so it seemed, to be embraced, caressed, played with, etc, and of course he was delicious, his charming little body warm and responsive in my arms.

This was my first all-male breakfast party on that scale, and I must say if all social life were cast in this mould, I would be a far more social type than I am.

More than his outings at the Arch, Arvin's "quite unexpected little affair" signified how far he was willing to go to have an active sex life in Northampton. He had brought home lovers before, but never strangers. Yet he was tired of depriving himself. Whatever his terrors, he apparently decided that in the privacy of his rooms he was still safe, and, anyway, nothing could be worse than more loneliness, reclusion, hiding, abstinence, and denial. In Hawthorne's puritan America, these were the "essential sin." Arvin, after years alone in his dismal chamber, no longer could abide his suffering and was willing to take his chances. As he wrote to Doughty, "S'il y a un risque, il le faut. [If it is a risk, so be it.]"

Arvin wasn't the first major writer to throw up his hands at Emerson. Hawthorne, his Concord neighbor, had called him "Mr. Emerson—the mystic, stretching his hand out of cloudland, in vain search for something real." Henry James, son of a friend, said, "He had no great sense of wrong—a strangely limited one, indeed, for a moralist—no sense of the dark, the foul, the base." T. S. Eliot called him "an encumbrance"; D. H. Lawrence, an "old drug"; William Butler Yeats, "superficial." Brooks put so high a stake in him, then found him so hard to pin down, that his failure to write a "perfect book" about him became not just a literary defeat but a moral one, an incitement to madness.

Arvin did not have it in him to devote a full-scale biography to a figure who inspired such criticisms, about whom he himself had become compelled to ask, "How can he be read with respect, or perhaps at all, in a time when we all seem agreed that anguish, inquietude, the experience of guilt, and the knowledge of the Abyss are the essential substance of which admissable literature is made?" Instead, in early 1958, he published an eight-thousand-word essay, unironically entitled "The House of Pain: Emerson and the Tragic Sense." In it, he channeled Emerson's life through his own recent past, and, as with Hawthorne, Whitman, and Melville, limned once again dark undercurrents that no other critic had seen.

In examining Emerson's life, Arvin discerned once more much that was familiar to him: the pale, frail, lonely intellectual who, escaping a dominant father, goes to Harvard, rebels, seeks a life of the mind, develops doubts about the church, and finally, heroically, hurls himself against the citadel of puritan materialism. There was no denying Emerson's historic contribution. Starting in the 1830s, he pleaded so powerfully in sermons, books, essays, lectures, and poems for a daring new brand of individual freedom that he provided the emerging American middle class with a new core faith: self-reliance. Arthur Summerfield was an Emersonian.

The problem was how to explain Emerson's relentless optimism, his endless hymns to joy, his abhorrence of suffering, all those "bland reassurances" about life's goodness that had allied him for more than a century both with charlatans who preached positive thinking and with businessmen who chastised the poor and denounced government relief programs as socialism. "We rub our eyes as we read," Arvin wrote, citing examples of Emerson's incomprehensible rosiness, such as "The less we have to do with our sins the better," and "I could never give much reality to evil and pain," and, perhaps worst, "Most suffering is only apparent." Arvin confessed his temptation to see Emerson as a Pollyanna, unshaken by life's horrors. "It is easy to get the mistaken impression that, for Emerson, there were indeed no Cape Horns in experience, no jungles, no Arctic nights, no shark-infested seas; only the amiable rustic landscape of the Concord fields and woodlots," he wrote.

How, he wondered in frustration, was it "humanly possible for a man to have so weak a memory of his own sorrows or so little compassion for those of other men?" To which he posited a novel answer: that Emerson's rosy optimism was "somewhat less the product . . . of a naively happy temper than it was an achievement both of intellectual and emotional discipline."

Emerson, Arvin discovered, in fact had suffered grievously, from early poverty and illness. His young wife, Ellen, died seventeen months after they were married. After growing so weak physically in his early twenties that he was forced to give up preaching, he wrote to an aunt, "He has seen but half the universe who has never been shown the House of Pain."

Emerson hadn't denied the existence of moral evil, Arvin concluded.

Nor was he blind to the pain of others. On the contrary; he had made himself rise in maturity above his youthful suffering by trusting boldly not in the power of God but of himself—of the individual.

After enduring the most painful decade of his life, Arvin now became, in the late 1950s—his late fifties—an Emersonian, defying intellectual fashion. He found in Emerson's "paeans of joy and praise" not superficial banality but a kind of grace—a rationale for his actions and path to self-acceptance, both of which had eluded him in church. Like Emerson, he had learned that the trick was to vanquish pain, believe in yourself, and survive. If one of the intrinsic blessings of his age was that there couldn't be much more of life, so much the better. In short, he decided, he would do what he wanted to do. He would no longer deprive himself.

Arvin and Ned began 1959 with a short New York holiday. They wandered around Greenwich Village, dropped in on the Christopher Street Bookstore, and saw old and new friends. Arvin wrote of Ned in his journal, "He fills my spirit too full for me to feel any other need. Have I ever cared for anyone more?" If not "this Thing" he'd once found with Capote, their friendship came as close to it as either felt he could hope for or expect, given what they'd come to agree was "the essential sadness of 'the life.' "

Then, a month later, Ned received an unexpected offer to teach at Amherst. "How painfully I should mind his not being in daily reach," Arvin told his journal. The invitation reminded them both that, although Arvin was stuck in Northampton, Ned wasn't, and might be lured away at any time. Helen Bacon got Smith to match Amherst's offer, and Ned decided to stay, but not before Arvin worried about losing him. Meanwhile, Ned befriended a new assistant professor in Arvin's department, a tall, stooped, sensuous-eyed Shakespeare man named Joel Dorius. Their budding friendship ratcheted up Arvin's anxiety. "Ned is silent and mysterious when I allude to Joel D," Arvin recorded on April 5. "Some concealment there that rather disturbs me."

As close as he and Ned were, unbridgeable gaps still divided them. Not least were their separate sex lives, about which Arvin, however proud of his conquests, still periodically panicked. "A bad day. Mea Culpa. Between 5 and 7:30, insane cruising. Playing with deadly fire. Alas! Alas!" he wrote a week later. And there was what Arvin called "this problem of the two orbits." Ned was young, proudly rootless, with a streak of irresponsibility and a passion for fun. He had his own life and plans, and Arvin feared he didn't have the pull to hold him. One day, Ned typically came up to borrow five dollars from him. Arvin tried to run off a new movie for him, but his projector failed to work. Then Ned told him about his adventure the previous night in Springfield, and Arvin was distraught. "Difficult to struggle against the suspicion that I am a convenience, to be used as such," he wrote in his journal. "Not the whole truth to be sure, but I'm afraid too much of it. Inclined at such time to withdraw from all relations with anyone under forty."

When Ned left in June to teach summer school in St. Louis, Arvin fell into loneliness and depression. He phoned Ned frequently and was crestfallen to hear students' voices in the background. Ned reacted impatiently, writing from Missouri:

> Dear Newton: You know too well that I cannot lift you out of despond for more than a few days at a time. And much as we need each other we ought not to pretend to ourselves that we make each other happy. Indeed, we usually see ourselves as the blind and the blind. This is crippling as well as comforting. And I love health, in others and in myself, and I take a favorite pleasure drawing it out . . . In short, there are sunny days, and there is memory, and— hardest of all—there is choice.

Wounded, Arvin went so far as to contact his old Harvard friend Bud Ehrensperger, his first love, with whom he'd lost contact more than thirty years earlier. Like Capote and Lilienthal, Ehrensperger had gone on to live a vigorous, peripatetic life. In the 1920s, he'd moved to Russia to study the Moscow Art Theater. He later traveled throughout the South Pacific, Latin America, Africa, and India, where he became friends with Mohandas Gandhi and helped found the country's first journalism school. A pioneer in combining religion and drama, he'd written widely and produced the original version of Arthur Miller's *The Crucible*. Knowing that Ehrensperger had never married, Arvin suggested a reunion. But Ehrensperger wrote back from Lake Forest, Illinois, where he was teaching, to explain that he would be traveling all summer. Maybe in the fall, he wrote.

Thwarted in his attempt to rekindle an old flame, missing Ned, Arvin plunged further into his secret life. He began to see more of his new acquaintances, who brought other men to Arvin's apartment, where they looked at films and pictures. A thirty-six-year-old car mechanic named Jesse Green visited several times for sex, staying an hour, then returning home to his wife and two young children. Arvin doubted how much he should indulge his desires, but his doubts dissolved the more he descended. At the end of June he wrote in his journal, "A suicidal day. Overcast, bleak, grey, humid. Saw no one except hard-faced, coarse, tough featured gangs of VFW men and their trollops here for a convention . . . A zoo of types." One day later, at "the lowest possible ebb," he phoned a UMass student who'd offered to visit him that day because his wife was in the hospital having a baby. There was no answer. "Consciousness," he wrote the following week, "is pure misery."

By the time Ned returned in August, Arvin's sexual life was more consuming than ever. Straight friends who knew what was happening sensed he'd become almost ruthless about it—predatory—especially in the way he set his mind for younger homosexuals on the Smith faculty, cajoling them, nudging them, it seemed, to participate. As ever, he was correct, mannered, well-behaved—nothing extreme or coercive—but he had apparently decided that he had denied himself too long. Whatever his desires, he would indulge them. Whatever his agonies, he had made his choice, as Ned had suggested, and would take others with him.

In mid-September he took the train alone to New York. After checking in, as usual, to the Hotel Latham on East Twenty-eighth Street, where Mary had lived during the winter of 1936 while he was working on *Whitman,* he had supper and then walked down the street to the Everard Baths. The baths were located inconspicuously in a Civil War–era three-story building in the flower district, between Broadway and Sixth Avenue, that reputedly had once housed a synagogue on the top floor. As its name more than implied, Everard promised inexhaustible activity, a sense of boundless possibility. Men came there from all over the world. The experience of walking in off the street was described unforgettably by the composer Ned Rorem in his *New York Diary*:

> You enter at any age, in any condition, any time of the night or week, pay dearly for a fetid cubicle, and are given a torn gown and a pair of mismatched slippers (insufficient against the grime that remains in your toes for days). You penetrate an obscure world, disrobe in private while reading graffiti, emerge rerobed into the public of gray wanderers so often compared to the lost souls of Dante.

Everard's windows were painted black, and the lights were a sulfurous yellow, like "a brothel lit like Guernica by one nude bulb," Rorem wrote. There were four levels, divided into cubicles and corridors and suites of rooms. The baths, such as they were, were in the basement, a large dirty pool and steam and massage rooms. Each level, roughly square, accommodated perhaps eighty men, active in full view. "At any time you may witness couplings of white with black, beauty with horror," Rorem wrote. "Your eyes widen as a faun mounts that stevedore, or when a mountain descends on Mohammed. Some cluster forever together in a throbbing Medusa's head; others disentangle themselves to squat in foggy corners, immobile as carnivorous orchids, waiting to 'go up' on whatever passes."

Arvin liked to wander—"hunt," as Ned said—which gave him freedom but also safety. Unlike those who lay passively on their stomachs, he could worry less about blackmail or getting beaten up when he was the initiator. He reveled in Everard's variety, finding it a sodomist's paradise, and wrote glowingly about his encounters in his journal, reporting after three straight nights, "Very tired when I got back to the hotel after midnight." Arvin loved the starkness, the abandon. Far from feeling ashamed or degraded, as Rorem seemed to, he was seldom so exhilarated. Sylvan Schendler, who was heterosexual and kept an apartment in the city, remembered picking him up after a few nights at the baths and asking how it went. "Oh, Sylvan," he said, "I feel so clean."

Arvin understood the grave risks he was taking. In late September he had dinner with Joel Dorius, who had come to Smith from Yale and was also homosexual, but kept it hidden—"a straight man with a homosexual private life," Dorius, thirty-nine, called himself. Arvin had met him the day after he met Ned, and though he had private reservations about Dorius's leadership and critical skills—Yale was a center of the New Criticism—he enjoyed the man's lively company. Dorius, uncharacteristically sad and subdued all evening, told Arvin he was distraught about reports of stepped-up vice squad activity in New York. As they had for decades with prostitutes, undercover agents were now actively soliciting homosexuals in known cruising spots, then arresting them. Similar crackdowns were under way around the country. Dorius, who had been raised to fear God's judgment and had got his Ph.D. at Harvard, poured himself out to Arvin about "the agonies of certain friends," Arvin wrote in his journal.

Arvin also knew of the latest professional literature regarding homosexual "perversion." A new book, published in early November, purported to explain the inherent, unquenchable self-destructiveness of the homosexual "lifestyle," and was receiving the sort of uncritical press attention then reserved for serious studies of society's more shocking ills. Written by a well-known New York psychoanalyst, Dr. Edmund Bergler, it was entitled *1,000 Homosexuals* and asserted that all sex between men was a form of "psychic masochism." Out-Freuding Freud, Bergler argued that homosexuals unconsciously try to turn the pain of being scorned and rejected into pleasure, but that such pleasure is a distortion—"counterfeit." Going further, he attacked sex researcher Dr. Alfred Kinsey's famous finding—that every third man in America had had an adult homosexual experience—as creating the "pitiful spectacle of the 'statistically induced homosexual,'" that is, millions of misguided and confused young men thinking it somehow was acceptable to have sex with men because others said they had done it.

Following Bergler's lead and capturing much of his flavor, *Time* addressed the topic in its next issue, in an article entitled "The Strange World." "The seed of self-punishment flowers in the conspiratorial world of the homosexual," the magazine reported. "Its life . . . is 'misery concentrated, guilt heightened, depression the order of the day.' Male homosexuals are pathologically jealous and 'unfaithful.' Some have relations with more than 100 males a year." Meanwhile, "the homosexual unwittingly yearns for exposure. His distorted pleasures feed on the allure of danger."

The "Liberals"

of Smith

By
ALOISE BUCKLEY HEATH

1.

2.

As the fifties dawned, America's anxieties about domestic communism and the postwar rise in sexual openness merged. At Smith, Aloise Buckley Heath (1), sister of William F. Buckley, Jr., organized an anti-Red campaign, urging fellow alums not to donate to the college while it employed five "pink professors." The five, including Arvin, were compelled to testify before a state commission. Meanwhile, Postmaster General Arthur Summerfield (2) launched a national crusade against what he called "pornographic filth in the family mailbox," persuading Congress to grant the Post Office sweeping powers to inspect and seize mail that Summerfield and his censors considered obscene. Following Summerfield's lead, many states including Massachusetts sharply increased penalties for possessing or distributing pornography.

1.

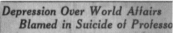

Depression Over World Affairs Blamed in Suicide of Professo

Matthiessen of Harvard Upset Over Setbacks to Socialism, His Sister Declares

Special to The New York Times.

BOSTON, April 1—Exhaustion brought on by literary research and depression inspired by world conditions were blamed by associates today for the suicide leap of Prof. Francis Otto Mattiessen of Harvard, authority on American literature and self-styled Socialist.

Professor Matthiessen, who was 48 years old, died soon after plunging from a twelfth-floor room at the Hotel Manger to the street at about 12:45 o'clock this morning. He had been on leave of absence from Harvard while writing a life of Theodore Dreiser.

In the hotel room which he had engaged yesterday afternoon police found a note stating: "I have been depressed by conditions throughout the world for many months. I am a Christian and I also am a Socialist. I believe firmly in international peace."

The phrase "I am a Christian and a Socialist" was one Mr. Matthiessen used last year when he was accused of supporting Communist-front organizations. The charge was made by Joseph B. Matthews, former research director of the

Prof. Francis Otto Matthiessen

of Social Studies. The Ada school was on the attorney's serverve list of the Attorney Gieral's office last year.

Howard Fast Hits U. S. Polic

In a statement issued here y

2.

3.

*S*tanding between fellow winners Wallace Stevens and Brendan Gill (1), Arvin received the National Book Award in 1951 for his biography of Herman Melville. Otherwise, it was a disastrous period, both for Arvin (3) and for the intellectual left. The previous year, Harvard's F. O. Matthiessen—like Arvin a leftist homosexual critic and key architect of American studies—killed himself just weeks after Senator Joseph McCarthy first attacked domestic subversion (2). A few months later Arvin tried to commit suicide, taking sixteen Nembutals. Soon he would receive dozens of electroshock treatments, which aged and addled him.

AMHERST COLLEGE ARCHIVES

FREDRIKS LAROCK, COLLEGE ARCHIVES OF SMITH COLLEGE

1.

2.

3.

As younger homosexuals flirted with greater openness throughout the Eisenhower years, Arvin—depressed, lonely, frail, unable to write, and feeling his life was all but over—yearned to join them. Despite the risks, he began to entertain a circle of younger colleagues in his attic apartment a few doors from the Smith campus, including Wendell Johnson (1), Joel Dorius (3), and especially Ned Spofford (2), a classics instructor half Arvin's age. "Have I ever cared for anyone more?" Arvin wrote in his diary, in which he recorded each encounter. As Arvin began to collect erotica, cruise, and occasionally have sex with men from town, his apartment atop what Sylvia Plath called the "odd Gothic blind stairwell" became a haven where Smith homosexuals could relax and drop their disguises.

1.

2.

Northampton Probe Deepens
Suspect's Diary Studied For Clues to Smut Traffic

BOSTON HERALD-TRAVELER

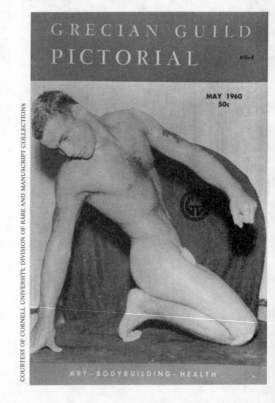

11 More Sought In Smut Probe

NORTHAMPTON—Two more men were arrested and at least 11 others were being sought Saturday night in a widening investigation of an alleged pornography ring in which two Smiht College faculty members have been arrested.

3.

On September 2, 1960, four months after Summerfield's postal inspectors seized copies of three "beefcake" magazines—*MANual, Trim,* and *Grecian Guild Pictorial*—for obscenity, Massachusetts state troopers mounted Arvin's stairs (1, 2) and raided his apartment on an apparent tip from the Post Office. They confiscated both his erotica and his journals, and arrested him for distributing pornography—a felony with a maximum five-year prison term. Shattered, Arvin surrendered the names of several friends, including Spofford and Dorius, then admitted himself to Northampton State Hospital (3, in the background) as Smith College reeled from the scandal. The "smut probe" engulfed the campus, quickly spreading to other colleges throughout the Northeast as word spread of Arvin's tell-all diary.

*A*mid fevered antivice efforts nationally, Arvin's arrest at first was reported simply as a pornography raid. But as six more arrests soon followed, police revealed that Arvin and all the other suspects, including three married Northampton men, were homosexuals. Arvin's diaries became instantly infamous. Though police had also confiscated 8-mm movies, male nudes, and pictures of men involved in sexual acts, the beefcake magazines and other "obscene" homosexual materials like the Mattachine Society publication *One* comprised the bulk of the evidence against him.

TRIM

Young America's
Favorite Physique Publication

MAY 1960
Number 17
50c

Northampton Diary Tells All

2 More Educators Facing Arrest in College Sex Ring

BOSTON HERALD-TRAVELER

*A*lthough all seven men were convicted and given suspended sentences, and Arvin, Spofford, and Dorius lost their jobs at Smith, the "Arvin scandal" also signaled the end of a decade of mounting police abuse and moral persecution by the federal government. Spofford and Dorius appealed their convictions and were later acquitted in light of a 1961 Supreme Court ruling barring illegal police searches. In a second ruling a year later, the Supreme Court held that although the pictures of scantily clad young men in the beefcake magazines were "dismally unpleasant, uncouth and tawdry," they were not obscene.

1.

2.

3.

4.

Smith's trustees "retired" Arvin on half salary in recognition of his prominent standing, emotional precariousness, and thirty-seven years on the faculty, but President Thomas Mendenhall (1) failed to persuade them that Spofford and Dorius, two known homosexuals, were fit to teach young women. Arvin's literary friends, despite their qualms, remained loyal. Joyce scholar Al Fisher (2) cared for him through three more state hospital stays, followed by prostate trouble, diabetes, and cancer. Malcolm Cowley (3) tried and failed to preserve his place on the Yaddo board. Lillian Hellman (4) offered to do "anything I could, anything," saying later, "The poor bastard. He panicked and ratted."

And, finally, "The homosexual's worst trouble comes when he starts to age. His craving is for youth and the weird youthful banter of the homosexual world. But the young do not want him; they have to be bought."

Whatever his reasons, Arvin curtailed his sexual activities during the next few months even as Ned's grew. According to his journals, he saw less of his new friends, and Jesse Green stopped visiting his apartment. He still went to Springfield to cruise, still traveled to New York, but the last time he had a group up to his apartment to view what might be considered erotica was a night in November when Dorius gave in to Arvin's urging and brought over copies of Etruscan tomb frescoes dating from the eighth century B.C. "Circulation of Joel's collection of prints," Arvin wrote; "some very beautiful."

Ned meanwhile took greater risks, one of which surely troubled Arvin more than the others. Ned started to meet men in the public restroom of Northampton's City Hall, a known cruising spot, and taking them back to his studio apartment a few blocks away on Green Street, a busy student shopping strip across from Smith. There was a streetside entrance to the men's room, and Ned would walk in, stand at a urinal, and glance at the person next to him. If the other man had an erection, they would leave together without a word. For Arvin, who for thirty-five years had been a model of propriety in town, known to shopkeepers and waitresses and bank tellers, Ned's indiscretion was horrifying. But he could do nothing to stop it, nor would he try. Ned had applied to graduate school at Harvard for the following fall and hadn't yet decided whether to go if accepted. Arvin, not knowing what he would do without him, kept his apprehensions quiet for fear of driving him farther away. On campus they acted toward each other, as always, like regular friends and colleagues.

Chapter Eight

ARVIN AWOKE TOO late for Holy Communion, so he stayed "chez moi" all day. He had spent the last days of the benighted fifties, now mercifully over, writing letters in his apartment, reading Proust in the afternoon, and savoring the echoes of two nights of debauchery in New York. With Ned still in the city, attending the American Philological Society annual meeting, he'd seen no one since New Year's Eve, when he'd dropped in on Al Fisher for a drink and returned home early.

Northampton—*his* Northampton—was a tomb this time of year, buried under a crust of blinding snow and crouched against Arctic winds that swooped down from the Yankee hills, rattling windows. The view outside his study was immaculate: the bleached whiteness of the Manse, Northampton's premier homestead, built by Jonathan Edwards's father-in-law and grandfather; the snow-capped slate roofs under a glaring sky, the snow-buried ground, the ethereal spire of Smith's chapel, a lone skeletal birch—wintry whiteness of an almost allegorical nature. In *Moby-Dick,* Ishmael says it was the whale's whiteness that "above all things appalled me." Arvin resolved to stay in, warm, reading by lamplight, safe, alone.

The radio reported that 150 miles east, in Hyannis Port, John Fitzgerald Kennedy had finally declared his candidacy for President. Kennedy's strategists had been working for months on a novel plan to enter him in up to a dozen state primaries. In the years before televised campaigning, these were grueling marches, with candidates driving hundreds of miles on bad roads to reach voters in groups of ten and fifteen. Most presidential aspirants spurned them, but Kennedy had no choice. At the age of forty-two, a Roman Catholic not well known nationally, he needed to show strength in all regions of the country. His announcement had been carefully delayed until after New Year's to draw his opponents belatedly into a costly spring campaign that he, with his father's money and connections and political brain trust, had been organizing since fall. Arvin distrusted the Kennedys, but with New York governor Nelson Rockefeller quickly fading from contention, the Republican nominee promised to be "that paltry Richard Nixon," as Arvin called him. Disgusted, he resolved not to vote.

Where was Ned? Ordinarily Ned called or visited every day, and Arvin expected him to be back by now from New York. He worried at his rear window, with the same ambivalence he'd awaited Capote years earlier.

Looking south through his porch screens, Arvin beheld much the same vista as he had then, though bleaker and denuded. Capote's mountains "burning green and blue" had lost their blaze and were ashen, a thousand-foot strand of rolling hills against which Main Street seemed shrunken, almost minuscule, in the snow. Arvin could see where Lambie's store had burned down in 1927, three years after he made his speech booming La Follette, and where Woolworth's, which had moved next door the following year, had recently built a modern, low-slung brick block with a new lunch counter. Otherwise, it all looked more or less as it had when he first came to town—indeed, as when Coolidge came in the late 1890s. Landlocked, staid, resolute, steeped in the past. The interstate highway penetrating north from Hartford remained well to the south, beyond the hills.

Ned arrived in the late afternoon and stayed for an hour, filling Arvin in on his doings during the past week. Just before both had left for New York, he'd been accepted at Harvard, but he and Arvin had yet to broach what Arvin called "the difficult subject"—whether he should go. As both of them knew, sooner or later, if Ned was to have an important career at Smith or any other good school, he would have to get a Ph.D. Everything had been up in the air when Ned left for the city, causing Arvin more anxiety than usual about his return. Now, Ned told him he was thinking of postponing his studies and living with *him*.

Arvin was touched—and stunned. He had long since given up the idea of greater intimacy between them, and of cohabiting with anyone. Could they live together? Ned "must have been crazy enough to think so," he recalled. Even as Arvin's most intimate friend, he couldn't know how vigorously Arvin would have resisted such a life of captivity, how deeply he needed to be by himself, how impregnable his inmost self had become.

Arvin made Ned promise that if he went to Harvard, he wouldn't stay more than two years. His feelings were genuine, but he also seemed to be plotting a reprieve for both of them. Later that night, he admonished himself in his journal: "I must face the certainty of [Ned's] not being in Northampton for at least a year."

In February, Capote phoned from western Kansas, where he was working on an assignment for *The New Yorker* about a grisly murder. Since the publication, a year and a half earlier, of *Breakfast at Tiffany's,* he had been celebrated by Hollywood, which optioned the book, and had been applauded by—of all people—Norman Mailer, who called him "a ballsy little guy" and "the most perfect writer of my generation." He'd become courtier to a bevy of international high society matrons—his "swans," he called them—but still hadn't, at thirty-five, fulfilled his promise as an author. *The New Yorker* had sent him to Moscow to write about Russia, but he found when he returned that he couldn't do it. Owing the magazine a story, he became interested, in late November, in a small item in the back of the *Times* about a farm family that had been murdered at home.

True-crime reporting was still a seedy literary backwater, and Capote was primarily a fiction writer. Still, he'd ventured by train from New York, beyond the corn belt, to the semiarid prairie near the Colorado border, a barren, forbidding region that even Topekans called "out there," as he would write. He told Arvin he was staying in the little town of Holcomb to find out everything he could about the story and that he planned to write a factual book about the effect of the shocking murders on a small town.

Arvin was intrigued. He also was worried. Capote had arrived at the county courthouse two weeks after the murders, while the town was still fearful and tense, wearing a small cap, a large sheepskin coat, a long scarf that trailed to the floor, and moccasins. No suspects had yet been caught in the case, and raw-eyed men stayed up all night behind bolted doors, cradling shotguns. Capote had taken a companion with him, Nelle Harper Lee, his childhood friend who had written *To Kill a Mockingbird*. Before they'd left New York he'd asked her to buy a gun and bring it with them. Arvin didn't worry, as Capote first had, whether he would penetrate the place. He feared what would happen when he did.

Even more than Capote, it was Lilienthal whose globe-trotting most reminded Arvin how mincing and circumscribed his own steps had become. After leaving Washington ten years earlier for New York, Lilienthal had gone to work for Lazard Freres & Company, the celebrated banking firm, taken control of a troubled minerals company in which the firm had a stake, and amassed a paper fortune of more than $1,600,000. Meantime, he'd started another company to export TVA-style programs and know-how, and now spent months each year overseas, brokering giant land-reclamation and energy projects. Far from being "soft on communism," Lilienthal fiercely promoted postwar United States policies that favored repressive regimes over local democratic forces if those regimes opposed communist influence in their regions. He was the Shah of Iran's favorite American businessman.

Lilienthal was currently midway through a two-month round-the-world business trip that would take him to Honolulu, Tokyo, Manila, Mindanao, Bangkok, Siemreap, Tehran, Ahwaz, Andimeshk, Geneva, Brussels, and Madrid before returning to his home, a capacious brick colonial in Princeton, New Jersey, which he and Helen had bought in 1957 after several years of living in Sutton Place in Manhattan. Well into his second life, he was still ranging about at a gallop and apparently relishing every minute.

And still revering Arvin. Though they had drifted into the well-worn comfort of old friends, Lilienthal had never got over his initial impression— boosted in college, when Arvin sent him long lists of vocabulary words to look up, and books to read, and articles and reviews to discuss—that Fred was smarter than he was. He still sent Arvin his speeches to critique, and Arvin, though he disapproved of some of Lilienthal's imperialist apologies, encouraged him. "One cannot wholly despair of the Republic so long as there are people in public life like you," Arvin wrote on February 20. As most winters, Lilienthal had invited Arvin to begin thinking about visiting him and Helen at Martha's Vineyard come warmer weather, but Arvin, typically, begged off. "I have taken a job of editing that will keep me rolling the rock of Sisyphus uphill during most of the summer, and I don't expect I shall be in any position to do much lotus-eating during those months," he wrote in the same letter, explaining wistfully:

> I dare say I get myself tied up with these tasks quite deliberately for the sake of having reasons for not getting out of my cave and seeing the world—before it is too late to see, or hear, or taste, anything. But, so far as I know, this sitfastness means no skin off anyone else's nose but mine—and the whole subject is of no importance anyway. Only I sometimes do have fantasies of what it would be like really to *see* Palermo, or Paestum, or the island of Delos, or Angkor-Vat, or Nukuhiva . . .

Nukuhiva was the South Seas island where young Melville had lived among cannibals.

Five years after his tactical retreat over *Lysistrata,* Postmaster General Arthur Summerfield's war on smut lurched to a climax in Washington. The Supreme Court had ruled in *Roth v. U.S.* that obscenity *was not* protected under the First Amendment, enabling a victorious Summerfield to step up his campaign of mail blocks, seizures, bannings, and prosecutions. In 1957, sixty-two-year-old Samuel Roth went to prison for five years, his publishing empire destroyed.

But Summerfield remained vexed by the High Court's failure to define what was obscene. Justice William Brennan had written in *Roth* that "sex and obscenity are not synonymous." That ambiguity suited Summerfield and his censors but also invited court challenges. Twice, recently, the Supreme Court had reversed postal bans—against the Mattachine Society publication *One* and the nudist magazines *Sunshine and Health* and *Sun*—because, the justices said, the publications failed to stimulate "prurient interest," the new post-*Roth* standard.

To Summerfield, who deemed all sexual material obscene, the courts had become dangerously lax. Like Anthony Comstock, who in the 1860s roamed the Capitol lobbies buttonholing lawmakers to show them a great cloth bag filled with marriage manuals, "fancy books," abortifacients, and other "abominations," he put his ultimate faith in Congress, which, after a year of public hearings, was to take up new legislation, the Granahan bill, which would allow the Post Office to seek a court order to open all letters and packages addressed to mail-order obscenity suspects.

Kathryn E. (O'Hay) Granahan was Summerfield's chief congressional ally, a Philadelphia Democrat who chaired the House Subcommittee on Postal Operations. A large-boned, matronly woman with a helmet of wavy gray hair who had first married when she was forty-nine, Granahan was now sixty-six, a childless widow who'd won a special election for her husband's seat, and a leading lay Catholic who had served on the national ladies' auxiliaries of the American Legion and the Catholic War Veterans. During her first term, she'd handled Summerfield's bid to have Congress close a loophole created by *Roth*. The justices had ruled that the definition of morally offensive wasn't a universal one but was, instead, whatever individual communities decided. Although Granahan had ushered through an amendment to the Comstock Act allowing the Post Office to prosecute not only at the point from where mail was sent but where it was received, the legislation had done little to staunch the flow of mail-order erotica. Summerfield believed that only by letting the department seize vital business materials—subscription cards, checks, paper, printing supplies, pictures, and manuscripts—could obscenity be curbed. Hence the Granahan bill. A retaliatory escalation in the spiraling war over obscenity, it aimed to put the mail-order sex industry out of business by embargoing its cash and supplies.

Granahan, like Summerfield, was a tireless moralist and crusader. She believed the "pornographic pestilence" that preyed on children represented a deliberate threat to the American way of life and was "part of an international Communist plot." Aided by crime statistics supplied by the FBI, she claimed that smut was the common link in virtually every juvenile arrest, and that every one of the underage inmates in juvenile mental institutions in Philadelphia "is there because they read this [lewd] literature." Generally supportive of her party's leadership, Granahan was instrumental in gaining support for Summerfield's agenda in the Democratic-controlled

House. Summerfield maintained, and gave guided tours of, a "Chamber of Horrors"—a locked room in the Post Office building exhibiting hard-core pornography. Urged by Granahan to visit, many of her colleagues did.

Every cause in Washington has its optimal moment; now, six years after inheriting the puritanical zeal of a spent McCarthyism, the drive to expand federal censorship reached its greatest strength in nearly a century. With a national election looming, and mounting bipartisan calls for stronger legislation against mail-order smut, Summerfield and Granahan took full, furious advantage. They crisscrossed the country, held public hearings, met with church, civic, and business groups, counseled PTAs, lobbied local and national politicians, and solicited newspapers, radio, television, and community agencies. They were offering to eradicate a scourge, and except those whom Summerfield called "merchants of filth" and their liberal "pawns . . . raising pious cries of 'censorship,' 'freedom of the press,' 'civil liberties,' and so forth," no one publicly opposed them.

Almost weekly, events boosted their calls for stricter federal action. Beginning in February, a new cancellation stamp—REPORT OBSCENE MAIL TO YOUR POSTMASTER—appeared on letters in thirteen cities, bringing fresh waves of complaints from concerned parents and fresh leads for postal inspectors. Ten days later, a postmaster in the Berkshire hilltown of Cheshire, fifty miles from Northampton, was arrested and charged with smut trafficking on the same day that a Cincinnati-based organization called Citizens for Decent Literature, led by a young conservative lawyer named Charles H. Keating, Jr., heard at its annual meeting that mail-order obscenity was reaching a million children a year. In early March, a man described by the Manhattan district attorney as "the largest producer and purveyor of pornographic materials in the United States" was arrested after a raid on his warehouse on West Twentieth Street. Five days later, Granahan's favor with the Democratic leadership paid off. House Speaker Sam Rayburn, speaking to a delegation from the Philadelphia chapter of the Catholic War Veterans, urged Congress to do "everything possible" to aid in the drive against smut. "I have great faith in the youth of this country. They should have clean books and clean literature. I think it's time that we do something about the problem," Rayburn said.

Then, on March 25, Summerfield was again rebuked by the courts. The U.S. Court of Appeals ruled that *Lady Chatterley's Lover,* by D. H. Lawrence, was not an obscene book and could be sent through the mails. Summerfield, who had banned the book personally, exploded. He fired the Post Office judicial officer, who had been hired the previous year to help quell complaints about the department's capricious standards of mailability—"Breasts, yes, nipples, no. Buttocks, yes, cracks, no," as the department's chief censor candidly confessed during the *Lysistrata* controversy. And he vowed to appeal the ruling to the Supreme Court, even though the Justice Department, which handled appellate work for the government, made clear that it had little enthusiasm for it.

"This decision is very shocking to me," Summerfield said in a statement. "It also must be highly revolting to mothers and fathers and unbelievable to countless members of religious and civic organizations dedicated to high standards of decency to learn that this court declared this book to be mailable."

Summerfield redoubled his attacks. On the same day the court reversed him on *Lady Chatterley,* postal inspectors in Alexandria, Virginia, confiscated 405 copies of three "beefcake" magazines, *MANual, Trim,* and *Grecian Guild Pictorial.* Published by Herman L. Womack, an enormous near-albino whose eyesight was so bad that he could scarcely see the pictures he put in them, the magazines contained photographs of muscular young men either posed with some object obscuring their genitals, or else with their buttocks to the camera. Each of the magazines had pictures of men with swords or other long pointed objects—a Womack trademark—or pictures of naked men wearing only shoes, boots, helmets, or chains.

Womack claimed the magazines were intended for bodybuilding enthusiasts, but the local postmaster sent them to Washington, where Summerfield's staff upheld the ban after psychiatrists explained how and why the poses used in most of the pictures, and the clothing worn by the models, would arouse "great" prurient interest in homosexuals. The psychiatrists explained that certain objects in the pictures—specifically, swords and chains—were primary symbols of sexual fantasies among homosexual "deviants." Meanwhile, a postal inspector reported that, under an assumed name, he had submitted orders to some of the photographers who adver-tised in the backs of the magazines and had received "hard core pornogra-phy," pictures of groups of nude males engaged in homosexual acts.

Summerfield lauded the ban, but, uncharacteristically, from a beach resort. Less than a week after the *Lady Chatterley* ruling, under orders of his physician, he had traveled to Florida for ten days of forced rest, to re-cover, his office announced, "from general fatigue and the pressure of work." Upon his return, he immediately plunged back into lobbying for the Granahan bill. A veteran political merchandiser, Summerfield sensed that the nation was ripe for a sale. Beset increasingly by unfriendly courts—and with Eisenhower soon to become a lame duck—he was running out of time.

APRIL 9, 1960

Ned was home alone in his apartment when he heard the downstairs buzzer. He opened the door and discovered Alan, an eighteen-year-old youth he'd picked up at the City Hall men's room in February.

Unlike the first time they'd met and Ned had brought him home, the youth's presence now made him nervous. As they sat together on the couch, Alan asked for a drink, and Ned poured him a glass of whiskey and fumbled uncomfortably with a cigarette. Finally, the boy reached over and put his hand on top of Ned's.

Ned was confused. He realized that Alan had come for tenderness, which in its way was much more complicated than if he'd come strictly for sex. Nothing like this had happened to him before. Not since college, and then only once, had he had sex with someone he had feelings for. Indeed, he'd come to believe that sex and intimacy were "almost mutually exclu-sive." To open oneself emotionally to a sexual contact was to risk becoming vulnerable: to exposure, rejection, blackmail, violence, or worse. To have sex with a friend might jeopardize the friendship and put each partner in the position of possibly betraying the other in order to protect his own se-cret. Ned had resigned himself to this implacable split, knowing that it meant he would never fall in love.

Then there was Alan's age. The boy said he was eighteen, and Ned believed him. But what if he wasn't? What if he was younger, and went away hurt, or malicious? Ned loved youth as much as Arvin did, but he worried about disgracing a young man whose sexual identity wasn't yet set, one of Bergler's "statistically induced homosexuals."

Ned was too nervous to allow himself to return Alan's affection. Although he was touched by the boy's feelings for him, he recoiled, and told him they shouldn't see each other again.

Later that afternoon, he visited Arvin; over supper, he told him about the incident. An indifferent cook, Arvin usually prepared Tempo, a popular meatloaf mix, or Mrs. Paul's fish sticks. Standing elbow to elbow in Arvin's galley kitchen, he and Ned would mock their lowbrow tastes by raising their glasses to Mrs. Paul. Now, as Ned told Arvin about Alan, Arvin was tender with him, and it brought them closer. Ned, Arvin reported in his journal, "says he is not in love, and I incline, perhaps wistfully, to believe him."

As spring advanced, Arvin struggled with his own familiar conflicts. Smith had granted Ned leave to attend Harvard; he would be leaving Northampton for sure now. At the same time, though both were involved sexually with others, they spent long, intimate hours together, talking tenderly side by side, almost in each other's arms. Once Ned kissed him, and Arvin wrote about it in his journal, the only time since his affair with Capote that he reported in his diary being kissed. On a few occasions he had other men to his apartment for sex, and he worried that a sore on his thigh was a chancre until Ned, who'd recently had gonorrhea, reassured him. So too, finally, did his doctor. Getting a fair amount of work done, Arvin felt, more often than not, that he had reached an acceptable accommodation with life, Ned, the college, Northampton, even himself.

Then something nettlesome would happen, and his equanimity would crack. Often, it involved teaching. After thirty-seven years at Smith and earning just $10,500, yet still eight years from qualifying for full retirement benefits, he doubted whether he could last. His bitterness spilled out, especially during "dreary" meetings with his colleagues. At the last English Department meeting, in May, he criticized several other professors so acidly that Elizabeth Drew, now chairman, reprimanded him in writing.

Even Joel Dorius, normally gentle, appears to have offended him. During a discussion of Smith's Great Books course, which Arvin had devised and was responsible for as director, Dorius challenged some of the readings, saying such choices as Plato's *Symposium* and Montaigne's essays were far too technical—"unteachable for girls." Arvin conveyed no public anger but afterward told a mutual friend about the incident in such a way that made Dorius think he'd been impertinent. "Academic timidity at very nearly its worst," Arvin snarled that night in his journal. "The tepid generation."

Approaching summer, Arvin fell into a jaundiced habit of becoming disappointed with his friends, especially Ned, then chastising himself for his disillusion. "Weary of all this," he wrote in his journal on May 23. "Upset too by Ned's wishing meanwhile to borrow still more money. Rather unhappy talk with him. Saddened by his putting risky strains on friendship. Well over $200 now." Four days later, after drinking too many Manhattans and losing his temper with Drew, he grew remorseful, and spent the next day cruising. "How trying. Spent most of the middle part of the day in Springfield, largely fruitlessly. One success, Peter Pan [bus] station. Satisfactory consummation. Took a taxi back, extravagantly weary and low in spirit."

JULY 2, 1960

WASHINGTON, D.C.

After six months of what *Newsweek* called "dawdling, desultory lawmaking," the Eighty-sixth Congress drove hard through a rare Saturday night session, pressured by the Senate majority leader, Lyndon Johnson, who needed a legislative recess so that he could fly to Los Angeles for the Democratic Convention. Kennedy's strategy of proving he could win primaries in every section of the country left him a hair's breadth short of the nomination. Johnson, still vying for the nomination himself, hoped to wreck that strategy by raising doubts about Kennedy's ability to win in November. Eisenhower, meanwhile, seeking advantage in the Democrats' split and Johnson's vulnerability, had sent an ultimatum to Capitol Hill: increase his power to cut sugar quotas to Cuba, or he would call Congress back into special session next week.

Johnson didn't want to deliver the White House a powerful weapon against Fidel Castro, whose recent embrace of communism was thought to help the Democrats, so he put off a compromise until the last minute. For twenty-three hours, as he and Eisenhower's advisers postured through the night and early morning, a barrage of other bills came to the Senate floor, each receiving only perfunctory attention. Controversial issues like medical care for the aged and increasing the minimum hourly wage to $1.15 from $1.00, both already passed by the House, were tabled. Noncontroversial ones, like overriding a presidential veto on election-year raises to federal employees, were swiftly adopted. Amid the tumultuous bickering, a few measures passed unanimously, without discussion.

Among them was the Granahan bill, allowing the Post Office to seize and detail the mail of anyone suspected of trafficking in obscenity. A compromise worked out in the House earlier that week, to require a federal court order before the Post Office could stop any mail, had been accepted by both anticensorship groups and Summerfield, who, having also won an extension of the stop orders to forty-five days, heralded the new powers as vital to his department's ability to curb obscenity traffic. Never would postal inspectors hold greater authority to invade what Summerfield liked to call the "sanctity of the sealed envelope."

With Johnson finally agreeing to extend the President's authority to fix Cuba's quotas only through the first three months of 1961, just after the inauguration, Congress recessed until August at eight A.M., Sunday. Church bells across Washington pealed for morning services as the legislators staggered from the Senate and House chambers. Three days later Eisenhower signed the Granahan bill into law.

Summer arrived in Northampton with a blast of dank tropical heat; "Singapore weather," Arvin called it. With the students and most of the faculty gone, Smith turned eerily quiet. Spreading copper beeches and steeplelike Chinese redwoods towered over exotic flower beds and fountains, maintained to perfection by stooping groundsmen in green uniforms. As Arvin walked across campus to the library and to his office, in a white clapboard house overlooking Paradise Pond, he saw next to no one. From his desk, he looked across Paradise to the state hospital, rising above the pines just beyond Smith's empty playing fields. In a few years, the house—the sort of "fragrant cottage" with its "rose-scented porch" that Henry James had found so inviting yet suffocating when he visited Northampton a century earlier—would be used as the primary setting for the film version of *Who's Afraid of Virginia Woolf?*, Edward Albee's monument to the rage, pain, and loathing underlying small-town academic life, rumored to be based on the life of a homosexual couple at Williams.

This was Arvin's world, a moist, protected setting designed to nurture young women through their most delicate transformations, a world from which many if not most emerged to become the wives of important men. A world that for Arvin and Ned alike made cruising and bars and anonymous sex not only appealing but somehow profoundly life-affirming.

To Arvin's dismay, Ned had discovered he liked "not rough trade exactly, but something like that," as Ned put it. His motives were personal and ineluctable. At the college, people who knew him were struck by his gentle decency, and he was beloved by his students. In April, on his twenty-ninth birthday, Ned had arrived at his office on the top floor of College Hall to find it filled with a profusion of forsythia and other spring flowers. Later, after he left for the day, someone came and removed the flowers as mysteriously as they had arrived. No one suspected that he possessed a dangerous secret side, especially now that he was going to Harvard, seemingly destined for a distinguished career.

What Ned sought, specifically, were young men who reminded him of the working-class boys he'd been cut off from when growing up in Lee. His closest friend in high school had been a girl, Joan Ford—Joanie—with whom he played piano duets. He'd been terrified of a hulking boy named Billy, a basketball star with smoky blue eyes and wavy black hair, who, Ned feared, would beat him up. When Ned had traveled to Springfield, it was as the best boy in Lee, one of dozens of decaying hill towns in the area. Now a man nearing thirty, looking for excitement, he was drawn to what he hadn't had—couldn't have had—as a teen: the Billys of the world. "It was finally," he said, "like making contact with kids my age."

Like Arvin, Ned relished asserting himself during these encounters, the surge of relief that comes with no longer having to hide and be proper, the wild prison break of emotions. Once, at Everard, he recalled, "I first gave a guy a blow job. Then I fucked him. It was somehow exactly what I wanted." For both him and Arvin, sex was like experimenting with strong chemicals. Combustibility was part of the thrill. Experimenting more or less in parallel, and talking about it afterward, added to their closeness. But power worked both ways, and Arvin had begun to fear Ned's indiscretion, worrying about him as if about a talented but undisciplined protégé, admiring his daring but also afraid of it.

Taking risks was one thing, courting them another. Once at the Arch Ned picked up a Negro and took him back to a room at a hotel. Mounting Ned from behind, the man suddenly twisted off Ned's wristwatch, a gift from his father, pulled up his pants, and fled. Ned followed him downstairs, threatening to call the police. The man punched him once, knocking him to the sidewalk. Ned seemed clueless about the larger dangers. He never considered how the episode was likely to be perceived by the police—a quarrel between a college "queer" and a black assailant who had sex with him and rolled him. Later, Ned was philosophical, rationalizing his abuse: "I guess I was glad that was all that happened."

Crossing back and forth between the sylvan world-within-a-world of Smith and the Springfield demimonde, Arvin relied on the serenity and seclusion of the former while craving the latter's frank pleasures. He found more excitement, more *life,* in five minutes of groping a stranger at a highway rest stop than in a year of faculty meetings. At least in Springfield, when buying a drink at the Arch for a man he never saw before and would never see again, he didn't have to pretend. The other person would see him as he was, a small, sallow, well-dressed older man in glasses, bursting with sexual needs. And so he continued his pilgrimages, momentarily ecstatic when he found a taker, scolding himself only when he was unsuccessful. "Spent most of the day in Springfield," he wrote in his journal on July 7, "an appalling waste of time. This must be the last such jaunt for many weeks."

Unlike the previous summer, when Ned was teaching in St. Louis and first broaching the idea of going to graduate school, Arvin tried to steel himself against the reality of Ned's no longer being nearby. Believing his life was set, tired of pretension, faced with loneliness and loss, he withdrew to the safety of his rooms, reading and editing. As always, he kept up his correspondence and daily diary, but he also began writing for the first time in a large clothbound journal. Perhaps because his life was more fragmented, Arvin found this ledger an extra channel for his thoughts and feelings, another ear not quite his own. Unsurprisingly, the voice in it was bitter. After a lifetime of trying hard not to offend so as not to draw attention to his secret life, he was suddenly free. "My distaste for social relations of the usual kind is rapidly becoming an obsession," he wrote on July 9. Two weeks later, after returning from a pleasant visit with Ned to Granville and Dorothy Hicks, he wrote:

> Reading of student papers, bluebooks, etc. a form of torture, though inescapable at best. What gives the extra turn of the screw is, of course, the debased English in which most of them are written. Reading them is a matter of rubbing an iron file over one's teeth, or holding urine in one's mouth, or having the racket of a bulldozer in one's ear for an hour or two on end. Physical tiredness inevitably ensues.

As the weather turned sultry, there emerged from within Arvin's concave breast the murderous heart of a full-blooded misanthrope. "Almost impossible," he wrote on July 27, as the Republicans poured into Chicago to nominate Richard Nixon, "to contemplate the political scene, the vulgar conventions and the like, without revulsion."

Two days later, approaching his sixtieth birthday, he summed up:

> Emerson is right about old age: one of its blessings is the knowledge that there can't be so very much more of this. The edge of disappointment in people, for example, is less keen, and even the withdrawal of friends and lovers seems less a torment than it does at forty or fifty . . . Would love to go to Africa just the same, and watch the waves of history tossing and turning in that tempest . . . Watch the Republicans at Chicago, dragging out old [Herbert]

Hoover, pumping him full of some artificial juice, and palming him off on the country as Lycurgus or Cato. A zombie if there ever was one. A ghoulish business.

By early August, Arvin was eager to get away. He and Ned planned a four-day car trip to Vermont and New Hampshire, a last vacation together before Ned left for Cambridge. They would be taking not Ned's car, an old Ford Falcon he'd bought for five dollars from the poet Anthony Hecht, to whom Smith had recently denied tenure, but Ned's father's Cadillac. The luxurious black car, Roscoe Spofford's one great indulgence, had a metal visor over the windshield, massive tailfins, and plush, dove-gray tuck-and-roll upholstery. The weather called for clouds and showers through Sunday, then clear and cool.

Ned arrived about four P.M., and they set out along the river. There were Jamaican and Puerto Rican men and a few university students in the fields, picking beans and shade tobacco at fifty cents an hour. As they approached Greenfield, the ground rose. The hills were bosomed high with trees, and it grew cooler. Across the Vermont border, they turned and drove to South Halifax, a cluster of picturesque dairy farms and vacation cottages too small to be listed on most maps, where an associate professor in the Smith English department, Ken Connolly, lived in a hilltop farmhouse. Connolly met them by the roadside and led them up the steep, rutted hill to his house, where they spent the night.

The very ordinariness of the trip accentuated its poignancy. The next day, in Concord, New Hampshire, the state capital, Arvin and Ned toured the senate chamber, then bought some gin at a state liquor store and some candy at a Fannie Farmer's. They sent off some postcards, climbed back in the car, and headed north to the lakes, in the middle of the state, driving through faded mill towns and along roads with broken views of woods and shorelines. Ned had already found a sublet in Cambridge for a year, and Arvin made him promise again not to stay at Harvard any longer than necessary. At Meredith, the highway descended a steep hill. They passed Lake Winnipesaukee and continued north to Center Sandwich, a lovely small settlement around a maple-encircled church that sat in a basin surrounded by mountains. Looking up toward the higher ranges, Arvin felt the blue air go light. It was four o'clock. Shadows already were descending in the deeper valleys.

Howard Doughty was home when they arrived. Arvin's enjoyment in mixing new and old friends was evident at once. Whatever their troubles, Ned was still something of a prize, and Doughty, especially, would have understood the pleasure and pain of their relationship. After Doughty's wife, Binks, arrived a little later, the four of them settled in for the night. Arvin was delighted by the evening's activities. "Very pleasant time," he wrote in his journal. "Ned very animated and sweet. Very helpful, too. A darling guest." Later he and Ned slept "separately and without incident" in Doughty's studio.

The next morning at nine, Arvin, Doughty, and Ned set out for the mountains, driving through the intervales and notches up to Wildcat Mountain, where they rode a gondola to the summit. As the three of them moved slowly up the mountain encased in the tiny swaying steel cabin, Arvin felt panicky. He hated these adventures, but went along because his friends prodded him to, or else because he wanted to keep up with his younger companions. At the top, they beheld Mount Washington and the rest of the Presidential Range—the premier mountain panorama of the Northeast. It was like being atop the dome of the world, where storms were born in an eerie quiet, and it seemed a sudden gust could carry you off. Arvin checked his foothold and stuck close to Ned.

Later, in his diary, Arvin described the mountain view as "uplifting," in quotation marks, suggesting that he had his doubts. It was a tired man's remark, and Arvin really was too world-weary to be much inspired by anything, least of all nature, that did not add form and clarity to his inchoate longings. Only words were still necessary to him, and even they were less reliable than they once had been. That night he and Ned retired early. Arvin experienced some hypnagogic images, heights and depths, but no dreams. The next morning he and Ned returned to Northampton, where, during the week leading up to Arvin's sixtieth birthday, they got together on two evenings and played old records. Ned brought over one of his favorite albums, Schubert's *Die Winterreise*, recorded by Dietrich Fischer-Dieskau. Arvin, who seemed deliberately to be cadging sentimental memories, reported in his diary that he thought some of the songs lovely.

AUGUST 20, 1960

Arvin wrote to Lilienthal, who had invited him to Martha's Vineyard, to say once again that he was too busy to get away and wouldn't be able to visit until Labor Day at the earliest. Lilienthal had asked in a previous letter whether Arvin had heard from the Century Club, the prestigious New York literary social club to which Arvin had been nominated and Lilienthal belonged. Arvin responded:

> I have never heard a word officially from West 43rd Street and imagine that some really judicious person . . . has . . . blackballed me as really not being the club type—which is absolutely true. In any case I hope this is what has happened: it would save me the embarrassment of having to write and decline membership, for no other, or more sinister, reason than that I simply can't afford this sort of thing for a minute—and if I had my wits about me I'd never have allowed my beloved Louis [Kronenberger] to go ahead and take the time and trouble, and involve others, like you . . . to press my case. Retirement draws so near and the financial stringency *that* is evidently going to mean (whatever Congress does) will be so real, that I must salt away every dollar I can possibly spare for the next eight years if I am going to be able to sit on in this apartment when the last class has got up out of their seats and shuffled out of Seelye Hall . . . I hope earnestly that both you and Louis— and Ben Wright and Malcolm Cowley, to go no farther—realize how very genuinely I appreciate your speaking up for me, and how much touched I have been by the whole procedure.

He added:

I do hope I can get to Princeton some time during the autumn or winter: I'd like to talk with you about those letters and my possibly borrowing them sometime—if, as isn't very likely, I take time off and write, mainly for the fun of it, and *not* for print, A Secret Autobiography.

MONDAY, AUGUST 29, 1960

Richard Stanley, a thirty-three-year-old printing salesman for the *Gazette* and principal of the church school at the Edwards Church, knocked on the apartment door of the man he knew only as John. Stanley had been a Navy pilot in World War II and had broken his back while teaching a class how not to go off the side of a ship. Before he worked for the *Gazette,* he had managed the Friendly's Ice Cream Store on King Street, a block from the Calvin Theater, and was well known in town. "Married straight," Stanley had a miserable home life, living with a woman he didn't love and two small children in a small house on Marshall Street, a block of bungalows near the Calvin Coolidge Bridge, which spanned the Connecticut River a mile from downtown. This was the fifth or sixth time he'd gone to John's apartment, "for lack of a better word, to get blow jobs," he said.

This time John invited him for a threesome. Inside, he was introduced to a short, bald, bespectacled older man with slightly protruding teeth, a Smith professor, John told him.

"I don't know whether I was homosexual or bisexual," Stanley would recall. "Male or female, it didn't make much difference. The only thing I admitted was I enjoyed it."

Joel Dorius's prize possession was a marvelous hi-fi speaker, a four-foot-high Voice of the Theater with a multicellular horn encased in heavy black plywood. It was a movie house speaker, and Dorius could sit in his tower apartment on Round Hill, overlooking the valley, with a record playing, and feel in his sinews the exquisite trills and heroic thunder of the European symphonies he loved. At such moments he forgot where he was and why he was there. Dorius lived on the top floor of a wildly grand Second Empire manse with a central tower. The prospect from his living room resembled a Flemish Renaissance painting, with layers of landscape, hills off in the distance, all beautifully green and exquisitely proportioned, the kind of view much admired by early American painters.

Dorius tried hard not to show it, but leaving Yale and coming to Smith had been a "disaster," from which he was just now recuperating, two years later. Desperate to stay in New Haven, he had restrained his desires while he was there, yet was shattered not to receive tenure. Then he had had to start over in Northampton while having to guard his sexual identity far more jealously even than Arvin.

He had ample reason for caution. He had grown up in a "wildly dysfunctional, superbly neurotic" Mormon family in Salt Lake City during the Depression, both his parents nearly the last children of polygamous families—for all intents, illegitimate—which left his mother, especially, with "overwhelming guilt which I richly inherited," he would say. As a young teenager, Dorius attended the Mormon-run Deseret Gym, where, in keeping with the sect's belief that each body is a temple of God, the men swam nude. "It was so strong, so healthy, so exuberant," he would recall. "No one planned that a sinister person like me would misuse that piety."

At Yale, Dorius had lived in constant terror of being exposed as a homosexual, was hardly sexually active, and found that he needn't be, so enthralled was he with being a college teacher. Since coming to Smith, where he had made several good friends, he'd kept "Eros at a distance." As Arvin suspected, he was deeply fond of Ned, but Dorius knew he could never indulge in Ned's brand of cruising and bar-hopping. "Absolutely fatal," he called it.

Dorius kept in an old suitcase at the bottom of his bedroom closet a collection of photographs that he seldom looked at and never showed anyone. Pornography didn't interest him, but he was enthralled with the beauty of male torsos, chests, thighs, buttocks. He loved men's bodies as well as their minds, though he was far more interested in their heads and faces than in their penises. In Europe, where such purchases were considered acceptable, he'd bought pictures of classical sculpture, of young Adonises. Why he kept them he wasn't sure, since he seldom looked at them, and was terrified of anyone knowing about them. He'd thought about throwing them out, but was afraid that someone might find them and trace them back to him.

After turning off the music, he hesitated as he took the suitcase from its hiding place and thought of what he was about to do: drive over to Arvin's apartment with it. Arvin had several times asked him to come, and Dorius thought it might be his last chance to see Ned, who was planning to go to Cambridge for a couple of days before moving there. Though the gathering seemed the "ultimate safety, with closest friends"—Ned, Arvin, another Smith professor, whom he knew to be discreet since their days teaching together at Yale, and this colleague's intimate companion: just the five of them—Dorius still worried that he was being incautious. Just two weeks earlier, on August 16, a federal court judge in Washington upheld the Post Office ban on Herman Womack's beefcake magazines. Only when he reached Arvin's foyer and put down the suitcase did he begin to breathe more normally.

It was a warm, soft, end-of-summer night. Dorius had worried ever since he'd challenged Arvin on the Great Books syllabus that Arvin was angry with him. But he had come to believe that Arvin was "very gentle," and that although he probably knew how Dorius felt about Ned, he would have realized there was no threat of their having an affair, since Ned was leaving in a week, and Dorius was too fretful to act on his desires. Arvin's solicitousness reassured him. One of the things Arvin did for his younger friends—particularly Smith colleagues who didn't have his connections, reputation, and job security—was provide them with the safety and materials to unbutton themselves, if only momentarily. As the five of them sat drinking Arvin's liquor and passing around some of Arvin's prints, Dorius felt accepted, albeit not relaxed.

There was laughter, led by Arvin, as they admired the muscular youths in the pictures. Later, Arvin drew the curtains, shut the lights, and showed one of his short, grainy movies. Though Arvin's fascination with erotica hadn't much rubbed off on him, Ned, too, enjoyed such moments, not just the danger but the way it loosened everyone up. Here was freedom, as much as one could hope for. Arvin had given Ned four pictures of male nudes, which he kept in his apartment—unconcealed—in a manilla envelope; the subjects all looked "about eighteen" and their penises were tumescent, hanging down, not erect. On another occasion at Arvin's apartment, Arvin had showed him a photograph, probably sent by Capote, of a Greek man with an enormous erection. There were not many times or places, especially in Northampton, where a group of such men could feel safe enough to share their sexual interests, and there was comfort in it when it occurred.

Yet despite the ribald conversation, Dorius suspected the others of feeling less at ease than they let on. There was something awkward and disturbing about five men, even trusted friends, huddling over pictures and joking about sex: it was embarrassing and unnatural. Dorius struggled to calm himself. He knew he was taking a huge risk, but so were the others, especially Arvin, who had exhibited his own collection—by far the most extensive and explicit—and who, by hosting such parties, invited the added attention of his neighbors and landlord. Of all the terrors of being homosexual, perhaps the gravest was the power delivered to others once they knew your secret. The only check on that power was that it went both ways; what you knew about friends and lovers could be as threatening to them as what they knew about you.

Finally, Dorius reached into his suitcase and showed his small collection, mostly amateur black-and-white stills of totally naked men sitting or standing. He also circulated five "action shots" of men involved in sexual acts. Arvin, with his jeweler's eye, adjudged some of them to have real quality. Such moments were supposed to induce exhilaration, by downing self-denial. When Arvin, three years earlier, had decided he could no longer stand reclusion and abstinence and embarked on an active sex life in Northampton, he'd written to Doughty that it was worth the risk. But Dorius, surrounded by close friends he trusted enough to show his troublesome pictures, felt, if anything, further—oceans—from a similar reckoning.

"I was ill at ease about the whole thing," he would recall. "It was too new for me. Sharing something so private was odd." Far from pleasurable, the gathering only reminded him how lonely and emotionally straitened his life had become. "There was no release at all."

WEDNESDAY, AUGUST 31, 1960

Arvin, for reasons he found obscure, was more tired than usual. He lumbered around his apartment, heavy in the bones. Tomorrow would be September, and the seasonal migrations that marked fall would begin. Families returning in their American-made wagons and sedans from the shore and the mountains. Children lining up for school. Canada geese alighting in the meadows headed south, honking like Shriners. The gangs of gray-uniformed men at the state hospital going out to pick cucumbers and the last of the season's corn. The circulatory motion of itinerant writers scrabbling for an existence by teaching college literature courses. Ned's leaving for Cambridge.

And then the wheel would start all over again. The students would return. Arvin liked the ones who were different, who had an edge, but most of them he found drearily the same: "swells" and "all-around girls." He liked the pale ones, the ones who haunted the library the way he did, whose minds were on fire. The others he mostly disapproved of behind a charade of donnish benignity. He was having a harder time concealing his disdain for the whole process.

He had taught for almost forty years, he had to admit, for the money and little else. And though he had to admit, too, that he had a pleasant enough life, a decent sanctuary, he had saved next to nothing—so little that he couldn't afford to join the Century Club, *if* they let him in—and would have to keep teaching and hoping Congress would pass legislation to improve the lives of "senior citizens."

He wrote in his ledger, "The thought of beginning the semester again makes me think of an old plowhorse being hitched up to the plow once more when he ought to be put out to grass . . ."

Arvin felt his life was over and that nothing could change it. Surrendering to age, he resigned himself, with some relief, not even to try.

Then came the deluge.

Part Two

Personality is a very mysterious thing. A man cannot always be estimated by what he does. He may keep the law and yet be worthless. He may break the law, and yet be fine. He may be bad, without ever doing anything bad. He may commit a sin against society, and yet realize through that sin his own perfection.

—OSCAR WILDE

Everything looks permanent until its secret is revealed.

—RALPH WALDO EMERSON

Chapter Nine

STATE POLICE SERGEANT John Regan drove, as always. Though his partner, Gerald Crowley, had been assigned first to the state police antipornography unit, where they held equal rank, Regan had taken charge, and Crowley deferred to him. Their Boston-based bureau had been formed in May, when Public Safety Commissioner J. Henry Goguen, a former U.S. marshal with ambitions for statewide office, stepped up the department's drive against smut, following passage of a new state law making it a felony to possess obscene materials "for the purpose of sale, exhibition, loan or circulation." Goguen, a dapper Quebec-born Francophile who spoke better French than English, was an outsider among the Irish politicians who ruled the Massachusetts State House, courts, and police. But Regan and Crowley had both been reared in that system. Under its rights and rules, Regan—bigger, older, tougher, rowdier, more assertive—did what he wanted. Crowley, a solid, athletic-looking thirty-two-year-old former GI who had once worked for the Bureau of Subversive Activities on Beacon Hill, watched out, filed the proper paperwork, and covered for Regan's excesses.

Regan took the Massachusetts Turnpike, pushing the unmarked Ford hard across the state's central plateau to Holyoke. Though they were primarily vice investigators, Crowley and Regan both were veterans of manhunts along this wide-open stretch of the "Pike," known, because of its lawlessness, as a proving ground for troopers. Like other new links in the interstate highway system, it had been blasted and bulldozed through the state's ghost country, and motorists often found themselves isolated at night along a dark ribbon of highway in small towns with little or no local law enforcement. Drivers routinely had tires shot out. They were robbed at gunpoint and kidnapped from their cars, leading to police chases and, occasionally, shoot-outs. It was after one of these high-profile chases, earlier in the year, that Crowley was brought up and reassigned to the antismut unit, followed by Regan.

Since then, both had been busy responding to more calls than they could handle—up to thirty a month. Most were political favors: a state representative was running for mayor or a district attorney was up for re-election; porno arrests made good newspaper copy for candidates who wanted to be known for cleaning up their cities. A few originated as bizarre tips: hotel crooks in Boston broke into the room of a Holyoke paper executive and, after inadvertently acquiring a suitcase full of sadomasochistic sex tools—hoods, gags, and whips—dropped it down a laundry chute, where an alert housekeeper found it and handed it over to a security guard, who phoned the bureau. Increasingly, they were getting postal cases, which Cowley resented. He thought postal inspectors, who acted as if they were G-men, ought to be doing their own legwork.

Regan, on the other hand, relished every arrest and went out of his way to solicit more. Though he was married, and he and his wife had adopted a son, he never stopped working. "His whole life was the state," Crowley would later say. Regan spent nights and weekends arranging stings. He advertised under fake names in the personals sections of the *Philadelphia Inquirer* and other newspapers for couples interested in wife-swapping. Those who wrote back, he arranged to meet in a motel room in Sturbridge, where, posing with a policewoman as a married couple, he arrested them. Crowley worried about Regan's zeal. Once, a "sporty little guy" in a checkered cap drove up in an MG from New York to Springfield in response to one of Regan's ads. After he was released on bail, he went home and killed himself. "What the hell are we doing, John?" Crowley asked him afterward. "But that's the law, Gerry," Regan said.

Other times, Regan laughed about it. "There better goddamn well be a hell," he told Crowley.

Regan pulled off at Exit 4 in Holyoke, where they followed the Connecticut River to the Troop B barracks in Northampton, a two-story brick facility three miles north of Main Street. The building, amid cemeteries and cornfields, was headquarters for all four western counties. There they met with a third trooper, Joseph Jagodowski, who'd graduated from the police academy with Crowley. Jagodowski, another plainclothes detective, was assigned to work with them when they were in the area and needed a conduit to the local police and courts. A blunt Polish Catholic, he'd grown up in a tenement in Holyoke, once the world's biggest paper-producing city, now decaying and depressed. He and his wife owned a small postwar house in Chicopee, home of America's largest Strategic Air Command base, where his neighbors flew B-52 "fail safe" sorties with nuclear bombs. Both were Troop B towns.

Regan and Crowley briefed Jagodowski on their assignment. The suspect was a homosexual whose name had come to them as a result of a postal investigation. Either federal authorities had got his name from a mailing list seized from a magazine supply house in St. Louis, they said, or else a package addressed to him had "broken open" in the Springfield post office, revealing obscene pictures. Crowley doubted the broken-package theory—smut marketers double-wrapped their wares in heavy-duty brown paper and tape, anticipating rough handling by Summerfield's inspectors— but he let it go. Jagodowski didn't recognize the suspect's name but understood from Regan that he was a "pretty important man" on the Smith campus. They'd be joined by a Northampton patrolman, who would coordinate with local police, and a Springfield postal inspector.

Jagodowski hoped the case, a routine "pinch," would allow him time to get home on the weekend, though with cool, dry weather forecast across the commonwealth through Labor Day, he doubted he would be leaving Northampton. Commissioner Goguen had announced to the press that even former troopers would be pressed into traffic duty along the Pike over the long holiday weekend. Aggressive public safety was hornbook local politics. The barracks was likely to be hopping.

Regan pounded on the door to Arvin's apartment. He believed sex deviants *wanted* to be caught. He'd found that most people involved in pornographic practices were "more sensitive, more educated, more to be pitied" than other culprits, and often were respected by their communities. "There's a tremendous potential for blackmail," he said. "But nobody will talk. The whole thing becomes a nightmare for them." He liked to think he was doing them a favor by exposing them.

According to Jagodowski, the search of Arvin's rooms yielded quick results; most of the material was "fag shit"—muscle magazines and copies of *One,* the "common denominator" in many of Regan's arrests. It was in Arvin's study that Jagodowski found the hard-core photographs that Arvin had shared with Ned, Dorius, and the others three nights earlier. Jagodowski was repulsed. He'd once helped in the arrest of a cult of flagellists in Framingham. He'd confiscated "stags," grainy black-and-white 8-mm Mexican movies in which prostitutes cavorted with skinny men in ankle socks and harlequin masks. He felt disgusted, physically ill, he later said, by a picture he found at Arvin's of "multiple buggering"—a daisy chain.

Arvin was ashen. He could hear doors banging shut, gruff shouts, booming footsteps, snickering murmurs—and sickening silences in between. It was in the closet in his study that Jagodowski found his journals. The twenty six-by-nine-inch clothbound daily diaries going back to 1940 were stacked neatly atop a built-in three-drawer bureau with brass pulls. Jagodowski hadn't been seeking them and had no inkling of their value, but added them to the cache, on the chance that they might be useful.

The sudden seizure of his secret history completed the shattering of Arvin's world. When he saw police returning with the slender volumes, opening them, flipping through their lined pages—beginning to decipher the penciled hieroglyphics that unlocked his inmost life—it was as if there was nothing left of him to take or preserve. He was in utter panic, shaking, his face fallen.

Hawthorne, interpreting colonial America, wrote that Hester Prynne's branding with the embroidered A "had the effect of a spell, taking her out of the ordinary relations with humanity, and enclosing her in a sphere by herself." Arvin knew, had always known, that the price of his secret life was extreme, enduring isolation. He had been locked in a sphere by himself his entire conscious life. And so it was not for the "intrinsic flagrance of the sin," he understood, that he was being punished, but for everything else, too. And the penalty would not stop at arrest and conviction. It would go on, taking the very last of what he hadn't already spent in trying to keep himself hidden. The pitiful portion that was left.

Regan, despite his menacing presence, often handled suspects fairly, "by the book." A practiced interrogator, he knew that with most smut offenders force was unnecessary. He relied instead on their guilt and fear to make them want to confess to him.

Looming over Arvin, he asked the names of those to whom he had showed his pictures. According to both Crowley and Jagodowski, Arvin didn't hesitate. With terror and great urgency, he named the names of others who had gone astray.

Ned pulled his beat-up Falcon into the parking lot behind his apartment. He'd been gone less than twenty minutes, accompanied by a friend from New York who had come to help him move to Cambridge. A woman who lived in the building rushed out and blurted, "You'd better go upstairs. There are strangers in your apartment."

Inside, Spofford found two men sitting on his couch, examining the pictures of nudes he kept in manila envelopes on a shelf at the top of his closet. They identified themselves as police officers. Another tenant apparently had buzzed them in.

Ned collapsed in a chair, more shocked than frightened.

"They aren't mine," he said defiantly. Besides the four pictures that Arvin had given him, he was safekeeping a cache of erotica for Wendell Johnson, who was out of town. Wendell had sublet his apartment for the summer and didn't want his tenants to discover his collection of photographs, prints, drawings, magazines, and typescripts.

"They're in your apartment, aren't they?" replied one of the officers, most likely Crowley, who had driven to Spofford's apartment directly from Arvin's.

"Yes," Ned admitted. Since the pictures were in no way important to him, he didn't think they could harm him. He acted as if he had nothing to apologize for or hide.

The officers, after informing him that he was a suspect in an obscenity probe, drove him to the police station, a former primary school behind the First Church. Along the way, one of them pointed to a coffeehouse where teenagers met and played guitars and bongos, and which some townspeople suspected of being a bad influence. The officers asked Spofford if he'd ever been there. He replied he hadn't.

At headquarters, they took him to a small room with a long table. Regan, taking a pencil drawing of "a guy masturbating" from one of the envelopes confiscated at Ned's apartment, led the interrogation.

"Who drew this, Professor?" he demanded.

Ned hesitated. "I'd rather not say."

"Was it Do-RAY-us?" Regan asked, mispronouncing Dorius's name.

"No," Ned said unequivocally. The mention of Joel's name made him shudder.

Regan kept calling Spofford "Professor" until Ned corrected him. He explained the academic ranking system in which he was at the bottom: professor, associate professor, assistant professor, instructor.

"Did you ever show this to anybody else?" Regan asked, waving one of the envelopes.

"Three or four people, my friends," Ned said, again thinking the admission harmless.

Up to that point, Ned had felt no real fear. Whatever the price of being found with smut, even homosexual smut, he could handle it, he thought. It just wasn't that important, wasn't *who he was*. But he also thought it vital to clarify exactly how much pornography he had. The small amount, he felt, and the fact that most of it wasn't his would favor him if the police tried to label him a pervert. Therefore, he volunteered that he had other pictures in his apartment that Crowley and his partner had missed during their search. At this, Regan interrupted his questioning, and Ned returned to his apartment with two officers to retrieve the rest of the material. When the officers discovered some pictures he hadn't led them to, Ned apologized; "Oh, I forgot about those."

Back at the station, Regan left him alone with Charley Lynch, the Northampton police sergeant, who struck Ned as less aggressive and more decent than the troopers. Ned thought they were "playing that very neat and very effective game of good-cop, bad-cop," so he remained on guard.

"Do you ever do the other thing?" Lynch asked. He meant sodomy.

Ned lied. "I did once in high school."

Lynch asked about the City Hall men's room. "You spend more time there than you need to," he suggested.

"No."

"You take boys up to your apartment, don't you?" Lynch said.

Ned froze. Realizing they might know about Alan, he felt a hard ball of panic rise in his chest. Suddenly the full measure of Regan's understanding, and malevolence, came clear. How they knew about his picking up the high school boy was too much for Ned to fathom. *Had they been watching him? Did they have Alan, too? Who else did they have? What could others say about him?*

It was Regan who inadvertently saved him. Returning before Ned could answer Lynch, he pointed to the material on the table and said, "This is the most disgusting stuff I've ever seen," and, turning to Ned, told him, "You're under arrest."

Ned said, "All right."

After they had Ned booked at the desk, two of the officers led him to a holding cell, which was bare and stank of bleach. Sitting on a wooden bench was Arvin. Ned wasn't surprised to see him. He didn't know how Arvin had got there or what he had done or said, but he assumed that any investigation in which one of them was a target would connect automatically to the other. Ned took from his wallet several pieces of paper with addresses and telephone numbers of men he knew. He tore them up, then chewed and swallowed the pieces.

Arvin stood up and paced nervously, beseeching Ned with his eyes, saying next to nothing. He was clearly upset but wasn't crying. At last, he suggested that they commit suicide together.

Ned "emphatically" said no. He had always known he might end up in the hands of the police. And Arvin wasn't anguished, just quiet and sad, when he made the suggestion. Ned thought Arvin was "infatuated with me. He saw more of me than was there." What cause, he wondered, could they possibly have to kill themselves?

Arvin's bail was set at $2,000; Ned's, $1,000. Neither of them had the money—Arvin's bank account held only about $1,500, and Ned owed him about $200, which he was unlikely to repay anytime soon—so they had to call friends to pay for their release. Ned would not recall what he and Arvin discussed as they waited, but he didn't suspect, nor did Arvin in any way suggest, that it was Arvin who had told the police about his pictures. All that was clear was that they should not talk to each other. The very fact that they were friends incriminated them. Anything each knew about the other could be used as a weapon by Regan. Any feeling each had for the other would only add to the picture of a depraved conspiracy.

Helen Bacon arrived and drove Ned back to his apartment. He knew he could rely on her and perhaps a few others, senior people at Smith and Amherst who may have suspected that he was homosexual but would remain loyal. As a department chairman and a woman alone, Bacon, forty-one, was brash, outspoken, independent, and enough of a force on the faculty to defend him at Smith. She also was a political progressive—a radical in her student days at Bryn Mawr—with a fire that others either admired or found unfeminine and reckless. She was sincerely fond of Ned and, Ned suspected, in love with Dorius.

Ned phoned his parents, telling his mother only that he had been arrested for possessing obscene pictures. Although she was mortified, she didn't sound terribly upset; he didn't speak with his father. Then he made two other phone calls. The first was to Theodore Baird, the influential Amherst English professor, and his wife, Bertie. The Bairds invited him to stay with them if he didn't feel comfortable remaining in his apartment. The second call was to a young man to whom Arvin had introduced him and with whom he'd had sex. He told the man to "stay out of sight."

That night he ate alone at the Northampton Diner, near the train station. Sitting at the counter, he imagined that others recognized him, people who might know his face because his grandparents had lived in town. Later, he got a call from a senior professor at Amherst who told him that he, too, had once been picked up by police while walking around Amherst late at night. The confession was reticent, indirect, cryptic. Ned didn't know why the man had called him.

Al Fisher paid Arvin's bail and took him back to his house. Arvin couldn't bear the thought of spending the night in his violated apartment, and Fisher was worried about his mental state. He and Dan Aaron, having each discovered Arvin after a suicide attempt, agreed that Arvin was a danger to himself and shouldn't be left alone. They thought he might survive, but probably not without first suffering a severe collapse.

After Arvin retrieved his diaries from the police, he summarized the day's events: "Day of the avalanche." It was the last journal entry he would ever make.

SATURDAY, SEPTEMBER 3

Northampton District Court—the "vulgar" court of low crimes, morals charges, petty disputes, and domestic rifts—was housed in a former boiler room in the basement of the old stone courthouse. It was dingy and cramped, with a polished wooden bar, stands, jury box, and benches. Daylight slanted in through several open windows high along one wall, which also let in traffic noise, bus fumes, and a view of the marquee at the Calvin, advertising *Bells Are Ringing* with Dean Martin and Judy Holliday.

The arraigning judge was former Democratic mayor Luke F. Ryan, a broad-chested jurist with gold spectacles and a sternly cherubic face. Ryan, fifty-two, a Columbia University Law School graduate, had been the first Eagle Scout in the county and was the father of eight. He was active in the Knights of Columbus, the Holy Name Society, and the Diocesan Committee for Scouting. He also was a former city solicitor, as Coolidge had been when, as Ryan liked to say, "the Republicans had everything."

Arvin stood, mute. For years he'd strolled by Ryan's house, reading as he walked. They'd recognized each other "downstreet," where one got used to faces. Arvin denied the felony charge and also a second count of being "a lewd and lascivious person in speech and behavior," a catchall misdemeanor usually charged to men who exposed themselves in public, especially public bathrooms, but applicable to anyone whose sexual activities violated common decency. His lawyer, retained for him by friends at Smith, was William Welch, a Harvard Law School graduate whose father was presiding justice of the probate court, upstairs. Like his father, Welch was a taciturn former commander of the local post of the American Legion.

Ned sat jumpily with Helen Bacon and his lawyer, Edward L. O'Brien,

202 / BARRY WERTH

a bullet-headed former district attorney and president of the county bar association. A college basketball star at Catholic University in his youth, O'Brien towered beside Ned as he quietly denied a single charge of obscenity.

When Arvin had come to Northampton thirty-seven years earlier, the men who ruled the courts and City Hall were stern Yankees. Now they were Irish—Ryan, Welch, O'Brien. Arvin thought them all the same; indeed, as Catholics, the new group seemed more inimical, since they'd been raised in the doctrine of sexual asceticism: celibacy for clergy, conjugal fornication mainly to propagate the faith, chastity for the unmarried. Homosexuality was an abomination to them. Ned, having grown up in Lee's Protestant minority, sensed that he was at the mercy of people who, however upright, could only despise him.

The proceeding lasted just a few minutes. Ryan rapped his gavel. He continued the case to September 10, and resumed his other business, issuing a suspended sentence to a thirty-two-year-old Elm Street man who admitted stealing an automobile and fining a forty-three-year-old Bondsville man $30 for speeding and driving without a license.

Around noon, Jagodowski and a Northampton police officer drove out Bridge Street, past the fairgrounds, and turned left onto Marshall Street, two blocks from the river.

Richard Stanley was home with his two young children; his wife had gone to the supermarket. When the police came to Stanley's door and arrested him, he asked whether they could wait until his wife came home. They said no. At the police station, they tried to get him to admit he'd performed sodomy with the man he knew as John, and to give them the names of other homosexuals.

Stanley knew no other names and had never had anal sex, but the police persisted. They knew he'd been at the man's apartment the previous Monday, along with a third man. They were nasty, suggesting the things that Stanley must have done with the men and threatening him with jail. When Stanley, struggling to understand what they meant to do with him, asked how they'd known he was at John's, he was told that the police had had the building under surveillance.

After charging him with sodomy, lewdness, and unnatural and lascivious acts, they took him to a four-by-eight cell with two other men he didn't
know. Stanley, principal of a church school, had never before been arrested.
He was mild and introverted, a good citizen, with standing in the community and a respectable job. He stayed in the cell overnight, until his mother-
in-law bailed him out. His wife, horrified at the charges, refused to come
to the station.

Arvin craved solace, a temporary refuge where he could avoid facing people he knew and the horror of having to explain himself. Ryan had ordered
him to stay in Northampton until his trial. With no place else to go, he
asked Fisher and Aaron to drive him up to the state hospital.

The hospital recently had begun quarantining acute patients instead of
mixing them with the chronically ill, as it had done to Arvin in 1940. After
being admitted, in a new, low-slung brick building, he was given a physical;
his head, eyes, ears, nose, heart, lungs, weight, and general appearance all
were sound. Next, he was given a mental examination by a psychiatrist, to
evaluate his appearance, mood, and affect. With only three full-time psychiatrists for more than two thousand patients, the interview was cursory.
The doctor noted that Arvin was depressed and anxious, and that his homosexuality may have been the cause of much of his unhappiness and underlying disturbance.

Despite his previous suicide attempts and the suggestion to Ned, Arvin
was placed in the less restrictive of two new men's wards. His belt, shoe-
laces, jewelry, and sharp implements—pencils, pens—were taken from him,
though he was allowed to keep his clothing and books. Because of his homosexuality, he was assigned a private room; it had lime-green cinderblock walls,
caged windows, linoleum flooring, a steel gym locker and bedstand, rip-proof
bedding, and a heavy wooden door with a double-thick window reinforced
with chicken wire.

Incapable of living in his apartment, unable to afford a private hospital
like McLean, estranged from Ned, encysted in Northampton, Arvin settled
grimly into the last safe place he knew—Dippy Hall.

SUNDAY, SEPTEMBER 4

Dorius awoke in the Provincetown inn where he and three friends were vacationing. They were on their way to breakfast when the desk clerk asked whether they'd seen that morning's *Times*. 2 SMITH TEACHERS HELD IN VICE CASE, the headline read:

> Northampton, Mass., Sept. 3 (UPI) An award-winning author and a Greek instructor, both male members of the Smith College faculty, pleaded not guilty today to morals charges in the wake of a police raid that police said uncovered thousands of pornographic pictures.
>
> Frederick Newton Arvin, 60 years old, Professor of English and 1951 winner of the National Book Award for nonfiction, and Edward W. Spofford, 29, were freed in $3,000 total bail after an appearance in District Court here today. Judge Luke F. Ryan continued their cases until Sept. 10 . . .
>
> The police said that the two had implicated other male faculty members at the school . . . but that no female faculty members or students were apparently involved . . .
>
> The state police said Professor Arvin, after his arrest, gave them the names of other faculty members who had been involved in his activities. The information led to the arrest of Mr. Spofford, they said.
>
> The police said Professor Arvin, a faculty member at Smith since 1922, admitted displaying the photographs at his apartment and swapping them with others.

Dorius buckled, but not from surprise. He had "a certain fatefulness" about one day being found out, and his doubts about opening himself to Arvin had never fully subsided. Then he thought of the suitcase in back of his closet and was suddenly sick with fear. He needed to get home, destroy its contents before the police found them. Frantic, he and his friends made plans to catch the earliest air shuttle to Boston, where he would pick up his car and race back to Northampton.

All Dorius had feared and more was now happening. Scouring for information, he learned that the *Boston Globe* had reported that Arvin had specifically identified two other faculty members, presumably him and the other colleague who had been at Arvin's apartment four nights earlier. While riding to the airport, he heard a radio bulletin announcing a warrant for his arrest. In forty-eight hours, the case had gone from routine to sensational. A smut ring involving male faculty members at an elite women's college was plainly big news. The involvement of a celebrated author and critic like Arvin guaranteed added publicity. Dorius was horrified about what awaited him.

So were others. Roy Fisher, a close friend of Dorius's, was rooming that summer in Cambridge at the home of Arthur Schlesinger, Jr., the historian and close Kennedy aide, while finishing his Ph.D. in fine arts at Harvard. Fisher knew about Dorius's pictures and that he was in Provincetown. After reading the story in the *Globe*, Fisher sped by car to Northampton in the hope of removing the pictures before police found them, but he was too late. He found Dorius's apartment ransacked.

Fisher, a rail-thin, high-spirited epileptic, told Schlesinger what had happened, and Schlesinger gave him the name of a lawyer, William P. Homans, Jr., a tenth-generation Massachusetts Yankee and Harvard Law School graduate regarded as the best young civil liberties advocate in the state. With Schlesinger's help, Fisher located Homans on Martha's Vineyard, where he was vacationing. Homans, outraged at the invasion of Dorius's home and privacy, agreed to take the case; he told Fisher to try to keep Dorius from returning to Northampton until he himself returned to Cambridge. Aware of Regan's reputation, Homans didn't want Dorius facing him alone.

Fisher knew Dorius had flown to Provincetown and planned to return through Boston's Logan airport. He consulted the plane schedule, determined which flight Dorius and his friends would probably take, and drove to the airport access road, where he stationed himself to intercept them.

It was already dark, in heavy traffic, when Fisher spotted the dim headlights of Dorius's Volkswagen and flagged him down. At the side of the road, Fisher explained Homans's instructions. Dorius was dazed, unbelieving. Fisher's intervention was almost as unexpected as hearing on the car radio that he was being sought by police. Dutifully, Dorius followed Fisher to a leafy street with big houses near Cambridge Common, where a sympathetic family named Sprague agreed to hide him until Homans's return.

The fear spread concentrically, in waves. There were those at greatest risk, like Dorius, who had shown their pictures to Arvin and to whom he had shown his, and whom Arvin, according to the news reports, had named. There were other homosexuals, at Smith and dozens of other schools, who understood their value—and weakness—in any investigation. There were friends, and friends of friends, who feared that their past connections might implicate them. And there were those heterosexuals who had erotica of their own and whom Regan was determined to find and punish. Most of these people were veterans of the McCarthy era, outsiders with unpopular politics and hidden pasts, liberal intellectuals who had seen their lives and communities ripped by this kind of thing before. They knew they would be pressed to name others to save themselves, and that everyone around them would be, too.

In the evidence room of the Troop B barracks, Jagodowski spent the day poring over Arvin's journals. In nearly a decade of vice probes, he had never seen such a thorough record—virtually a log—of the crimes under investigation. Names, dates, activities; all meticulously documented. He was searching in particular for evidence of child pornography, although other than Arvin's description of seducing an eighteen-year-old "buck" at Everard the previous fall, there was no trace that Arvin or anyone he wrote about was involved with underage boys. He also had obtained a faculty list from Smith and compared the first names and initials in Arvin's entries to those of professors, deepening the probe—and the climate of fear—at the college. He typed up his comparisons and passed them on to Regan, who had worked nonstop since Arvin's arrest.

Regan, intent on exposing what appeared to be a major conspiracy, didn't rest. He knew he had a juicy story, in which the villains were a secret society of perverts at a fancy women's college, and there was, all told, including Arvin's personal papers and Dorius's artwork and old love letters, enough filth to fill a police van. He knew he was going to attract major press in Boston, where such accomplishments were noticed and rewarded. He also knew the investigation had the potential to go well beyond Massachusetts. Arvin's network included big names in publishing and at the country's top colleges. Regan may have cracked a national porno ring linking other well-known figures, fish much bigger than Arvin.

Regan's nose for the larger prize led him, almost at once, to Henry-Russell Hitchcock, Arvin's equal—and, in many ways, opposite and rival—at Smith. The pre-eminent architectural historian in the country, Hitchcock was a high-toned WASP with Rabelaisian appetites who had arrived at Harvard in 1920, just as Arvin was leaving, and had helped forge one of the most remarkable groups in its history, a circle of brilliant young modernists—Virgil Thomson, Lincoln Kirstein, Philip Johnson, among others—who were homosexual and who regarded Hitchcock as their model. Hitchcock openly entertained a large circle of young homosexual faculty members from area colleges who idolized him. "That pig," Arvin called him in his journal.

Hitchcock was traveling in Europe, as he did every summer, when Regan phoned his house and asked for him. A young UMass instructor who was house-sitting took the call and, realizing that Hitchcock's closets might be filled with the same sort of material that the police had found at Arvin's, tried to avert him. Fearing that Regan would come to the house anyway and that Russell, as friends called him, would be implicated while he was overseas, the instructor, William Kornegay, frantically searched the dwelling. In the basement, he discovered a footlocker filled with muscle magazines, mostly *Tomorrow's Man* and *Strength and Health*. On Hitchcock's bureau he found explicit love letters from "Buck," an English car salesman. Later he would realize that in Hitchcock's files were graphic letters from Virgil Thompson about his own sexual exploits in Paris.

Kornegay hurriedly filled a laundry bag with pictures, letters, and documents, backed his car up to Hitchcock's rear door, loaded the bag in the trunk, and drove twenty miles into the Berkshires. He dumped the magazines in the Westfield River, making sure not to be seen and pleasantly imagining their being discovered downstream by fishermen. Then, because the letters had Hitchcock's name on them, he took them into an open field and burned them. As with many others, he now saw his and others' private lives through Regan's eyes, and therefore tried to destroy whatever the most zealous inquisitor might think obscene. Another young professor burned in his fireplace, in addition to hundreds of letters, several Goya prints.

Around the time on Saturday when Jagodowski arrested Stanley, police picked up Arvin's friend John Goss, a former private-school music teacher, who was so distraught at his arraignment that the judge ordered him committed to the state hospital for observation. Goss's arrest heightened the apprehension in Northampton. It was whispered by unnerved men that Arvin had given police dozens, maybe scores, of names. Many people stopped using their phones, on the chance that they were tapped. Others abruptly left town, hoping the hysteria would end before the term began. Wendell, who had given Ned his erotica for safekeeping, passed on a typewriter case full of muscle magazines to a friend, instructed him to dump them, and then took off to a destination unknown.

Jagodowski, noting several references in Arvin's journals to someone named Jess, identified for possible suspicion a Smith professor named Jess Josephs, a straight-arrow physicist who worked on secret defense projects and had eyes-only federal government clearance. When Regan brought him to the police barracks for questioning, Josephs demanded, "Where is this leading?" After Regan told him about the investigation stemming from the raid on Arvin's apartment and the confiscated private diaries, Josephs again cut him short. "If you have any more questions about me, contact the FBI," he said. Josephs, a heterosexual, left unperturbed, but by the end of the day, as word spread at Smith about Arvin's journals, new fears rippled through the male faculty. *Am I in his journal?* Arvin's colleagues asked. *How? In what context? When was the last time I visited his apartment? Who else did I talk with there? What did I say? Who could I be confused with?* "The diaries," recalled Vincent Brann, then a young theater instructor, "were instantly infamous."

Forty-eight hours into the investigation, Jagodowski understood that Arvin's journals were far more explosive evidence than the load of mail-order pornography in his closets and the names he'd blurted out under questioning. Because of the diaries, the case would make headlines and keep the investigation going full throttle for several more days at least. But

Jagodowski felt none of Regan's exhilaration. The journals had clearly helped bolster the government's case, but reading them made him "suffer with disgust." Arvin had been "just a name," but his need to write down every intimacy had yielded a galaxy of new names all over the Northeast. As long as the troopers were busy chasing down new leads, Jagodowski was eager to be involved. But he knew that even the suggestion that a man consorted with known homosexuals could be "quite a stigma." That night, alone, he felt sickened by Arvin's frank admissions of perversion and the damage they would do. Finally, he later said, he retched, but it did no good.

MONDAY, SEPTEMBER 5

Regan liked to feed information to the *Boston Traveler,* the boisterous evening companion of the Republican *Herald,* the Democratic *Globe*'s archrival in the city's newspaper wars. All the city's papers except the *Christian Science Monitor* bowed to the powerful Catholic archdiocese and its recently named cardinal, Archbishop Richard Cushing, the gaunt, beloved leader of a million and a half Catholics throughout New England. The *Herald* never rose to the blaring pitch of the New York tabloids, but scandal sold in Boston, as elsewhere, and Regan's exploits made good copy. NORTHAMPTON PROBE DEEPENS, the *Herald*'s second-day lead-in read:

SUSPECT'S DIARY STUDIED FOR CLUES TO SMUT TRAFFIC

The *Herald* reported that Regan and his investigators had spent Sunday combing a suspect's diary for clues about a pornography "exchange" involving people in Massachusetts, Vermont, Connecticut, New Hampshire, New York, and California. No associates were identified, but police appear to have considered suspicious Arvin's links with Ken Connolly, who lived in Vermont; Brooks, who lived in Connecticut; Doughty, who lived in New Hampshire; Hicks and perhaps Wilson, who lived in New York; and Berkeley's Henry Nash Smith, who six months earlier had invited Arvin to fill in for him during the academic year. The paper also quoted Regan as saying that the diary contained nicknames or code names of associates, and that at least eight more men involved in the activities in Arvin's apartment were being sought.

Regan also told the paper that a quantity of photographs, literature, and art objects had been seized from the apartment of another male professor wanted for questioning, and that "all the suspects arrested so far were present at a gathering at Prof. Arvin's home on the night of Aug. 29." He described the gathering as an "orgy."

Though the last statement was untrue—Stanley had never been to Arvin's apartment, nor was Goss there that night, and none of the five men present had had sex—Regan's allegations seemed to confirm that Arvin was connected to a depraved conspiracy. The college and the community "reeled under the impact of [the] scandal," the *Herald* reported. "It makes me ashamed," a member of city government told a reporter from another paper, "ashamed to be a man."

As thousands of racing fans crammed the barn-board grandstand for the opening day of parimutuel betting at the Three-County Fair, police arrested two more Northampton men in their homes. Michael Howard, a married twenty-nine-year-old siding installer, and Jesse Green, thirty-six, the mechanics helper with whom Arvin and Ned had had sex months before, were charged with lewdness, though not with possessing obscene pictures or sodomy. The arrests brought to six the number of local men connected by the probe—seven with Dorius, who remained in hiding in Cambridge.

From the police station Howard phoned Ned, whom he hardly knew. Spofford urgently called Helen Bacon, telling her she had to pay Howard's bail. Bacon, who had never met Howard, agreed without hesitation.

"I told her," Ned said, "he could put me in jail."

Chapter Ten

SMITH'S PRESIDENT, THOMAS Corwin Mendenhall II, was vacationing on Martha's Vineyard when news of the arrests reached him. A bald, bearish, imposing man, Mendenhall, forty-nine, had come to the college from Yale the previous year and, although popular on campus, wasn't yet widely known—or trusted. He postponed his return to Northampton until the next day. He and his wife, Nellie, were expecting several old Yale friends that night for an end-of-summer party, among them Yale's president A. Whitney Griswold and his wife, Mary, a Smith trustee. Mendenhall wanted the Griswolds' counsel.

At Yale, Mendenhall had been the most energetic member of "Whit" Griswold's "kitchen cabinet," doing what needed doing most—revamping the history curriculum, chairing numerous governing boards, serving as master of Berkeley College. Striding about campus with a great loping gait, he was legendary for his Yale partisanship—he wrote a book about its 1956 crew team—and wore loud-checked tweeds so disreputable that Griswold accused him of aging his sports coats in a manure pile. When Mendenhall, a Rhodes scholar, had announced that he was leaving for Smith, a crowd of rambunctious Elis held a mock protest with placards saying TAKE US WITH YOU, LEADER!, then drove en masse to Northampton to demonstrate again in the Smith quadrangle, hoping to impress the girls.

But Smith wasn't Yale. Women were strong here; the campus was liberal and democratic; power devolved from committees, not clubs; the moral protection of students was held vital; scandal was feared above all. If Mendenhall was to hold Smith together, as Ben Wright had done during the Red hunts, the Griswolds told him, he would need to assure Smith's faculty and students that he would defend their liberal traditions and freedoms. Academic and personal liberty were watchwords on a campus long on talent and short on salaries.

In the past, when there was trouble with teachers facing morals charges, the college had been able to dispose of matters quietly, usually with the cooperation of local authorities. Barely a month before Mendenhall's arrival, a male teacher in the education department was caught having sex in a car with a boy who may have been a minor, and the police threatened to charge him criminally if he didn't leave town within twenty-four hours. Friends advised the shaken man to get a lawyer, but he went instead to Wright, who, staring at his watch, told him he had fourteen hours left and better get packing. Since it was the end of the school year, the disappearance of a mid-tier faculty man was easily explained away. Few people outside the administration ever learned the real reason for his departure.

Mendenhall regretted that he had no such recourse now. With the story already in the press, Arvin's prominence, the journals, the arrest of Spofford, the police interrogation of faculty members, the search for Dorius, reports that the probe had spread to other colleges (including Yale), and the fact that within weeks parents would be driving their daughters to campus for the fall term, he would be lucky just to keep up with events.

His first task was to secure the college. On arriving at his office in College Hall, he informed the campus police not to let Regan and his men on the grounds without a court order. Then he turned to the nettlesome issue of Arvin's and Spofford's teaching status. Arvin was tenured; Spofford wasn't. That meant that Arvin had job guarantees, and presumably faculty support, and Spofford did not. At the same time, Arvin had been named publicly as a pornographer and kingpin, his apartment virtually a den of illegal activity. Spofford was assumed merely to be an accomplice. Even if all the seized material wasn't homosexual in nature, as was rumored but hadn't yet been confirmed in the press—even if Arvin was innocent of all charges—his further association with the college could be ruinous for Smith.

Mendenhall worried about how long the Affair, as he and others at Smith began calling it, would continue and where it would lead. But he had no choice except to convey a strong public message that whatever evils lurked on campus would not be allowed to threaten young women—even as he understood that students and their parents had far less to fear from male homosexuals on the faculty than from heterosexuals or lesbians. Within days, the University of Massachusetts would announce its plans to suspend immediately any staff member named in the investigation. Mendenhall, mindful of Smith's tolerant and genteel traditions, opted for a more flexible course.

After consulting with Smith's lawyer, he wrote to Arvin:

Dear Newton,

In light of the charges under which you have been arraigned, the college has concluded to relieve you of all academic responsibilities and to grant you a leave of absence, with pay, until a judicial decision has been reached in your case.

He prepared similar letters for Spofford and Dorius, wondering how many others he might have to send.

Bill Homans arranged the details of Dorius's surrender—bail terms and the like—by phone, from Cambridge. He already believed that Dorius's and Spofford's cases might yield a new national standard about a key constitutional principle still in dispute—whether illegally seized materials could be used as evidence in criminal cases, particularly against those from whom they were taken—and he wanted a "clean" record on which to appeal.

Dorius marveled at being in such sure, deliberate hands so soon after feeling violently upended. He believed he was the "worst person" to be swept up in a scandal like this, since he had never intended his homosexuality to be anything but the darkest secret, a private suffering, and therefore could feel nothing but shame and horror at having it exposed.

Yet here was Homans, rescuing him, handling it all. He was a towering man, six feet four inches, weighing two hundred pounds, with a lumber-jack's hands, black hair, and what one newspaper called a "giant Apache face." Chain-smoking vigorously, he was a fierce, down-to-earth champion of both his clients and the law, yet disarmingly humble, an enigmatic Boston Brahmin who had graduated from Harvard in 1941, volunteered for the Royal Air Force six months before Pearl Harbor, and then, when he couldn't squeeze into the cockpit of a British Spitfire, joined the Royal Navy and fought in the Pacific. Since graduating from Harvard Law School, in 1948, he'd won dozens of notable civil rights and free speech cases, both in private practice and as counsel for the Civil Liberties Union of Massachusetts. Homans's reluctance to charge his clients had got him into financial crises so severe that they ended his marriage and his law partnership.

Homans had expected, as soon as he read about the raids on Ned's and Dorius's apartments in Sunday's *Globe,* that one or both of them would probably contact him, even though he was relatively inexperienced in criminal matters. The problem was, he couldn't represent them both, and their arrests raised different issues. Spofford's presented the legal point most starkly: the search of his apartment was plainly unconstitutional, since the police had no warrant. But the seizure of Dorius's pictures, letters, and sonnets had what Homans called the "trappings of legality," because Regan had obtained a court order. More excited by the issues raised by the raid of Dorius's closet—if his pictures weren't obscene, or if he had the legal right to possess them, what did that do to the legality of Regan's warrant?—Homans had decided to represent Dorius and find a sympathetic lawyer for Ned.

Dorius himself agonized over whether to challenge the law. He already felt like a criminal, afraid that every time he went out he might be stopped and seized by speeding police cars, sirens screaming. And this was Massachusetts; retribution for sin and temptation was mythically harsh here. The penalty for adultery from the beginning of the Massachusetts Bay Colony had been death. For seducing an Indian, a woman of the Plymouth Colony "was sentenced to be whipt at a cart's tayle through the town's streets, and to weare a badge with the capital letters AD cut in cloth upon her sleeve . . . and if she shall be found without it abroad, then to be burned in the face with a hot iron." With his homosexual friends urging him not to do anything that would invite further attention, Dorius shuddered to think of taking a stand that would publicly identify him as having committed crimes against morality far more unspeakable than adultery. "A white hot cauldron," he called it.

And yet what choice did he have? The police had legally seized more than enough material to convict him. They had the names of his friends, which they had furnished to authorities in New York and Connecticut, where local police were beginning to question former Yale colleagues like Roy Fisher. His only defense was that he was within his rights to possess that material in the first place and not be incriminated by it; that, and the sanctity of home.

Dorius was slightly encouraged by seeing Regan for the first time, at the courthouse on Wednesday afternoon, September 7. Homans had warned him that Regan was mean and clever and that "no one should trust himself with him." But as Dorius surrendered to police with Homans beside him, Regan seemed "thrown off," he recalled. Regan "uttered something literally filthy," but suddenly grew quiet as he realized that Dorius, unlike Arvin, meant to resist him in court. So far the Northampton probe had all gone Regan's way. The district attorney and the local defense bar were cooperative, and Smith's refusal to let police on campus hadn't kept him from following up other leads. Homans's pleas indicated the first real challenge to Regan's methods and aims.

Dorius denied a single charge of possession of obscene pictures for the purpose of exhibition and was released on $1,000 bail, pending arraignment later in the day. Afterward, he received a troubling phone call from Al Fisher, who told him he had got the names of all of the homosexual men on campus and had discreetly called and instructed them to destroy their pornography. These men shared a sense, which Fisher helped foster, that he was not acting independently but at Smith's behest, and that the college wanted privately to know who they were in order to help them. Dorius was alarmed. Like most homosexuals, he believed that if Smith or any employer knew about him, he would lose his job at once. And he wasn't sure whether he should trust Fisher, perhaps Arvin's closest heterosexual friend, whose willingness to drive Arvin to cruising spots and interest in what Aaron called "kinkiness" were common gossip within the department. Fisher apparently tried to calm him by reminding him that everyone who had any pornography was equally vulnerable and by saying that he had contacted married friends at other campuses with similar instructions.

"I hear," Dorius would recall Fisher telling him encouragingly, "that there are many, many fires all over New England, in every valley, as people are burning the contents of their bottom drawers."

The *Boston Herald Traveler* continued to trumpet Regan's probe. NORTHAMPTON DIARY TELLS ALL, the paper announced on the day Dorius returned to Northampton:

2 MORE EDUCATORS FACING
ARREST IN COLLEGE SEX RING

Citing Regan, the paper reported that police had now culled more than twenty names from Arvin's "sordid 'tell-all' diary" and were in contact with police in other states. It added that the large quantity of obscene materials seized in the case were "mostly photographs of males."

This last, picked up by the wire services, began to circulate at once in other papers, including the *New York Times*, hinting publicly for the first time that the men involved were homosexuals. A certain prudishness and self-restraint, however, kept any explicit references to their sexual orientation out of the news accounts.

In perhaps this one way only, the Northampton defendants were lucky. As an erupting national security scandal simultaneously grabbing page-one headlines made clear, homosexual perversion was again being identified as a subversive menace. On the day before Dorius surrendered, two young code clerks for the top-secret National Security Agency who had defected to the Soviet Union appeared in Moscow to condemn United States spy flights over Russia. In Washington, HUAC chairman Francis Walter, a Democrat, promptly denounced the Eisenhower administration for "gross dereliction" in hiring the duo in the first place, since it was "common gossip" that one was a "notorious homosexual."

Eisenhower, head of Allied military forces in Europe in World War II, was forced at a press conference to defend his record in cleansing America's defenses of such "sick" individuals. "I have possibly been more sensitive to the dangers to our country as created by this kind of weakness, human weakness, than have most people," Eisenhower said. "This incident should be a lesson to all of us that we must never cease our vigilance in the large and small places at any time."

FRIDAY, SEPTEMBER 9

A week after his arrest, Arvin assumed a routine in the Haskell building that outwardly resembled his life in his apartment and at Smith. He read in the library, wrote letters, received visitors—mostly Fisher and Aaron, who once again were his conduits to the outside world—and talked quietly with one or two other patients, principally Goss. He dressed carefully, concealed his agitation behind a practiced politeness, and kept to himself. The other patients, he discovered to his relief, had their own problems and little interest in sharing—or judging—his.

He heard from scattered literary friends. Malcolm Cowley, the first to write, urged him "at the first unencumbered moment [to] plunge into some *work* . . . our only justification and refuge." Cowley, a visiting professor at Stanford, was convalescing in Connecticut, having just had part of his prostate removed. He pledged in his note to stand by Arvin and volunteered to do "anything I can," although privately he was conflicted. "I am shocked and disturbed about Newton," he wrote to Dan Aaron the next day. "Why did that discreet and in most ways cautious man let himself be so indiscreet and uncautious in one direction? Why did he give names? . . . Existing as he does on the edge of a nervous collapse, will this push him over the edge?"

Capote, having moved to Spain to write his "Kansas book," counseled Arvin, "Well, what's happened has happened; and it has happened to many others—who, like Gielgud, took it in stride and did not let it be the end of the world." Seven years earlier, after being arrested for "persistently importuning male persons" on the streets of Chelsea, the English actor John Gielgud told a London courtroom, "I am sorry. I cannot imagine that I was so stupid." Five days after his conviction, he received six curtain calls at the opening of a new play. Capote continued:

All of your friends are with you, of that you can be sure; and among them please do not count me least. Aside from my affection, which you already have, I will be *glad* to supply you with money should the need arise. This is a tough experience and must be met with toughness; a calm head, a good lawyer. This combination has won out over and over again for those similarly involved. I am certain it will all blow to sea; but meanwhile I am most awfully concerned for you.

The playwright Lillian Hellman, who famously refused to name names during the Hollywood Red hunt, wrote similarly from Martha's Vineyard:

I would like to do anything I could, anything, and I hope you feel friendly enough towards me to tell me what I could do . . . Please don't feel too bad. I know that sounds silly, but please don't. There was a time when I thought the world had gone to pieces for me, but it didn't, and it's our duty to see that it doesn't. Just you be sure that many, many people admire you and respect you.

Arvin's literary friends knew his history. Many were veterans of the left, survivors of McCarthyism, or sexual outcasts themselves. In their view, Arvin's persecution by the police in Massachusetts was punishment for his lifetime of courageous defiance, going back to the Sacco-Vanzetti case, itself a prime example of antileft bias in the state's courts. He was a victim, no different, it seemed, from countless other radicals who for centuries had defied the state's religious puritanism, conservative politics, and stern judiciary, and had been harshly branded for it. What they read in the press about his giving the police names was excused, by all except Cowley, as an unfortunate but understandable reaction by a sensitive, scared man to brutal, repressive, and ultimately overwhelming government force. As the writer Martin Duberman later put it, Arvin was driven by the state to choose between his friends and his own survival. At sixty, facing old age with little money and no immediate family, and after a lifetime of fears, he "panicked and ratted," Hellman said.

Or so it seemed. Among the generation of liberal intellectuals who had made "naming names" the defining test of individual conscience, honor, and morality during the McCarthy era—Arvin's generation—his surrender of others was surprisingly well tolerated, perhaps because his friends believed that it was still safer to be revealed as a communist than as a homosexual. Arvin himself confessed remorse, but vaguely, leaving uncertain exactly what he regretted. "The pain of the pain," he wrote back to Cowley, "is the bitter sense of the hurts one has given to other people."

Which other people he meant—whether the friends he betrayed, those he simply embarrassed, or those like Aaron and Fisher whom once again he was encumbering with his problems and putting in the awkward position of having to defend him—he didn't specify.

With the district court trials of all seven defendants scheduled in less than ten days, beginning on September 20, Arvin anguished over how to plead. He couldn't bear to think of admitting guilt and, as appeared likely, going to prison. And yet if he chose to fight the state's charges, he faced the spectacle of a full public trial. Either way, he believed, he was through. He was taking Meloril, a powerful antipsychotic, in low doses, mainly to sleep, and it left his mind sluggish. He shuffled miserably through his daily routine on the ward, keeping to himself, then anxiously asking visitors, "Will people still like me?" His friends hedged their answers. They knew that others at Smith, particularly friends of Ned and Dorius, were disgusted by the degree to which Arvin had already capitulated and would never again like him no matter what he decided to do.

Arvin's lawyer, Bill Welch, was an able, taciturn attorney whose main goal was to become a judge, like his father. Unlike Homans, he was no ideologue. As Cowley wrote to Hicks, Welch favored a quiet resolution:

It seems that Newton's lawyer thinks he should plead guilty & hope he comes before a sympathetic judge—not the local Irish puritan who recently sentenced a citizen to thirty days in the workhouse for taking a leak in his own yard. A sympathetic judge would give him a suspended sentence in view of his psychiatric record. The lawyer says that if Newton pleaded innocent & appealed the case to a higher court, it would almost certainly be won there, in view of the lawless actions of the investigators, who probably made their search without a warrant. But they're terrified of having Newton on the witness stand, & he's terrified too—the "obscene pictures" are few, but the investigators seized Newton's diary and his entire correspondence with Truman Capote.

Arvin's closest friends were torn. They wanted to protect him but didn't know how to do so. Aaron in particular understood that if Arvin pleaded guilty, his academic career was over, since no board of trustees could tolerate such an admission. He avoided raising the subject with Arvin, however, because of Arvin's fragile state. Aaron disagreed with Welch's expediency, but he, too, feared a trial. Arvin had "simply collapsed," he'd recall. "There was this feeling of complete shame and guilt . . . 'Here I am alone. What a disgusting specimen I am.' All these kinds of self-repudiations." Testifying could destroy him. On the other hand, Arvin's friends believed, the invasion of his private life should not go uncontested. "The police completely smashed into his nest," Aaron said. "What happens when something like this is suddenly spread all over the country? You want to do something. You want to rally around and protect. You want to make sure that all his friends know. You want to make sure that he's not getting thrown out."

As the trial loomed, fears spiked at Smith and elsewhere that more arrests were imminent. As the main contacts for Arvin, Ned, and Dorius, both Aaron and Helen Bacon received desperate, late-night phone calls from panicked acquaintances at other campuses begging to know what to do. Many of the callers were anonymous, friends of friends, frantic that they may have been implicated. There were hushed, cryptic confessions and terrified talk of tapped phones, secret mail blocks, more police raids, more lives ruined. Aaron and Bacon expressed sympathy, but probably less than the callers craved, since the specific secrets for which they feared being exposed were only hinted at. Both heard stories of people fleeing the country and would, in time, hear of suicide attempts.

Aaron, at Welch's urging, solicited written character references for Arvin from his fellow literary critics, who responded unstintingly. Again, Cowley answered first. "I want to express my admiration for Newton Arvin as a writer and a critic," he wrote on September 11, nine days after Arvin's arrest. "I have known him for nearly thirty years, and he always impressed me as being a shy, modest, and highly scrupulous man, deferring politely to the opinions of others, but standing by his own convictions. I find it hard to credit the charges against him, considering I have never heard him utter so much as an indecent word."

Arvin's will to live, all but spent before his arrest, was negligible. His friends worried that any more bad news would cause him to suffer a complete, perhaps final, collapse. But his spirits now lifted slightly as, one by one, his fellow critics rushed to his defense, confirming that those whose good opinion he valued most intended to stick by him. Indeed, if nothing else, he appeared to have the unanimous support of the elders of the literary left, which, in view of his shattered friendship with Ned, vilification among his younger colleagues, and raging self-contempt, seemed little short of miraculous.

Within the next two days, Lionel Trilling responded from New York: "I should like to record my opinion that Professor Newton Arvin is one of the most distinguished and devoted college teachers of our time and one of the most notable of American scholars and critics. In the more than twenty years I have known him, he has shown himself to be a man of perfect probity and the most delicate sense of personal honor." Granville Hicks wrote similarly from Grafton: "He is a man of unusual erudition, high perceptivity, and unflinching honesty . . . I should say that few critics are more respected." Even Van Wyck Brooks, whose reservations about countenancing homosexuality remained entrenched, steadfastly supported his old friend. He wrote:

I have known Newton Arvin for about forty years, and I have always greatly respected his moral integrity, not to mention his intellectual ability . . . What has always impressed me most about him has been the sincerity of his convictions. I have always felt that he was a very courageous man, ready to stand by his beliefs, which I have largely shared, and extremely sensitive and honorable as well.

It was Edmund Wilson who was most outraged and whose encouragement, as during Arvin's crises in the early and mid forties, supplied the greatest strength. Since the suppression of *Hecate County* by what Wilson called the "censor morons," Wilson had suffered his own public agonies. After enduring several highly publicized trials, during which he, too, was characterized as lewd and obscene, his annual income had dropped as low as $2,000 and he'd neglected to file federal income tax returns from 1946 to 1955. Chronic money problems kept him writing and teaching ceaselessly—at sixty-five, he had just finished a term at Harvard—while fending off the Internal Revenue Service, which was suing him for tax evasion. Full as ever of bile for the hated state, Wilson wrote from Wellfleet:

I regard Mr. Newton Arvin as one of the two or three best contemporary writers on American classical literature . . . I have been struck not only by his sensitivity but also by his excellent judgment and by his obviously high principles in both his personal and professional life. I am unable to believe the charges against him which have been printed in a story in the *New York Times* and which sound like a fantasy of the local police distorted by an incompetent reporter.

Those who knew and admired Arvin professionally couldn't conceive that he was the leader of the small-town homosexual smut ring described in the headlines. The character identified by police was not—could not be—the man they knew. And yet the headlines, though exaggerated, reflected a truth about him that many had failed to recognize, that Arvin wasn't just homosexual but a sexual adventurer. Most of them absorbed the contradiction privately and went on from there. Such was the obtuseness of public life in the Eisenhower era—and so profound the sense among liberals that the state's bullying of a harmless homosexual signaled a dangerous resurgence of McCarthyism—that even some of the period's most famously perceptive public intellectuals could be shocked by the private behavior of a man they thought they understood, yet still defend his probity, honor, courage, and morality. Arvin, sustained by their sympathy and refusal to judge him, rallied as he realized he still had friends who believed in him.

On September 12, as Aaron and Fisher scrambled for testimonials, Hicks wrote to Arvin at the hospital from stormbound Grafton. A giant hurricane, Donna, had slammed into the East Coast, paralyzing the coast from Miami to Maine. "Dick Rovere called almost as soon as telephone service was restored," Hicks reported encouragingly. "He is deeply concerned and has offered to help in any way he can. He said that Fred Dupee and Saul Bellow were disappointed at our not getting down over the weekend, because they had hoped to talk with us about the situation. You have more friends, Newton, than you can easily imagine."

Three days later, Arvin wrote back with an unexpected burst of hope and equanimity:

> Life here at the hospital is very tolerable—with some really good personal relations as always. Letters from friends, and visits, have been like warm but bracing water on a bitterly cold day. Coraggio! Good may somehow emerge from all this distress, and my own personal fortune is of minor importance, even I think to me. But what you tell me of Dick R., Saul, Fred D., etc. affects me to tears.

It was in this mood of fatalistic optimism—and perhaps with a sense that if he was to have a future at all, it would be at the favor of those who might still feel kindly toward him—that Arvin belatedly answered Mendenhall's letter four days before his trial. However he pleaded in court, he realized, the problems for Smith were just beginning. And, in the balance, the college held his livelihood. Whatever he decided, he would need Mendenhall's continued help and support. He wrote:

> Dear Tom,
> I have no proper note paper or pen here at the Hospital, and that is one reason why I have not written to you before. But I cannot

delay longer to send you a brief message of thanks for your very generous letter . . . and the magnanimous arrangement you suggested in it. I find it quite impossible to say how much I appreciate this—or how excruciating has been the constant sense of distress I have caused to my friends, and to the college. You will have to try to believe that this has been far more painful to me than any shock or shame I may have felt on my own behalf.

Chapter Eleven

*A blessing on the righteous colony of Massachusetts, where
iniquity is dragged out into the sunshine!*

—BAILIFF'S CRY, FROM *THE SCARLET LETTER*

TUESDAY, SEPTEMBER 20

ARVIN ENTERED THE basement courtroom flanked by Dan Aaron and Al
Fisher. He wore a gray suit they had brought him that morning before
driving him from the hospital to Welch's office. Hawthorne wrote in *The
Scarlet Letter*, "In our nature, there is a provision, alike marvelous and merciful, that the sufferer should never know the intensity of what he endures
by its present torture, but chiefly by the pang that rankles after it." He was
describing Hester Prynne's bearing up "under the weight of a thousand unrelenting eyes" as she was led from the prison door to the marketplace,
where she was to stand pilloried. Such was Arvin's suspended state as he
took his seat in the gallery.

The lawyers for all the defendants but Goss, who remained "under observation," were cloistered in chambers. Presiding Justice Charles O'Connor, another Irish Catholic former mayor, had sent each a summons to
meet with the district attorney, a stocky, disheveled, soft-spoken man
named Sanford Keedy. Because of the attention the scandal had generated,
and for other reasons less apparent, Keedy was prosecuting the cases himself, and he hoped to contain the proceedings before they started.

Keedy was a vigorous trial lawyer with a keen legal mind. Like both
judges and the local defense lawyers in the case, he was born to the county
bar, his father having been district attorney before him. But Keedy,
forty-nine, was Protestant, not Catholic; Republican, not Democrat; from

Amherst, not Northampton. He had attended Amherst College, to which he was fiercely loyal, and, while precise and deliberate in the courtroom, "was not too well-organized domestically," a friend noted. Before he married, later in life, Keedy's car overflowed with neglected laundry, and he once wore a piece of evidence, a pair of galoshes, home on a snowy night. Keedy believed in the rule of reason as much as in the rule of law, and he was apparently troubled by bringing harsh judgment to bear on men whose harm to the community he felt had not been proven by the state's probe.

Despite the publicity, few people gathered in the dim courtroom. There were no "stern-browed men and unkindly visaged women," Hawthorne's proxies for a reproachful public—just a scattering of nervous summer-clad defendants, their lawyers and friends; Donald Sheehan, Mendenhall's assistant, who quietly took notes; Regan, Crowley, and Jagodowski; a couple of Northampton police; and two or three local newspaper reporters. None of the defendants had family present, and the jury box remained empty. A large carton, allegedly containing obscene literature and pictures seized during the raids on the defendants' homes, sat unopened in a corner of the courtroom.

Ned, first on the docket, glared hatefully at O'Connor as the bailiff announced his charges. Since his arraignment, he had retained a new lawyer, a Boston civil liberties attorney and friend of Homans named Harold Katz. Like Dorius, Ned planned to appeal, but unlike him he refused to conceal his contempt for the proceedings against him. He continued to fix O'Connor with a hostile gaze even as Keedy stood up and quietly explained, ignoring the unopened carton in the corner, that he would not be introducing any evidence in court, because Ned, through his attorney, had already conceded that the state had enough material to convict him.

This was the deal Keedy had offered all six defendants, including Arvin, and that their lawyers had indicated during the pretrial meeting would be acceptable—no direct testimony in exchange for what amounted to a submission to a guilty finding. The defendants would all be subject to suspended jail terms and fines but no prison terms. Nor would they be forced to endure the spectacle of a full-scale trial in which the exact nature and the extent of their activities were exposed and dissected. As for Ned and Dorius, the agreement didn't require them to retract the innocent pleas necessary for their appeals, which Homans and Katz planned to litigate, not by contesting the evidence against them or the trial outcome but on constitutional grounds.

O'Connor, as arranged, accepted Ned's admission of guilt. He sentenced him to a year in the House of Corrections and fined him $1,000 for illegally possessing obscene pictures and literature. But he refrained from suspending Ned's sentence, because, Ned believed, of his defiant gaze.

Ned was shaken but unbowed as the charges were read next against Jesse Green. Green was charged only with lewdness, a misdemeanor. The mechanic had been to both Arvin's and Ned's apartments for sex, but was not implicated in the obscenity traffic at the heart of the state's probe. Yet his role in the investigation was more than tangential. Regan, during Ned's interrogation at the police station, had told Ned that he knew Green had gone to his apartment, and that Ned had taken Green's clothes off and "given [Green] a blow job." At the time, Ned was reeling, too thunderstruck to wonder how the police already knew about him and Green, who hadn't yet been arrested. Now, however, Green's lawyer, who had accepted Keedy's offer like all the others, allowed Regan to testify "informally."

Without being sworn in, Regan stood up and read a signed confession from Green that he had committed homosexual acts with both Ned and Arvin during the past two and a half years.

Arvin and Ned buckled as Regan read Green's statement. They had been assured by their lawyers that no evidence would be introduced at any of the trials, since "submitting to facts" precluded the need for testimony. Ned believed Regan demanded to testify in order to thwart Keedy's attempts to dispense quietly with the scandal, and perhaps to punish him—Ned—for his boldness. It scarcely mattered. Suddenly, it was public knowledge that he and Arvin had had sex with men from town. The obscenity charges, though more serious legally, paled beside the shock of this new disclosure.

Ned's bravado vanished as Green was sentenced and O'Connor called a short recess. He knew now that what would hurt him most wasn't the pornography charge, which had never seemed important to him, but the fact of his homosexuality, gratuitously announced by Regan. He also knew that all of the defendants were equally dangerous to one another, and that the deepest betrayals usually came not from one's enemies but from one's friends and associates.

Staggering from the courtroom, Ned was appalled to see Arvin chatting with Charles Lynch, the "good" Northampton cop who had questioned Ned at the station house prior to his arrest. "Don't *talk* to him!" Ned screamed, hurtling past a reporter who wanted to know if Ned planned to appeal. Having, he felt, been betrayed in court, he feared further collusion.

Arvin and Ned had not spoken since they'd been jailed together at the police station. Moving to a bench, they were careful not to touch each other or sit too close or in any way hint at their former affection—lethal gestures, in view of Green's statement. Arvin started to say something, but Ned "immediately cut him off," he would recall. "I cared so much about Newton that I couldn't press him about whether he had given the police my name."

Unasked questions haunted their brief encounter. Since his arrest, Ned had struggled to believe that Arvin had protected him, that the police had taken his name from Arvin's diary. He refused to accept Regan's statements or the rumors that Arvin had turned him in, although logically he knew that the police were at his apartment too soon after they had raided Arvin's to give them time to identify him simply from the journals, in which he'd been referred to as "Ned" or "N." The police would have had to trace their relationship back almost three years to his and Arvin's first meeting at the faculty club and their first few meals together to learn Ned's last name, and still would have had to know where he lived and about the pictures in his possession. For a minute Ned sputtered, trying to prevent either of them from saying anything that would estrange them further.

But Arvin persisted, dolefully. He had long ago connected, if not equated, confession and absolution: "All that associates, saves. All that isolates, damns." Whether or not he was soliciting Ned's sympathy, or exorcising his shame, or trying to expunge their common secrets, he blurted out, "I couldn't go through this alone."

It was the only time Arvin would try to justify his capitulation, to Ned or, it seems, anyone else.

Arvin stood stiffly as his own punishment was read. He was given a suspended one-year jail term and fined $1,000 on the obscenity charge, an additional $200 for being a "lewd and lascivious" person, and placed on probation for two years. He knew that he would have to borrow from friends to pay his fines and would need the court's permission to travel, but the legal penalties were not unduly harsh, nor would they destroy him as, say, prison might. Indeed, his sentence was relatively light in view of the fact that his crimes were regarded as depraved by society and that Regan had characterized him as a smut lord.

It was the larger sentence of *living* that Arvin now would confront. The verdict affirmed him as a criminal. Cast out of the ordinary life of society, he faced not the comforting exile of a dark dungeon, but the searing punishment of relentless sunlight. As Hawthorne understood, this was the supreme punishment in Calvinist America—to live out one's disgrace in public—a punishment Arvin had foreseen with fearsome clarity. He would be pilloried when the gallows might be preferable, and he didn't need to be informed how the ugly machinery of his ruination would work.

First he would lose his job. Smith would drop him, and no decent school would dare hire him. Cowley, at Stanford, thought the left-leaning New School for Social Research, near Greenwich Village, "might tolerate a guilty plea," but otherwise, Cowley told Elizabeth Ames, Arvin's "academic career is at an end."

Next, his writing income—occasional royalty checks of $250 or less from his books; similarly modest fees for introductions, editing jobs, articles, essays, and reviews—would dry up. Already, he had asked the publisher of an anthology of American literature, for which he'd written a chapter on Emerson, to advance him $500 to help defray Welch's fee. But the company, Harcourt Brace, refused to pay until Smith ruled on Arvin's status. Its corporate directors feared another round of bad publicity if the college dismissed him or forced his resignation.

As his career fell to pieces, Arvin could see himself tumbling inevitably, invisibly, into poverty. Old people were America's poorest, most forsaken cohort. Arvin imagined losing everything, including his home. He had health insurance, but expected to lose that, too, when Smith let him go.

Without his salary, he might spend all he had before he was well enough even to return home, and then struggle to keep a roof over his head. Not that he wished to return to his violated apartment. But what choice did he have? Arvin suffered to think of himself—old, sick, alone, frightened—subsisting on the generosity of friends like a broken pensioner.

And yet that was not the worst of it. Above all, he dreaded the thought of venturing out, of being seen. Now that he was sentenced, literally, to stay in town, and was long past moving elsewhere, he would have to face at last the full censure of a place he had always hoped to leave but never could, a place whose people had learned of his shameful iniquity.

In *The Scarlet Letter,* Hawthorne reviled the pillory as the most evil instrument of social control and reprisal ever devised, "as effectual an agent in the promotion of good citizenship," he wrote, "as ever was the guillotine among the terrorists of France." Designed to lock the human head in an upright position and "thus hold it up to the public gaze," it forced the wicked to face the admonitions of the righteous. "The very ideal of ignominy was embedded and manifest in this contrivance of wood and iron," Hawthorne wrote. "There can be no outrage, methinks, against our common nature—whatever the delinquencies of the individual—no outrage more flagrant than to forbid the culprit to hide his face for shame; as it was the essence of this punishment to do so."

Northampton was more than two centuries removed from Hawthorne's colonial Boston, but there remained in town, as in most American small towns, a puritan severity, a solemn intolerance of heterodoxy "as befitted a people amongst whom religion and law were almost identical," according to Hawthorne. Arvin had violated local morality. More, he had crossed the liberal ethos of many of those at Smith as well, by surrendering his friends.

Sitting in the courtroom, he had been condemned to wear not one scarlet letter but three—for smut fiend, homosexual, and informer. Aaron, sitting next to him, feared the strain would amount to more than he could bear.

Homans had moved to have O'Connor declare the search of Dorius's apartment illegal, but O'Connor refused, requiring only that the state produce a list of the allegedly obscene materials seized by Regan and his men. Although no such bill of particulars was presented now, Dorius, like Ned, accepted a guilty finding in order to expedite his appeal.

He stood numbly with Homans beside him. He was fined $1,000, his one-year sentence in the House of Corrections was suspended, and he was released on $1,000 bail, pending trial in Superior Court, some time in October. Helen Bacon paid both Ned's and Dorius's bail by cashing in her World War II bonds. She had never written such a large check.

First bemused, then frustrated, Regan and Crowley sat impatiently as O'Connor plowed through each submission. Regan especially wanted to present evidence to buttress the state's case, but Keedy and O'Connor ignored both him and the large cardboard evidence carton Jagodowski had hauled over from the barracks.

Fulminating, his face red, Regan shifted in his seat. He and Crowley had cracked an interstate smut ring, made several high-profile arrests, and were still tracking down fresh leads. They had delivered a van-load of evidence to local prosecutors. But Northampton was not Boston. In the schema of Massachusetts politics, towns west of the central hills generally distrusted—and felt neglected by—Beacon Hill, and responded by doing things their own way. With each new submission of facts, Crowley realized that the exigencies of local justice would prevail over the state's need for high-visibility arrests in its war on pornography. He also knew that Regan was unlikely to tolerate such a brusque dismissal after the recent triumph in the press.

In fact, Regan's version of events was crumbling, revealing a gauze of half-truths stitched together by an overzealous investigator. Since the arrests, he had trumpeted the existence of a homosexual smut ring in Northampton centered on Arvin, who had been nabbed by a vigilant postal service and had named all the other defendants, plus up to a dozen other men. But that no longer appeared true or even plausible. It was clear that Arvin and his friends weren't trafficking in smut; they were, instead, showing each other erotica for private pleasure. And Arvin was not the lone, or even the key, informer; he may have been partly a victim himself.

The next defendant was Richard Stanley. Of all the accused, only Stanley had been charged with sodomy, which, like bestiality, was classified under Massachusetts law as an "abominable and detestable crime against nature." The charge bore the harshest stigma, if not the steepest penalty, of all the counts against the various defendants, and Stanley was terrified that he would be convicted and sent to prison as a buggerer. He also had the weakest connection to the other defendants. He had not met Arvin, whose name he hadn't known before his arrest and who most likely hadn't known his, before their one encounter a few weeks earlier. Still, the court complaints against both him and Goss, which Regan signed, were filed on August 29, four days *before* the complaint against Arvin, indicating that police were investigating them before, not after, the raid on Arvin's apartment.

During Stanley's arrest, when he'd asked Regan how the police had found him, Regan told him they had been watching John's apartment, and Stanley, who was married and had two children, quickly had come to fear that Regan accused him of sodomy mostly to bully him into informing on others. Crowley would deny any such surveillance or deal, but Regan often acted independently, without informing Crowley what he was up to.

Proceeding quickly, O'Connor now dismissed the sodomy complaint against Stanley; Keedy didn't press it, and Regan wasn't invited to testify. Stanley then submitted to guilty findings on two counts of committing an unnatural act and one count of lewdness, and was given a one-year suspended sentence, two years' probation, and a $200 fine.

More serious and disturbing questions about Regan's case and his actions arose during the day's next and final hearing. Court records showed that Regan filed a complaint against Michael Howard for lewdness, though not obscenity, on August 8, more than *three weeks* before police raided Arvin's apartment, but that they didn't arrest him until September 5, three days after. Fearing suspects may flee once they know they're being sought, police usually file court complaints only when they're about to make arrests. Regan claimed repeatedly that Arvin had led officers to the other defendants—indeed, that all six of them were at an "orgy" at Arvin's apartment the night Dorius brought over his pictures—but what appears far more likely is that they picked up Howard first and turned him or Goss, or both, in on lewdness charges before zeroing in on Arvin for obscenity traffic. Either way, Howard submitted to a guilty finding and received a suspended six-month jail term and no fine—the lightest sentence of the six.

Altogether, the legal proceedings shattered the state's claim of an organized smut conspiracy in Northampton. What Regan had depicted as a predatory "college sex ring," with Arvin, its leader, cravenly naming two dozen names, was revealed as something much more recognizable and natural: a small-town homosexual demimonde where frightened individuals could easily be intimidated into trading one another's secrets for a promise of leniency. Arvin clearly had led police to Ned and Dorius, but he apparently was not the only one who couldn't bear to undergo his ordeal alone, nor was the distribution of obscene material the real target of the investigation. Whatever the original basis for the obscenity probe—whether the stepped-up vigilance of Summerfield's postal inspectors following passage of the Granahan bill and the ban against Herman Womack's beefcake magazines, or a random sweep of the City Hall men's room—Regan and the state police simply had dragged a net through the underside of Northampton, entangling seven unfortunate men. "We caused a lot of goddamn misery," Crowley would say.

Outside the courtroom after the hearings, Regan told reporters that the Smith-Northampton probe was continuing and would result in "many more defendants being brought to court." But the case had crested and was fast unraveling. Keedy's sober prosecution had squelched the affair in court. Harold Katz, Ned's lawyer, announced that afternoon that he was preparing to protest Regan's investigation to the attorney general's office on the grounds that Ned's civil rights had been violated. More than two weeks since the last arrest, none of the out-of-state suspects promised by Regan had been apprehended. Anyone who feared being discovered with obscene pictures had had ample time to dispose of them; the trail, such as it was, had grown cold. Barring spectacular new revelations at Goss's trial, scheduled for October 3, the five-month-old bureau's flagship probe had reached a dead end.

Back at the state hospital after court, Arvin huddled with Aaron and Fisher, who promptly reported the session in a letter to Hicks:

> We went to see Newton almost at once. And I had the unpleasant duty of suggesting that he consider the kind of letter he thought he should (and soon) write to the administration. He took it hard,

poor thing, and immediately began to think of reasons for not writing it, or, if so, putting it off. He wanted us to tell him what kind of letter to write, but we did not do so . . . It wouldn't take me by surprise if, presently, he had a rather sharp collapse from which, I believe, he would recover, if he had news of *security*. Dan and I did *not* speak of the Yaddo possibility.

It was Malcolm Cowley who had first suggested that Arvin might find a few months' sanctuary in Saratoga Springs. Hicks, too, hoped Yaddo would take Arvin—but he anticipated stern resistance. Stung by the Robert Lowell–Agnes Smedley scandal of more than a decade earlier, some of Yaddo's corporate officers, especially President John Slade, feared further embarrassment. Hicks and Cowley, like Arvin, were directors, but Hicks also served on the executive committee, which would have to approve any invitation. Like Fisher and Aaron, he feared stirring Arvin's hopes, and therefore did not mention Yaddo in his letters to him.

More urgent, as Fisher noted in his letter, was Arvin's standing at Smith. Now that he had agreed to a guilty finding, the college would want to know, before making its own ruling, whether he, like Ned and Dorius, planned to appeal, or whether he accepted the verdict. College bylaws were vague in cases like his, and there was no precedent at Smith for firing a tenured professor for "cause"; that is, for a reason other than professional incompetence. Smith could ask him to resign, but Arvin was unwilling to do that. Desperately, he put off a decision until morning. Though he knew Smith's choice could "be only one," as he soon wrote to Hicks, part of him believed the college would stand by him.

Like others in Ned's hometown of Lee, his parents learned that their only son was a homosexual from an article in the *Berkshire Eagle*. The paper included a summary of Regan's testimony in the Green case in its coverage of the hearings. "We didn't know it was anything like that," his mother told Ned on the phone. Ned "bullied [his] way through." He told her, "That wasn't evidence. He was not under oath." He maintained the fiction with his mother and sisters that the case was solely about pornography. He avoided speaking with his father.

After court, he couldn't stop thinking about Alan, the eighteen-year-old. On hearing Regan reveal what he'd done with Green, Ned convinced himself that Regan also knew about the youth. He grew frantic, pacing incessantly until late that night. Finally, he called Ted Baird, his mentor at Amherst, and confessed, "There's a high school senior. It would destroy his life if this came out."

Baird demanded to know if there were others, and Ned told him no. There was a pause. Baird was the reigning figure on the Amherst faculty, revered by two generations of students, for whom his word was all but law. Amherst was Keedy's beloved alma mater. Baird instructed Ned to come over, saying he would take care of the situation. "I'll call up Sanford Keedy and tell him, 'No more.' "

Whether Baird called Keedy and Keedy complied, Ned never knew, but he soon calmed down. That night he slept in the tiny guest room of the flat-roofed, one-story Usonian house behind a grove of trees that Baird had commissioned Frank Lloyd Wright to design for him in South Amherst. Baird's wife, Bertie, made him cookies and gave him a *Peanuts* comic in which Snoopy laments, "Cats hate us. Other dogs bark at us. Thank heaven for human beings."

The next morning the Bairds made him breakfast and sent him off, telling him to "go back and face the music." Ned did as instructed. Within days, he packed up the last of his things, moved into a basement sublet in Cambridge, and began his graduate studies in the Harvard Classics Department. His department head there told him, "We won't do anything until your final appeal. If you're guilty, we'll set up a committee to deal with it. No guilt, no committee."

Unlike Arvin, Ned was young, a likable and talented man with a promising future. He had the support of a confident institution, anonymity in a new setting, much to gain, and little, presumably, to lose. Seeing a way ahead, he resolved to start anew. The leap from his arrest and conviction to Harvard, he would recall, "couldn't have been timed better."

Chapter Twelve

ARVIN WAS STILL in the hospital when Smith reopened the following Tuesday with the annual president's address in John M. Greene Hall. After his trial, he'd written to Tom Mendenhall, "I shall gladly abide by any decision the college arrives at concerning my future," and Mendenhall had responded that although the "good book"—Smith's bylaws—was "not completely clear" on the handling of cases like his, he had asked the Committee on Tenure and Promotion to review Arvin's "status as an individual on tenure at the College." Arvin was heartened by the decision. Tenure and Promotion, T&P, was the senior committee of the faculty, ruling on all reappointments. Arvin had served on the panel the year before and knew that the Board of Trustees commonly rubber-stamped its recommendations. No one could remember a teacher at Smith ever having been formally let go without T&P's approval, which, since Arvin's more radical days, had always given him comfort.

Arvin had found Mendenhall's first convocation speech, a year earlier, "a thoughtful, modest and frank one, though he has greater expectations for female students than I can any longer share." Since the arrests, Mendenhall had maintained a discreet official silence, reassuring alarmed local leaders, parents, and alumnae only that "the appropriate college authorities" would consider Arvin's case, and withholding comment on Ned and Dorius, pending their appeals. Privately, however, the Affair was dragging him away from other duties. No incoming freshmen had withdrawn, calming initial fears, and the enrollment unexpectedly rose. In Smith's "houses," maids' rooms were hurriedly converted to singles and singles to doubles as underclassmen doubled up. Paradise, which had been drained during the summer for dredging and was no longer a sylvan pond but a winding brown sluice banked by mudflats, looked "like the River Styx," reported the *Sophian,* the college newspaper. The campus was in "a state of embarrassment," it said. Students and their families who hadn't heard back home about the three professors convicted on sex charges learned about it as soon as they arrived for orientation.

Hoping to quell rumors, and ease any doubts that he was fully in charge of a campus well prepared for the fall term, Mendenhall used his speech to Smith's twenty-three hundred undergraduates to make his first public statement on the scandal.

> There is a confused image of the professor, the academic . . . Somehow society expects the teacher, like the priest, to be a nobler, finer being, somehow above or not subject to human frailties. This unfortunately is not the case . . . In spite of and often because of the academic role he is called to play, his character and conduct are as fallible as anyone else's.
>
> It is in this light that we must face the fact that three members of our academic community are charged with moral offenses. Until the courts have had their say and the evidence is in, we must suspend our own judgment and comment, public and private, in keeping with the central tradition of our personal liberty: a man is innocent until he is proved guilty. But already the affair should have impressed upon us the need to bring modern medicine, contemporary morality, and the laws we must live by into more reasonable harmony.

He referred to Arvin, Ned, and Dorius, in Smith's spirit of semifamilial understanding, as "our unhappy friends and colleagues."

Few Smith students could be expected to understand the behavior Mendenhall was asking them not to discuss or judge. Sex was a subject

very few knew about firsthand, and male homosexuality was all but un-
fathomable. Publicly, America remained prudish and sexless. Those students who were whispered to have "done it" were generally considered
fallen creatures by their classmates. Meanwhile, Smith, like Mount
Holyoke, Wellesley, Harvard, Yale, and other leading schools, still made incoming freshmen pose for "posture photos"—full-length nude views, front,
back, and rear—as part of a secret eugenics experiment aimed at correlat-
ing body types with intelligence. Although that exercise, now going on before classes began, was often traumatic, no one on campus discussed *that*.
Not even those who wondered snickeringly why the female gym teachers
who ran the project seemed so interested in it could imagine three of their
male professors exchanging pictures of naked men.

As to Mendenhall's larger point—Smith's "public responsibility" to act
cautiously and fairly—there seemed little risk of outcry. American college
students had only just begun to recognize institutional injustice, albeit
mainly in the racially segregated South. Even the most radical activists had
no inkling that "civil rights" might soon extend to others also mistreated:
women, homosexuals, the mentally ill, the aged; any people whose privacy,
dignity, and safety were violated or denied. Whatever Mendenhall's concerns, an inflamed student body challenging Smith's handling of the scandal wasn't one of them.

It was Arvin, surprisingly, who questioned whether he should lose his
job because of what he'd done. Writing to Mendenhall two days after the
latter's speech, he repeated his willingness to accept the college's decision
and again expressed his gratitude. But, he added,

> it also seems to me possible that a real question, not of academic
> freedom in the usual sense, but of the civil liberties of the individ-
> ual, is involved, and the college might not wish to sever my con-
> nection with it solely on the official basis that I have been
> convicted by District Court on the basis of evidence gathered by
> methods which violated my civil rights.
>
> The general question for American colleges and universities of
> what is to be the treatment of individuals similarly arrested and

tried seems to me far more important than that of my merely personal future.

Arvin, by raising the same literary and political themes he'd long advocated in his writings—privacy, individual rights, the mind's lonely struggle to prevail against a repressive society—now challenged his "colleagues and friends," as Mendenhall had called them in his letter, to discuss in the same terms whether to fire him.

"Am holding on grimly," Arvin wrote to the New York novelist Leonard Ehrlich. His depression had not lifted, and though he talked freely with the hospital staff about his unhappiness and homosexuality, his days were lonely and tedious. He was unable to write more than a few short letters a day, and work was impossible—harsh punishments in themselves. For Arvin, self-expression was life, and feeling too "dazed and benumbed" to put things properly into words was both crippling and painful. What little he wrote to friends was steeped in apology and self-mortification. "The torment of thinking what this has done to other people is inexpressible," he wrote to Ehrlich, an old Yaddo friend who, like Doughty, emulated him and with whom he had long suffered common miseries.

He was given a battery of personality tests, revealing what psychiatrists deemed a classic homosexual profile. He was fixed at a prepubertal stage of development and consequently sought solace in an inner world, the tests showed. He was insecure as a result of early parental conflicts. He had a strong affinity for his mother but resented her dominance. At the same time, he had an indifferent and inexpressive father to whom he yearned to be close. Incorporating his mother's femininity, he suffered from a "repetition compulsion," by which he tried to capture the affection and succor he never got from his father. This compensatory longing for affection from other men, he was told, was the chief source of his depression.

Arvin, who was in no state to argue, accepted the results whole. Though this analysis was too formulaic to explain all his recent behavior, he believed that his present crisis had been somehow preordained, that he was acting out a drama written for him long before he left Valparaiso. "One's nature asserts itself appallingly early," he would soon write, recalling one formative incident he thought especially ominous.

He was twelve, almost thirteen, and had recently got a secondhand bicycle and happily learned to ride it. One day his father, observing that the seat was too low for him, raised it. After riding the bike all one July afternoon, Arvin felt pain and started limping. Although a few days' rest should have had him back on his feet, instead, he "fell into a wholly 'unnecessary' slough of nervous anxiety, irritability, and dejection."

During the next few days, Arvin suffered "a tiny and premature 'nervous breakdown,'" his first. Moping about the house, he lay for hours on the davenport in the parlor clad only in a nightshirt. He stopped eating and sleeping; he lost weight, turned pale and peaked, and presented all the symptoms of real illness, until the doctor had to be called for. "Had an awful night," Arvin wrote in his journal.

Here were all his masculine weaknesses revealed, Arvin believed. His propensity toward "crackups and breakdowns." His physical weakness and cowardice. His neuroses, hypochondria, and hysterical self-absorption. Even the symbolism of the sexually injured, father-hating hero, like Ahab himself. And yet the attack had served its purpose at the time. "I had succeeded in getting attention of a concerned and kindly sort from my father," he would write, "and that, no doubt, was enough."

Whether his present troubles were the result of a "repetition compulsion," Arvin readily, even eagerly, accepted the hospital's assessment. All this heightened his distress. He was in no hurry to leave the hospital, but knew he eventually would have to, and, anticipating his release, feared that he would never again find solace, not even in his "inner world."

"In my weak periods," he wrote to Hicks, "I find myself uncontrollably thinking of it all as somehow inescapable, even fated."

His most urgent problem was deciding where to go after his release. "I feel that I cannot and probably ought not (for the time being) to stay in N'ton—solus in my apartment—as before," he told Hicks. "I am tired, terribly tired, and pretty sore all over, and I wonder whether I can possibly face a strenuous and problematic way of life for months to come."

As when he was twelve, Arvin suffered awful nights, and he systematically alerted those around him of his incapacity to endure many more of them.

Hicks didn't say so to Arvin, but he was afraid that Yaddo might not take him in. John Slade, the seventy-eight-year-old president, was "violently opposed because he thinks it would be a mistake in respect to public relations," Elizabeth Ames told Cowley. Some of the trustees had strong feelings that Arvin should step down from the board at once to spare Yaddo further embarrassment; others believed that Yaddo's history as a haven for artists called for it to stand by Arvin through his ordeal. Still others were undecided, and worried that no matter what they did, Yaddo would suffer. It was Slade, a lifelong Saratogan, a "lawyer's lawyer," and perhaps the city's most respected, civic-minded, and powerful citizen, who would do the brokering among the three groups.

Arvin's own connection with Slade and his wife, Caroline, went back nearly thirty years, to the time Caroline had offered to put five or six bedrooms at the Slades' thirty-two-acre estate, Chestwood, at Arvin's disposal for his wedding guests. Arvin had seldom visited Yaddo during the fifties, when, reeling from his crises and stalled writing, he had little use for the hothouse life of the colony. But he had remained active on the board, reading applications, attending meetings, and humbly apologizing, as ever, for his inadequacies. "I am much pleased," he had written to Ames two years earlier, "to be reinstated as a director despite my lapses."

Ames, who knew Arvin's past, was deeply concerned about him, but couldn't invite him to stay at Yaddo without the executive committee's approval. Having been suspect herself during the Smedley-Lowell affair, all she could do was to follow Slade's direction to poll the directors about their feelings toward a visit by Arvin, and relay her findings to Cowley and Hicks, who, like Aaron and Fisher, remained deliberately vague with Arvin about his chances. But Arvin was desperate. Three days before he was to be released from the hospital, he proposed to Hicks "a crazy thought": that Ames put him up at her own residence, Pine Garde, where he and Mary had been married. Whether he believed such an arrangement—he vowed to work for his room and board—would obviate the need for the board's approval, the suggestion apparently was never discussed. And so, after a month at Northampton State Hospital, Arvin was released on the morning of October 4 and, with no place else to go, returned to his apartment on Prospect Street.

Never had as familiar a place seemed so alien to him. When Fisher brought him home, he appeared not to recognize it. He was in no danger of being evicted, as he had earlier feared; his landlady, a widow who lived in the basement, sympathized with his problems and felt he'd been mistreated. But even that shred of security offered little real safety. As he paced from room to room, Arvin observed the same peaceful and unchanged panorama beyond his windows—Smith, the town, the settled valley, the Manse. But in those moments, when there was no bottom to his loneliness, the walls pitched in on him. Arvin's adopted name for the demons he had first encountered fifty years earlier, as he lay on the davenport in his parents' house, hysterical for his father's sympathy, was the Enemy. It was that Enemy, even more than society, that he now feared most.

Not that he could leave, either. Though the hills were burning with Capote's "green and blue," and the beautiful autumnal light was Northampton's most inviting, the thought of going out and being seen was shattering. Other than at the trial, Arvin hadn't had to face society in the month since his arrest. He didn't know if he could do it. With Dottie Hicks and others sending food—brownies and casseroles, mostly—and Fisher and Aaron coming regularly to his apartment, he found it easier to stay in. What business he had to do he conducted either by letter or through his lawyer. The Tenure and Promotion Committee had authorized Mendenhall, an ex-officio member, to meet with Arvin to discuss his case. As he now wrote to Mendenhall, "Though on purely personal grounds, I should very much like to have at least a brief talk with you, I do not myself feel that it is officially necessary for me to take part in a formal discussion of my case . . . Mr. Welch will, I believe, call your office."

Seeking solace in an inner world, Arvin retreated to the last haven he knew: books. He read until his eyes gave out, and he drank heavily. Goss's trial yielded no new revelations, meaning that Arvin's role as a potential witness against the other defendants was soon ending. Ahead lay Ned's and

Dorius's Superior Court trials, scheduled for the following week. Beyond that Arvin, seeing no light, hesitated to look.

A few days later, he received a letter from Capote, reacting belatedly to news of his trial:

> Well—at least it's *over*. If, as you say, you must resign from the college, I hope it is not without compensation—that would be most unfair; after all, in a few years you would have retired. And am I wrong in thinking you will receive other teaching offers? Being "on probation" doesn't mean you have to stay in Northampton, does it? . . . If you need money, *please* say so; I have some, I really do, and it would not inconvenience me at all. Everything will sort itself out soon. Meanwhile know that I am thinking of you and love you very much.

◁━▷

"The best that can be said of this court," a state inspector had written about Northampton's Superior Court chambers in 1957, "is that it is not quite as bad as Taunton, and being in a smaller county does less harm." The one huge courtroom on the second floor was "archaic," its dry, high-studded floorboards croaking feverishly with each footstep. The drafty, underheated jury rooms were "dreadful," crammed onto the third floor of a nineteenth-century granite tower. Ned had been there once before, in high school, when he was selected to represent Lee in Boys' State exercises.

The three weeks since the district court trial had been explosive for Ned. In Cambridge he fortunately was unknown, but those who knew him at Smith had been shocked and startled by his behavior, since it had never occurred to most of them, even friends, that he was a homosexual. Much of the energy Ned had spent on keeping the parts of his life separate and "not letting the mask slip" now surfaced as corrosive tension, and his friends worried about his rashness and volatility. "He is burning with suppressed (not always) rage," Al Fisher wrote in his journal, a Joycean monologue he started keeping after his third wife, Madeleine, left him.

Ned's and Dorius's trials were held separately; Dorius's was first. There were two main witnesses against him. Regan, under questioning from District Attorney Sanford Keedy, testified that he and his men had seized "152 pictures as well as one magazine . . . two pamphlet stories, two greeting cards, a number of letters and one faculty administration book" from Dorius's apartment. The magazine, he explained, contained photographs of males, and the photographs and drawings each depicted one or more males, "some of them nude or semi-nude." Homans, conceding that five of the pictures were explicitly sexual, objected to the introduction of all the other exhibits, on the grounds that drawings of photographs of barely clad or unclad men could not be construed as obscene, but the judge, August Taviera, overruled him, allowing them into evidence.

The state's second witness was Arvin. Keedy had called him to help the commonwealth prove that Dorius had shown his prints and photographs to others, and Arvin had agreed—apparently without being coerced—to testify.

For radicals of Arvin's generation, turning state's witness against former friends and associates was considered the ultimate capitulation. The agonies of the Red scares were still fresh and unambiguous. Arvin himself had anguished repeatedly about being "turned." He appeared, however, not to be aware of what he was doing, or if he was, was so desensitized and self-absorbed that he failed to fathom what for Dorius was a crushing betrayal.

Keedy, having first established that Arvin and Dorius had known each other for about two years and were colleagues in Smith's English Department, questioned Arvin for several minutes about their activities together.

"Have you been to his apartment?" Keedy asked.

"Yes," Arvin replied.

"Now, has he, on occasions, shown you certain pictures?"

"Yes."

"And during the months September, August, and July of 1960," Keedy continued, "has he shown you these pictures?"

Before Arvin could answer, Homans objected. "This is leading. This is the Commonwealth's witness. I think an appropriate question is as to when and where." Homans assumed Keedy meant to have Arvin say that Dorius had brought pictures to Arvin's apartment for the small gathering on August 29, the one that Regan had labeled an "orgy," and he didn't want Arvin to answer the question. With Taviera excluding it, Keedy continued his examination.

"*When* has he shown you these pictures?"

"I couldn't possibly date the occasions," Arvin said. "It was more than a year ago, I think."

"More than a year ago?" Keedy sounded surprised.

"Yes." Somehow Arvin recalled only the occasion, in November 1959, when Dorius first brought his art prints to show him and he had judged some of them "very beautiful."

"And is that as nearly as you can place the time?" Keedy pressed.

"I'm afraid so, yes," Arvin said, hoping to demonstrate his cooperation.

"And where was it that he showed you these pictures?"

"I think at my apartment," Arvin said.

"In your apartment," Keedy repeated. "And do you remember the nature of the pictures?"

Up to now, Arvin's compliance had perhaps helped Dorius as much as it hurt him. He recalled that Dorius had brought pictures to his apartment, but not when. He had diverted attention from the alleged "orgy."

But as Keedy began to show Arvin various exhibits, Arvin suddenly turned more assured—and damaging.

"Did he show this to you, Mr. Arvin?" Keedy asked, offering a picture for examination.

"Yes."

"Did he show that one to you?"

"Yes."

"Did he show that to you?"

"Yes."

"I assume," Homans interrupted, "all these questions relate to this one occasion."

"Yes," Keedy said, and turned back to Arvin. "Was there ever another occasion, other than this one time you told about, when he showed pictures?"

"No," Arvin said.

"That was the only occasion?"

"Yes."

Whether Arvin couldn't recall the night six weeks earlier, when Dorius had brought his pictures to the apartment, or he was lying, Homans was encouraged as he began his cross-examination. He pressed hard to discredit Arvin's memory, which Arvin himself feared had been eroded by his shock treatments. First Homans asked whether Arvin was certain that the pictures Keedy had shown him were the same ones Dorius had brought to his apartment almost a year earlier. Arvin said he wasn't sure. Then Homans asked how he had been able to identify them as the same in answer to Keedy's questions, and Arvin replied that it was "just a general impression." He said he had done his best to remember and to distinguish between those he'd seen and those he hadn't. He was less than convincing.

Dorius sat as if in a trance all through Arvin's testimony, too stunned to comprehend or even listen to everything being said about him. He felt as if he had fallen off a high precipice, crashing through the "thin line between security and utter ruin," between being a professor at a good school and "a criminal." During such a cataclysm "one works on one or two pistons," he later said.

Taviera ruled shortly after Arvin finished his testimony. He found Dorius guilty and delayed sentencing for one week. Later that day, Dorius retreated to the "safe house" in Cambridge, where he'd been staying since before his arrest, to await his punishment. Homans immediately requested documents and transcripts for his appeal, including, prominently, all of Arvin's psychiatric records since 1941. He planned to use them to discredit Arvin as a witness if Dorius's appeal on constitutional grounds was rejected by the state's highest court.

Arvin was excused from testifying at Ned's trial, two days later. According to Ned, Arvin was asked to identify certain nude pictures as belonging to Ned; when Arvin pleaded with Taviera not to make him do so, Taviera agreed. But Arvin's belated loyalty did little. Ned, like Dorius, was tried quickly, found guilty, and received a sentencing date, although he suffered no added sense of betrayal. After the trial, he told his lawyer, Harold Katz, "to make as broad a legal issue as possible" in mounting his appeal, to which Katz responded that Ned "probably didn't need to worry about that."

With Helen Bacon and others urging a full public fight, Ned had become furious at the police invasion of his apartment, the violation of his privacy, and Regan's abusive treatment of him and the others, and he was determined to press his case, if necessary, to the U.S. Supreme Court. He didn't see what he had to lose.

Dorius was less sure. Smith had indicated that it wouldn't rule on his or Ned's teaching status until each had exhausted his appeal, but Dorius doubted Smith could afford to retain either of them even if they were cleared. All he had ever wanted to do was teach, yet he was unsure whether he could face students, and worried that he might never again have the chance. He didn't know how he would support himself.

Like Ned, he hoped to be exonerated in the Supreme Judicial Court, but as he wrote to Aaron from Cambridge, "the final decision may not be until March or April and I must, meanwhile, be thinking of alternate ways of life." He continued, grimly:

> I have been wondering about how best to speak out about the law, the press, the police, and social custom, as these have recently cut across my life. I would appreciate any suggestion from you. If I were a professional writer in any sense, I think I would try to subsist, somehow, by writing . . . I think it important for myself and others like me that I don't let a sense of being broken or crushed overcome me. . . . If [pornographic] pictures of any sort had ever occupied a central place in my consciousness; if I had thought my now celebrated pictures, as Homans (with about four exceptions) did not, obscene, well enough said . . . You don't happen to know of any teaching jobs abroad for any part of this year, or next summer, do you? I am no authority, but I could "make out," even with American literature.

⇥

As the election campaign—and the Eisenhower era, which began so darkly for Arvin and others—hastened to a close, never was Arvin more severed from world events. Public opinion polls, which earlier had favored Nixon, had swung to Kennedy during a three-week visit to New York in October by Soviet premier Nikita Khrushchev. The first televised debate between Kennedy and Nixon, watched in black-and-white by eighty million people, had revolutionized American politics, but Arvin, in the hospital, had missed it. He had no interest in television and didn't own a set.

The whole political colloquy was alien to him. Just as in 1924, the main question was which candidate would stand more firmly against communism, but the country was increasingly more susceptible to imagery than ideology. Indeed, what seemed to matter was which candidate *looked* more like what the country needed after Eisenhower. "Isn't he marvelous!" the newspaper columnist and dean of the brilliant, foreign-policymaking "Georgetown set," Joseph Alsop, gushed about Kennedy's cool masculinity during the first debate. "A Stevenson with balls."

There was simply no political framework for Arvin's suffering; in historical terms, the Affair was a decade or more ahead of its time. Homosexuality, other than that of the NSA codebreakers who had defected to Moscow, wasn't a topic for presidential contestants but for vice squads and mental hospitals. Taking care of the Constitution, the Supreme Court vigorously debated the definition of obscenity and the rights of individuals in their homes, but so reluctantly that several justices refused to look at evidence in cases brought by pornographers like Roth and Womack against Summerfield's Post Office. The sexualization of American politics and culture that would begin a few years later, and overtake both by the end of the century, remained undiscernible, beyond imagining.

And yet these were the issues of Arvin's life; in the end, it seemed, all that was left. A double life had been his means of survival, as it was for almost all homosexual men in public life, with rare exceptions like Capote. Joe Alsop was a dazzling example. The reigning host of Georgetown, an informal adviser to every President since Franklin Roosevelt, Alsop was also a daring sexual adventurer. He took extraordinary risks; in 1957, the KGB tried to blackmail him into becoming an agent by photographing him in bed with a young man in a Moscow hotel, and he lived in fear that the photographs would turn up and be used against him. Yet Alsop remained the country's leading private voice on state policy, architect of the fictive "missile gap" that Kennedy used so effectively against Nixon. Perhaps no one proved better that America tolerated, even prized, homosexuals who led double lives—as long as those lives remained separate.

However hard to keep in place, Arvin's mask had been a necessity. Now that it was shattered and he was exposed, he could see no future without it. *What was he supposed to do? How would he go on?* There was no precedent for what would later become an industry: public atonement and redemption. Once a man was ruined, he was ruined. There were those marginalized young radicals from the Mattachine Society and the Daughters of Bilitis who marched in front of the White House with pickets demanding "First Class Citizenship for Homosexuals," but Arvin was old, sick with himself, and too weak to fight. He had failed at religion, which had no place for him.

On October 20, two days after Ned and Dorius received suspended jail terms and were fined $500 each, Arvin re-entered the state hospital. He complained of feeling severely depressed. He told a psychiatrist at his intake examination that he was "lonely living by himself," but that venturing out was worse. He felt people watching him, staring at him. He was agitated and suicidal and had begun talking to himself. The doctor, concluding that he was "obsessed" about his homosexuality, changed his prescription from Meloril, an antipsychotic, to Stelazine and Tofranil, potent tranquilizers. Securely back on the men's ward in the Haskell building, Arvin brooded about his problems and kept to himself, but he apparently had no delusions or bizarre ideas. He soon stopped talking about killing himself, despite, as he'd once written to Aaron, feeling "nearer death than life."

The Smith trustees met in emergency session the next day. It had become clear, seven weeks after the arrests, that the police investigation would not engulf the faculty, as some had feared, and the board hoped to resume the college's educational mission by putting the Affair quickly behind it. T&P had ruled that Arvin's arrest and conviction, while deeply troubling, did not disqualify him from teaching, although its members noted privately that, for the good of all, he should not be in the classroom. Several trustees, angered by the trouble Arvin, Ned, and Dorius had caused the college, thought all three should be asked to resign. Mendenhall struck a compromise. Mindful of Arvin's prominence and distinguished contributions to Smith, and the faculty's insistence on protecting tenure, he proposed that the college "retire" Arvin while continuing to pay half his salary—about $5,300 a year—until his scheduled retirement in 1968. He advised that the college make no comment on the two cases under appeal.

Arvin, immensely relieved at the outcome, wrote to Mendenhall a few days later from the hospital: "I . . . wish to thank you for the kindness which you have shown throughout and the generosity of the conditions you have specified for my future financially. I hope to be able to prove not unworthy of the liberality of those conditions." In truth, he knew the college had done him a favor, mercifully terminating his troubled thirty-seven-year career as a "schoolmaster." Ned and Dorius, who still hoped to teach elsewhere if not at Smith, took the trustees' silence as a positive indication that the college would abide by due process. When the decisions were presented at the next faculty meeting, there was little sense even among progressive members that Smith was proceeding in any way but honorably.

Arvin's return to the hospital and swift removal from the college did trigger concern, however, among his literary friends, who worried about his health and welfare. As a group, these writers and critics were famously competitive, jealously obsessed with one another's success and buoyed secretly by others' failures. But they were also accustomed—after decades of alcoholism, divorce, insanity, and political persecution—to mobilizing when one of their own was in crisis, and to view attacks on one as an attack on all. Arvin, though little known to the public, was a large enough figure in their world so that his arrest and conviction sent shudders throughout the literary left, and his friends responded by spontaneously rallying to his side.

While Arvin remained in the hospital for another two weeks, Kronenberger wrote letters to those who had offered Arvin financial help. Arvin, he said, was in no serious need after Smith's decision, but would be "very much upset" unless he could pay back the money that Aaron and Fisher had borrowed from a local bank to pay his fines and legal fees—about $1,500. "I imagine that anything given would be something that Newton would hope to repay," he wrote to about twenty of Arvin's friends, including Hicks, Capote, Brooks, and Lilienthal. Meanwhile, Hicks and Cowley continued to press Arvin's case for sanctuary at Yaddo, where the crisis had begun to preoccupy Elizabeth Ames. Somewhat misinformed, Ames wrote to Malcolm Cowley:

> The matter most on my mind is the tragedy and ruin of Newton Arvin. This matter has been reported all over this country, and also in the European capitals. He will soon be dropped with (I am told) some financial settlement. There is said to be great bitterness against him among Smith faculty people for the ruin he brought to two men so much younger than he. These two are now in jail.

Cowley responded:

> I've been thinking a great deal about Newton's tragedy and its bearing on Yaddo . . . If we invite Newton for the winter, we do run some risk of unfavorable publicity (though not a great risk, I think). If we don't invite him, then members of the literary and artistic public will accuse us of cowardice and disloyalty. Balancing the two dangers, I think the second is the worse, especially as inviting Newton would be the courageous and honorable thing to do.

Arvin's friends—his "carapace," as Aaron called them—once again shielded him as he faced a future he knew he could not survive alone. Even Carson McCullers, disabled by strokes and alcoholism, wrote fondly from Nyack, New York, "Newton Darling: This is just a note to tell you that I love and admire you and will do so always." Realizing that he was still loved, Arvin left the hospital for the second time on November 10, more optimistic than at any time since his arrest. He spent the night alone in his apartment. Early the next day, after he received permission from his probation officer to leave Northampton for the weekend, Father Cochran drove him for two hours across the gray-brown hills to the Hickses' farm.

"I can't tell you how I long to get over to Grafton and have a few days with the two of you," Arvin had written in advance of his arrival; "better than all these tranquilizers."

Chapter Thirteen

MEETING IN SARATOGA Springs on the same afternoon Arvin left the hospital—but without his knowledge, since his friends feared a rejection might destroy him—Yaddo's executive committee voted three-to-two to invite him for the winter. John Slade pressed Ames, past seventy and almost deaf, to consider whether she would be willing to accommodate Arvin, given his actions and state of mind. She said she would, "chiefly because it may be almost a life-and-death situation."

"I don't see how he will put his life together again unless he can take up his writing," she told Cowley, "and this he would be more likely to do in the ordered atmosphere of Yaddo."

Ames's handwritten invitation to "join the pleasant and interesting people who will be coming to Yaddo after the holidays" awaited Arvin on his return from Grafton. He responded at once, "I should love to do so, and earnestly hope I shall not be a problem to you while I am there."

The problem was, studio space was sharply limited during the Small Season, when the mansion was shuttered and guests stayed in outlying cottages, and Ames could offer him a residency only for January through March. That meant that Arvin would have to remain in Northampton for almost two months, and he doubted he could last that long. Outside, the days were growing short, dark, and cold. The holidays, with their familyness and false gaiety, would be hard enough to bear under any circumstances. His rooms had become an echo chamber for his fears, especially his study, which was separated from the stairwell by a thin plaster wall that shuddered when anyone entered the building and amplified each mounting footstep.

Also in his mail were letters from Capote and Lilienthal, who'd been abroad throughout the crisis and were hearing about it in installments, amid oft-repeated rumors, a week or two after events. Capote had moved in October to Verbier, a "very pretty, very remote, very healthy, extremely snowbound, and unalterably *boring* village" in the French Alps so that Dunphy could ski while he toiled on his Kansas book, now titled *In Cold Blood.* "Do hope this finds you free of the hospital—and, perhaps, free of Northampton," he wrote, "for I think you will feel very much better once you breathe a different atmosphere." More than Arvin's other friends, Capote hoped the experience, however painful, might liberate him, not only from Smith but from the torments of his shadow life. "You will certainly have to take up book reviewing in a serious style," he wrote. "But at least, and at last, your time is your own; and as you have wonderful work ahead of you, that is most definitely the other side of the coin."

Lilienthal had told Fisher that he was "baffled and grieved" by Arvin's troubles and that "so ugly a charge shook me as greatly as it puzzled me." During a short layover in New York between business trips to Patagonia and Persia, he wrote to Arvin:

> I can only say, at this point, that I have never, in a long life, known a more creative intelligence, and that now that this grievous crisis is behind you, you will be full of hope of what you can do in the field of writing and criticism; there is no one in America of greater talent and literary comprehension. To see you return, full time, to such a life of writing will give all your friends and those who know the distinction of your mind great joy.

Among all his friends, Arvin found it hardest to explain himself to Dave, who sent a $500 check toward Arvin's fund, although his hurt and confusion were keen. All his life Lilienthal had believed that Arvin possessed a special intelligence and creative gift. He failed to understand how his brilliant, delicate friend had led—and concealed—so dark, mysterious, and shameful a double life, and his encouragement to Arvin belied a gnawing anger and bewilderment. Lilienthal, who'd known Washington's best-kept secrets, hadn't a clue about his oldest friend's.

Arvin acknowledged in his return letter both the breach and Lilienthal's pain at discovering it through the headlines. "It must be very difficult, if not impossible, for you to understand what has happened, or to comprehend all the behavior that led up to the crisis," he apologized. Arvin didn't deny the specific charges; indeed, he didn't address them at all. He thanked Lilienthal profusely for his loyalty, insisted that his "munificent gift" be treated as a loan, and said he hoped someday—"when a certain crust has perhaps grown over the wounds of both of us"—to tell Lilienthal some of the truth about himself.

> For the time being, perhaps you will just have to set it down to the well-known contradictoriness, indeed perverseness, of human behavior generally. The last few years (in spite of what may have appeared outwardly) have been full of conflict and unhappiness for me—which I have not wanted to burden most of my friends with—and what came finally at the end of them was probably inevitable: indeed in a sense I foresaw and dreaded it unspeakably. Well, it is, again in one sense, over, and shattered as I feel, I am not quite destroyed; I can pick up some of the pieces and try to fit them together and as you are good enough to suggest, go on from here to do whatever is left for me to do—and in my power.

Capote was right; Arvin would have to write reviews. But he also hungered for a book-length subject in which to lose himself, and decided, shortly before Thanksgiving, on Henry Wadsworth Longfellow. It was an odd, unfashionable choice—even Arvin considered the author of "Hiawatha" a dated, lesser poet—but Longfellow, he wrote to Hicks, suited him. He had been enthralled by Longfellow ever since he was a boy of eight or nine, when his father had bought a cottage in a Christian summer colony on a lake, and each night a traveling band of Indians performed a play based on "Hiawatha." So transfixed was Arvin by the handsome youth in the scant native costume who played Longfellow's "culture hero" that he persuaded his parents to buy him an Indian suit and went chasing after squirrels with an imaginary bow and arrow. Besides, Longfellow, as a secondary figure, meant a smaller, less ambitious book, which, after Arvin's experience with Emerson, appealed to him.

He diligently began reading and taking notes and "feeling a little stronger every day," he wrote to Hicks on November 23, ten days after returning home from Grafton. Otherwise, he said, he had no real news. He ate dinner once with Fisher, saw Aaron, and was reassured to find that he "could make out in company," although he feared he was a "very problematic guest." He gathered the strength to go to the bank and one or two other places and found it less difficult than he imagined. Remarkably, he convinced his doctor to give him a prescription for tranquilizers, which he'd been cribbing from the Hickses since his release from Haskell. Though the doctor, Hugh Tatlock, warned him not to take more than one or two a day, "I was surprised and pleased that he yielded the point at all," Arvin wrote.

Within a week Arvin received his strongest encouragement since his arrest. It came, as so often, from Edmund Wilson, whose own legal troubles had climaxed earlier in the month. Wilson had won dismissal on three of four federal tax evasion charges but had pleaded guilty to not reporting $17,000 in income and was fined $7,500. He still owed the government $68,500, which he didn't have. "I hope this episode will not discourage you but perhaps in the long run prove stimulating," he wrote defiantly from Wellfleet. "It will not detract in the least from your literary reputation. If it is impossible for you to teach at Smith, you ought not to have any difficulty in publishing reviews and articles. Would you like me to speak to the *New Yorker* and the *Nation?* I have always thought you didn't write half enough . . . Goddamn all this interference with people's personal affairs!"

Seeing Wilson overcome his legal troubles, Arvin resolved to do the same. "I believe I am holding my own, though not much more than that," he wrote to Hicks on November 30, "getting a little work done every day on HWL and venturing into places like the library, which I dreaded, but which has proved at least bearable." And yet his traction was weak, his grip faltering. To Wilson, he wrote the next day, "So far I have been able to work only fitfully and for short stretches . . . I feel very much as if I had been involved in a violently destructive automobile accident that had no intelligible meaning, only a shattering one." As Arvin and his friends understood, his great—his paramount—need was for uninterrupted work, and he might well have fine work ahead of him if he could find a way to concentrate. But for that, they all agreed, he needed Yaddo.

The next morning, after a dreadful night, Arvin stayed in bed. He was panicky and disconsolate, muttering to himself, terrified of being alone. Al Fisher came and, after a brief talk, gathered some clothes and books and drove him back to the state hospital. "For the first time," Fisher wrote in his journal, "I feel rather discouraged about his future." It was now clear that Arvin was scarcely more ready to live in the world than he had been two months earlier, when he was released from the hospital the first time. Even his three time-honored remedies—work, friends, and books—had failed. Only the hospital's regimen of supervised sedation, comforting anonymity among strangers whose problems weighed as heavily as his own, and forced tedium seemed to steady him at such moments, indicating that he probably couldn't leave Northampton even if he wanted to.

When they didn't hear from him, Arvin's out-of-town friends feared why. Afraid he'd re-entered the hospital, or worse, they phoned or wrote to Fisher and Aaron for reassurance. Fisher tried to conceal the depth of his concern, but now it leaked out, causing Hicks, especially, to become alarmed, and requiring Arvin to calm those who were trying to calm him. "Al tells me you have been troubled by not hearing from me," he wrote to Hicks on December 12, two weeks after his last letter. "It was really only that there was so little to say except that I had gone into another tailspin and felt that I ought to return to the hospital. I now feel ever so much better, however, and am leaving on Thursday on a 'visiting' basis." The hospital had decided again to release him, but, expecting him back, not to discharge him, which would ease the paperwork if and when he returned.

An early snowfall blanketed the valley with several inches before Christmas, further restricting Arvin's ability to go out. He didn't mind the tedium of the hospital life when he was low, but now that he felt better, he reassessed what he ought to do and where he ought to be, and he questioned the wisdom of going to Yaddo in January. He'd planned to spend Christmas with Capote's editor at Random House, Robert Linscott, and

Linscott's wife, Elizabeth, at their country house in Ashfield, a picturesque hill town not far from Northampton, but even that short excursion now seemed risky. Apologetically, he wrote to Hicks, canceling his visit to Saratoga:

> I dislike to seem ungrateful to you and the others who spent time and energy to get me invited: in fact I was deeply touched by all that, and will not forget it. But it seems to me unwise for me to be at Yaddo, set up as it is, so long as I am in any danger at all of having a setback . . . I cling to the idea of going ahead with the book about HWL and, the fact is, it would not be at all easy to do so at Yaddo. The problem of books, reference works, etc., is a serious one there, and I know it would mean one frustration after another. Here I can use my office as I have always done, take books out of the library, borrow books *through* the library, etc. This is what I strongly feel like doing. I can easily see how people feel that I ought to get away from Northampton, and indeed I feel something of that myself. But here is where I have got to be, sooner or later, and if I can stand the gaff, perhaps it is just as well for me to be facing up to it now. In some respects it has already proved less grim than I feared it would be.

Arvin's Smith friends made sure he wasn't alone and idle through the holidays. Bob Petersson, another English professor and a friend of Dorius's since graduate school, invited him for Christmas Eve and gave him a paperback Fannie Farmer cookbook as a gift. Christmas Day he spent with the Aarons; it was, he wrote to Hicks, "tumultuous but cheering—and in any case familiar and homelike." There was caroling through the quiet and lovely neighborhood north of the campus where married professors and their families lived alongside Northampton's lawyers and bankers. The town never looked more luminous than at this time of year, in this light, in the snow.

Arvin would have liked to be with Ned, just the two of them, as in past years around this time. Two years earlier, Ned had come up to his apartment, and they'd opened their presents beside Arvin's Christmas tree. Ned had given him a volume of Flemish art, and they were tender and affectionate with each other. Last year, they'd exchanged gifts again, then went separately to New York for a few nights at Everard while Ned weighed whether to go to Harvard and Arvin pondered what it would be like not to have Ned close by.

Ned had called a few days earlier to say he would be in Northampton between Christmas and New Year's and suggested they get together. It was the first time they had spoken since Arvin called him from Al Fisher's, more than a month before, when Ned had been petulant and angry and didn't know what to say to him. Each was forbidden, under the terms of his probation, from associating with others of "bad character," which included each other. But Ned sounded well and told Arvin that, in fact, he was, and Arvin was hopeful. Then Ned called back to say he wasn't coming after all.

Thus Arvin faced a new year as he had in 1960 and many years before that: alone, in Northampton, in his apartment, with scant hope of ever leaving. In that one way, at least, little in his life had changed, and that continuity gave him surprising comfort, if not strength.

"Dear Granville," Arvin wrote to Hicks from home on January 11, 1961, a month after leaving the hospital for the third time and nine days before Kennedy's snowy inaugural:

> I have ventured more and more into public places, including the college library, and though it is painful enough sometimes, I gain a little strength by doing so. So far as I can intuit people's attitudes, they are mostly friendly or at least tolerant: I have not yet encountered any real rebuff anywhere, and some people have gone out of their way to be kind—sometimes surprising people. So in one sense I may "live it down" ultimately—though in another sense, subjectively, I never can. The imagery for a nightmare will always be there.

Having found that he could face people, Arvin equated his colleagues' civility with forgiveness, but many of them, not only friends of Ned and Dorius, were disgusted with him. They regretted his ruin, pitied him, but didn't excuse him. "That he was so tough at the center, yet could be such a shit, was very disturbing," Petersson would recall. "He drove into my whole system thoughts about where weakness ends and evil begins, and those thoughts were made more complicated by his being capable of such ruthless indifference to other people." Like many who knew Arvin, Petersson believed he had been in such terror when the police entered his apartment that "it just ripped everything apart." But those who had earlier detected selfishness in him now blamed it for what they considered his immoral surrender.

Aaron, especially, was conflicted. He regarded Arvin—as Emerson had said of William Ellery Channing, and Arvin of Emerson—as his "bishop." But after twenty years of friendship, he also thought him "remorselessly selfish. There was something hard and resolute about him underneath all his softness. When it came to his own feelings and desires, he was very hard—ruthless." Aaron sympathized with Arvin's "failure, his timidities, his fears, his anxieties," but being Arvin's friend meant feeling, too, that one's efforts were never quite enough. Whether Arvin could eventually "live down" the Affair, he was right in sensing the sadness and anger he had brought on others.

He had begun to write. Smith allowed him to keep his office, and most mornings, despite frigid temperatures and drifting snow, he battled across the campus, hung his coat and hat behind his door, removed his galoshes, and settled down to concentrate on a piece about Longfellow's "The Saga of King Olaf." "I am not writing like a burning building," he wrote to Hicks, "but it is encouraging to find that I can write at all." At Wilson's behest, *The Nation* had asked him to do book reviews "from time to time," and he was sharply relieved to learn that he was still employable. "I don't see how I can ever make any considerable addition to my income either by reviewing or writing articles," he told Hicks. But, he added, "real idleness would be a horror—and fatal." As Arvin saw it, he was no longer writing because he had to and because it was what he did. He was writing to save himself.

He began fitting together a new life from the shards of his old one, but unevenly. On January 31, three weeks after telling Hicks that he was feeling better, he readmitted himself to the state hospital. Fisher, who drove him up, wrote in his journal, "After a bout of some days drinking and general psychic grief and 'panic,' [he] began babbling to himself in a somewhat 'new' way." Arvin had now received a full diagnosis—"psychoneurotic disorder" (homosexuality) plus "reactive depression"—and though he was taking tranquilizers, he again felt shattered. "I am sorry to be (or rather seem) so unfriendly and unhospitable [sic] just now," he wrote to Ehrlich the next day, his normally slashing handwriting so shaky as to be almost illegible, "but I am in the hospital again and feeling too miserable to talk." By now, Arvin's pattern had become clear. He struggled until he gave out, and then fell back on the hospital for a period of enforced rest and isolation until he could gather enough strength to try to work.

Arvin's Smith friends, not surprisingly, were drained from helping him. Even Fisher, who had started a secret affair with a student, seemed put out at having again to go to the hospital regularly to see him. "It took me a two-hour stretch to visit Arvin (via delayed taxis) . . . ," he complained on February 5. "As I say, the weather stinks. Aaron thinks Arvin should be visited less frequently."

Barely a week later, Arvin was again ready to return home, part time. "Being now a parolee," he wrote to Ehrlich on February 12, "I am allowed to go out in the middle of the day for an hour or two." He was fully released three days later, went home, and threw himself back into his routine. The weather remained blustery, but the days were lengthening, the sun was higher in the sky, and the streets were streaked with melting snow—harbingers of a thaw. Arvin made plans to have Janet Aaron, Dan's wife, drive him to Grafton as soon as the weather let up.

He continued to visit the hospital as an outpatient, complaining to a psychiatrist that he felt old, impotent, and unattractive. During one visit, he expressed guilt about involving others in his morass, then softened it by recalling the badgering and aggression he'd been subjected to by Regan and his men. Whether these guilty feelings were explored further is unclear. Arvin had been told what was wrong with him, and his treatment was aimed at that. As far as the hospital could see, he was in a constant state of conflict because of his homosexuality, not because of any secondary remorse he might feel at having informed on friends. Driven by unwanted sexual impulses, he was desperate not to be controlled by them.

The Smith trustees met annually in Northampton in February. They were a lively group, sharp-minded and sharp-tongued, a cross-directorate of several powerful elites. There were rich alumnae from interlocking blueblood clans (Constance Morrow Morgan, Laura Cabot Hodgkinson); distinguished academics (former Harvard provost Paul Buck, Bryn Mawr Dean Dorothy Nepper Marshall); Eastern Establishment wives (Mary Griswold, Ellen Zinsser McCloy); and nationally prominent businessmen (advertising executive Robbins Milbank; Kuhn, Loeb partner Frederick M. Warburg). With their three daughters away at boarding school and college, the Mendenhalls had several of the trustees stay overnight in the large—and largely ceremonial—president's house, a secluded, elm-shaded Georgian mansion with six whitewashed chimneys. Nellie Mendenhall, adjusting to Northampton after New Haven, came to regard the entertaining as one of her happiest duties—a gay couple of days of financial business, enlightened conversation, formal dinners, and martini-drinking.

Since Ned's and Dorius's superior court trials, T&P had reviewed the cases, keeping the trustees informed of its progress. Unlike with Arvin, the committee's course had been uncertain. Smith's "good book" laid out no directives for dealing with nontenured faculty who were arrested, particularly on morals charges. Yet Ned and Dorius were popular young teachers with promising careers, and their departments both unanimously had voted to keep them. At the same time, many faculty members were upset and angry at the sexual revelations, especially about Ned. Ned heard through his lawyer that Mendenhall had received a disturbing phone call from the father of a boy at Northampton High School who said the youth had tried to kill himself after the arrests. Ned feared it was Alan. Petersson and other faculty members had come to believe that they could support Dorius, but not Ned. Meanwhile, the legal appeals were advancing, but slowly, meaning that it might be two years before a final court ruling.

Mendenhall had waited until the February meeting to bring T&P's recommendation to the board. The trustees met, as always, in a small paneled meeting room upstairs in Alumnae House, a whitewashed Georgian-style reception facility handsomely, if oddly, festooned with art deco and Swedish Modern accents. A gift from the graduates to the college, the building was a shrine to Smith's most self-conscious aspirations. Down the marble hall from the boardroom was a full-scale replica of the Victorian bedroom of Sophia Smith, the founder.

After reviewing the case, Mendenhall told the board that T&P unanimously favored reappointing both Dorius and Spofford to the faculty. He explained the committee's reasons: members felt strongly that an individual's personal life need not affect his teaching; the evidence used in court was second- and thirdhand, obtained by questionable means; and Smith was strong enough to resist outside pressure and public opinion.

The trustees disagreed vehemently, on all points. They told Mendenhall that parents expected members of a college faculty to be above suspicion in all ways. Spofford and Dorius had been legally convicted, their fitness for teaching gravely undermined. Smith should not have felons on the faculty, they said. Further, they reminded Mendenhall that they, not the faculty, were responsible for weighing the future of the college against the future of the two individuals and had a legal and moral obligation to protect Smith's reputation.

Mendenhall defended T&P's recommendation as being in Smith's best interest, but the trustees overruled him. On February 17, two days after Arvin left the hospital, Mendenhall wrote to Ned and Dorius, notifying them of the college's decision not to reappoint them. Technically, they weren't fired—they were being let go at the end of their terms—but the effect was the same. Smith had deemed them unworthy of tenure. Even if they were acquitted and stayed on, they had no future at the college.

Ned was in Cambridge when he received the news. Cushioned by Harvard's willingness to let the courts decide his future, he was upset but not devastated. "I think it would have been very hard for me to go back to Smith with people knowing I was gay," he later said. He had done well at Harvard, had the confidence of his department, and was living comfortably in Cambridge. He knew he faced a year in jail if he lost his appeal, but Homans and Katz thought the case could be won and might even make important new case law supporting individual rights. After writing Mendenhall a one-sentence reply, thanking him, Ned went out for dinner that night with friends. He cried in the restaurant but without the least sense of being derailed, either in his life or his career.

Not so Dorius. Teaching was his life. He had moved back to New

Haven to be near friends, especially Roy Fisher, who'd rescued him after his arrest and whose epilepsy had worsened during the crisis. Jobless, too anguished to work, Dorius brooded ceaselessly about his future. Encouraged by Bacon and Homans, he had refused even to consider that he might lose his job, especially so soon after Yale had let him go. As low as he sank, he clung to the hope of returning to the classroom, the one place where he thought he might, in time, redeem himself.

Being fired unexpectedly by Smith thus shattered him. Helen Bacon raced down to New Haven to comfort him and to take charge, but by then Dorius was inconsolable. "I expected never to teach again," he recalled. "I had no future, no life." The next day, after a harrowing night, he told Bacon he had better go to a mental hospital before he tried to "hurt someone." She took him to Yale Hospital, but Yale's psychiatric beds were full, so she arranged for him to be admitted to a center for schizophrenics across the street.

Dorius received tranquilizers but no treatment at the hospital. His friends came regularly to visit, though he couldn't hold his head up to face them. Roy Fisher, more ill than ever and distraught over the pall that the Affair continued to cast on the lives of Dorius and other friends, dropped by at first twice a day, before and after teaching his art history classes at Yale. Then, on the third night, Fisher failed to appear. When Dorius couldn't locate him at the university, he begged the doctors to let him leave so that he could go to Fisher's apartment to check on him. He finally became so frantic that they released him with a nurse and an ambulance. When Dorius and the nurse arrived at Fisher's apartment, they found him lying in bed, unconscious—breathing, but faintly. An empty bottle of phenobarbital lay on his nightstand.

Fisher was rushed to Yale Hospital and survived. But the "double shock" of his suicide attempt and Dorius's being fired plunged Dorius into a yawning despair. He had lost all hope. Bacon, by comparison, got furious at Fisher: "I thought it was unforgivable for Roy to carry on like that. It was an attack on Joel when he was down. I don't know what attention he was trying to get." She was even more outraged at the trustees, whose treatment of Dorius and Ned she considered "disgraceful." Bacon was up for tenure, but as she returned by car to Northampton she resolved to fight to get them both reinstated. "I was mad," she would say. "You get reckless. I said, 'Either I'll be fired or I'll have tenure.' I didn't care."

Mendenhall informed the appropriate department heads, including Bacon, of the trustees' decision, and waited until the end of the next regular faculty meeting, on February 22, to announce it officially. Facing Smith's 240 teachers in a low-rising semicircle in the Alumnae House conference hall, he hoped to avoid any rancor that might prevent him from completing other business. The trustees, he explained, had decided not to reappoint Ned and Dorius because they "felt it was not in the best interests of the college to do so." A brief, sharp exchange ensued. Someone rose to ask why the trustees hadn't waited for a final legal ruling, as Smith's previous statements had suggested the college would do. "The college," Mendenhall answered, "has never considered that it was bound by a decision of the courts." Then, realizing that his continued presence at the meeting "was a hindrance rather than a help," he asked that the faculty go into executive session, allowing him to leave. He returned to his office, where he informed the editor of the *Sophian* of the faculty's recommendation and the trustees' decision in time for the next day's edition.

Smith's faculty knew it needed to act. Most members agreed that the essential issue was whether Ned and Dorius were fit to teach. Yet even among those who professed loudest that a person's private life should have no bearing on an assessment of his or her professional competence, many were privately repulsed by the two men's behavior, especially Ned's. The conflict between their principles and their aversion to homosexuality put most faculty members on the spot and made them less-than-vigorous advocates. Those who were untenured, or secretly homosexual themselves, feared speaking out entirely. The Affair left most of Smith's famously outspoken teachers publicly tongue-tied. Like Aaron, they lacked the understanding, moral vocabulary, and intellectual certainty even to discuss it.

Only Wendell Johnson had no such hesitation. Many on campus knew that Johnson was a homosexual, but not how narrowly he himself had escaped arrest. It was Johnson's pictures the police had seized in Ned's apartment, and after the arrests he had passed a trove of muscle magazines to a friend and left town while the probe unfolded. Most of his colleagues knew Johnson as a popular teacher and prolific critic, if a bit of a showman, who, despite a second-rate educational pedigree, had worked hard, published like a demon, and was on the verge of getting tenure. For whatever reasons—guilt, his friends suspected, or a sense that after the Affair his days at Smith were numbered—Johnson now stood up near the front of the hall and called for Ned's and Dorius's full reinstatement. Upset, he denounced the trustees as "craven cowards."

No one rose to second Johnson's statement. His sincere cry, so rash and perhaps even foolhardy, elicited only stunned silence from the majority of the faculty, who didn't know how to react. Instead, the meeting was adjourned until the following Wednesday, when the faculty would again take up the trustees' decision.

Bacon left the meeting in a rage, feeling that Mendenhall had betrayed them. He had promised, she felt, to follow the wisdom of the courts, but had collapsed in the face of the board's opposition. Faculty meetings were confidential, but Bacon resolved to expose what Smith had done. On her own, she began to put pressure on the board to reverse its decision and on Mendenhall to reassert his support for the faculty's recommendations. With "fire springing out of her head," Dorius later said, she issued several urgent new appeals: to Homans, Katz, and the ACLU to explore any legal recourse; to distinguished friends and allies at Harvard, Yale, and other campuses to write letters of support; to the American Association of University Professors to push for some kind of public sanction against Smith; to sympathetic alumnae, who, she hoped, would restrict their donations in protest; and—an extraordinary breach of Smith decorum—to undergraduates.

Mendenhall would later denounce this last as "disgraceful and unpardonable," but it yielded prompt results. Ned's and Dorius's students loved them. Ned's classes had made Roman feasts for him, feeding him elaborate meals as for an emperor; and Dorius had sent his students out after his lectures reciting passages from Shakespeare and exalting life. "The best professor I had at Smith," the children's book author Jane Yolen later called him. Bacon, too, was a favorite of the fiery, studious girls who took her ancient fiction class, known as "Miss Bacon's course in pornography" because of her intimate readings of the *Satyricon* and *Daphnis and Chloë*. All told, a couple of dozen students now resolved to protest Smith's decision.

A week later, faculty members again poured into Alumnae Hall to resume their discussion. With Mendenhall away, the dean was in the chair. By all accounts, the meeting was calm, thoughtful, and temperate. The faculty unanimously voted to express their "regret" that the trustees "found it possible" to overrule a unanimous vote by T&P. "While recognizing the complexity of the situation and realizing that the Board of Trustees has already devoted much attention to these cases," they urged, "we earnestly request that it reconsider its action in consultation with the Committee on Tenure and Promotion." Later, nine members wrote to Hazel Coe, the board's outgoing chairman, dissociating themselves from the statement, and another minority favored a stronger line, but, in all, the faculty had spoken; the great majority favored a cordial meeting to try to get the trustees to reverse their stand.

As Smith braced for a showdown, the trustees' executive committee decided to consider the question at its next meeting, in New York, on March 15. But before that, on March 7, the *Sophian* published a sharply worded broadside headlined WE ACCUSE and signed by sixteen students, mostly juniors and seniors. Denouncing "all those who condone the Trustees' decision," the group threatened, "We will not sit back and passively accept this action."

Mendenhall, trying to appease both sides, was stung by the attack, which was picked up by the wire services and resulted in a few papers making something of Smith's "family squabble," as he called it. He summoned Bacon to his office in College Hall, where, she recalled, "he asked me to stop agitating and assured me that everything would be all right." Mendenhall was under great pressure to keep Smith together, and Bacon thought he felt guilty about the trustees' actions and frustrated by the role he'd been forced to play. She believed Mendenhall was "tweedy" but honorable. After their conversation, there were no further student protests, and Mendenhall quietly resumed arranging a joint faculty-trustee meeting in Northampton on April 5.

APRIL 1, 1960
WASHINGTON, D.C.

In the great marble chamber of the United States Supreme Court, Felix Frankfurter jousted with an Ohio assistant county prosecutor in a case that stood to bear decisively on Spofford's and Dorius's appeals. Around the country, civil liberties lawyers like Homans and Katz had paid close attention to the case, *Mapp v. Ohio,* since late October, when the Court first announced its intention to review it.

In May 1957, Cleveland police had broken into the home of a divorcée named Dollree Mapp to look for gambling paraphernalia. During their search, they also found some pornographic books and pictures that Mapp said belonged to an absent roomer. She was acquitted on the gambling charge, but convicted of possessing obscene material and sentenced to one to seven years in the penitentiary. Unlike Massachusetts and most other states, Ohio law made *mere possession* of an obscene work a crime if the person knew it was obscene. Although a majority of Ohio Supreme Court justices thought Mapp's conviction was unconstitutional, they couldn't overturn a statute unless all or all but one of the justices agreed, so her conviction was affirmed, leading to the U.S. Supreme Court review.

Aside from the legality of the search—no search warrant was produced at Mapp's trial—the question before the High Court was whether a state can punish a citizen for having obscene material in his or her home with no intention to sell or exhibit it. The justices were skeptical. Ever since *Roth,* they had moved to narrow the definition of obscenity. And although Frankfurter himself favored a restricted role in ruling on oppressive state statutes, and was so repelled by pornography that he had his clerks read it for him, he was plainly troubled by the breadth of the Ohio law.

Suppose, Frankfurter challenged the prosecutor, Gertrude Bauer Mahon, he "was a bibliophile—I collect first editions, and I have an obscene book—not for that reason, but because it was printed in 1527. Am I guilty?"

Mahon stood at the counsel's rostrum in front of the nine justices. "Any collector of obscenity would be guilty," she explained.

"Mark Twain," Frankfurter interjected, "was one of the biggest collectors. I can tell you right now where the collection is—but that is outside your jurisdiction."

Laughter trickled from the gallery.

Frankfurter continued. He asked whether Mahon had examined university libraries in her state. He said he knew for a fact that they had copies of pornographic works "known to literary history," but added, "I shan't mention them here lest people run to the bookstores."

Mahon answered, unambiguously, "I can't believe that any of those libraries have material of the kind in this case. If they do, someone should be prosecuted."

Well, then, what about psychiatrists? Frankfurter asked.

Mahon said that if she found a psychiatrist possessing obscene literature, she would do her duty as a prosecutor.

"I'm not stimulating you to any prosecutions," Frankfurter said drily.

Frankfurter's amusement aside, the Court had become less patient in recent years with those who resisted its efforts to restrict police power and safeguard individual rights, and all of the justices seemed reluctant to accept Mahon's central argument that obscene matter, like narcotics, was outside constitutional protection. When Justice Potter Stewart noted that the Ohio statute also made it a crime to possess contraceptives, there were murmurs all along the bench.

Homans, hearing the news accounts the next day, was sharply encouraged. He and Katz were working to have Dorius's and Spofford's convictions overturned by any means possible. He had recently gone to New York to consult with the aging civil liberties lawyer Morris Ernst, who had defended James Joyce and Random House in the *Ulysses* case, and was preparing a "nonobscenity" brief for Dorius. But he also intended to argue that the search of Dorius's apartment was illegal because the warrant gave Regan and his men unlimited discretion as to what could be seized. He hoped that the justices' skepticism about the Ohio statute in the *Mapp* case might lead to a wider ruling on the rights of police to enter people's homes, search them, and seize whatever suited their purposes. Calling Dorius at the mental hospital, Homans reported the good news and told him, again, not to worry.

Arvin muddled through as before, oblivious of the events around him. A disappointing squabble with the editors of *Commentary* over a reviewing assignment flustered him but failed to send him back to the hospital. He felt the magazine was imposing a "neoconservative" party line on him because he had been kind to Louis Auchincloss, a liberal author. Arvin swore off writing for the journal until "I get it straight that I have a reasonably free hand," he told Hicks. Otherwise, he endured, grimly and beyond public view. "I get through the days as best I can," he wrote to Ehrlich on April 13, "seeing almost no one and reading till the pages swim before my eyes. I hardly know how time passes, but looking back on it, as usual, it seems to have flown . . . I need you worse than ever."

As the one arrested professor remaining in Northampton, Arvin found his presence tolerated on campus as if he were a poor, disgraced uncle, to be treated with wary respect, embarrassment, and pity. He no longer presented a danger—although others did. Later that day, Fisher received an unexpected visit from Don Sheehan, Mendenhall's chief emissary to the faculty during the Affair. The college, having become sensitized to the risks posed by its professors' sex lives, discovered that he was sleeping with a student and strongly suspected that there had been other indiscretions. Sheehan warned Fisher, who was fifty-seven, "that the whole thing might become a matter for the President's office, and that the girl ran a risk of not getting her degree," Fisher wrote in his journal.

Fisher was appalled. "The incredible and nasty smallness, the meanness, of certain institutional gossips," he wrote. Believing the informer to be an "unhappy lesbian" on the faculty, he defended his relationship as "gentle, delicate, loving and altogether decent" and insisted that no harm had come to the girl, apparently not considering that his journals, in which he wrote about their "fantastic sexual joy with each other" and graphically described her "violently tender and tenderly violent" orgasms, might well ruin her if they fell into the wrong hands. Nonetheless, he complied with Smith's wishes. According to Fisher, Sheehan "said that the matter was known to persons in her house and (I'm not clear about this) perhaps to the 'Judicial Board.' He suggested, but ever so gently, that the matter be 'terminated' at once. I've 'terminated' it."

Unlike Arvin's, Spofford's, and Dorius's private behavior, which posed no direct threat to Smith undergraduates, Fisher's sexual interests apparently caused no great concern about his continued presence on the faculty. He remained at Smith until his retirement, in 1967, one of a number of male professors well known among the faculty for sleeping with students.

Chapter Fourteen

SMITH'S "SQUABBLE" CONTINUED through Lent. Across America, it was an anxious time. Kennedy's popularity, which had soared during the first three months of his term, convulsed abruptly when, on April 12, the Russians put a man in space; four days later, a U.S.-trained invasion force landed disastrously at Cuba's Bay of Pigs. Meanwhile, Smith was confronted by its own new crisis. On April 14, the forty-four-year-old director of the college art museum, Robert Parks, was arrested for committing "unnatural acts" with a seventeen-year-old Amherst youth in a car behind a popular pizza restaurant. The *Gazette* reported Parks's arraignment in its roundup of court news, but the *Springfield Daily News* carried it on page one, next to a story about cosmonaut Yuri Gagarin's post-orbit press conference: SMITH PROF ACCUSED IN MORALS CASE. Abruptly, Smith faced another round of scandalous publicity.

As the college and the town reeled from the latest news, Mendenhall worked through the weekend to assure the trustees that there was no connection between Parks's arrest by a state trooper and the arrests of last fall. Homosexuals on area campuses again lay low, fearing another sweep. Arvin could only have been horrified by such an ill-timed indiscretion, but, still terrified of the Post Office, he avoided mentioning Parks in his letters. Fisher called Parks to offer help, but unlike in September, he apparently was alone. A sexual suspect himself, he was hardly in a position, however, to defend Parks publicly.

Arvin departed the following Wednesday, as planned, for Grafton, one day before the trustees were scheduled to meet in Northampton. His determination to be involved in the affairs around him had long since dissipated, and if he was at all concerned about Parks's arrest or the spike in world tensions, he didn't show Hicks. Unlike his previous visit, when he read *Evangeline* aloud after dinner and talked excitedly about his idea for a Longfellow book, he was, Hicks found, intermittently sociable and withdrawn.

"Newton is far from well . . . ," Hicks wrote to Cowley. "At first we were struck by the great improvement from last November, and indeed at his best, to which he rose several times during the week, he seemed quite himself. But he could fall woefully low. He spent one whole day in bed, only getting up now and then to get a drink. (By fits and starts he drinks quite heavily all day long.) He is doing only little pieces of work. I am afraid the future is dark." Like a man rowing disconsolately away from the scene of a shipwreck he had helped cause, Arvin was unwilling and unable to look back.

The trustees arrived at Smith on April 20, one day before Good Friday; several of them again boarded at the president's house. However conflicted they may have been about the Affair in private, Nellie Mendenhall would recall "an extraordinary degree of congeniality" among them. By now most board members had narrowed the issues to just one—Ned's and Dorius's homosexuality. The executive committee had decided that, because of the disputed nature of the "obscene" material and the circumstances of its seizure, the trustees shouldn't discuss the pornography charges, but should leave those to the courts. Having twice heard the case for reconsideration, the issue before them was plain: were Spofford and Dorius, two known homosexuals, morally fit to teach at Smith College?

The board met privately throughout the afternoon. Mendenhall argued that both teachers should be kept, and that he feared a major rift with the faculty if they weren't. Privately, he hoped that most of the women on the board saw what Nellie Mendenhall would later call "the big picture"—that Ned's and Dorius's sexuality was no threat to the students—and would side with him against the men. But the men, with one or two exceptions, saw another "big picture" entirely, one that loomed larger and more menacing in light of the shocks of the past ten days.

The conflation of Robert Parks's arrest and the abrupt entry of the Cold War into a dangerous new phase had revived, for some of them, the last shadow of McCarthyism—the dark connection between subversive politics and abnormal sexuality. Homosexuals were ultimately weak, abominable, predatory creatures, several of the trustees believed. Like communists, they preyed on America's youth and were unreliable. Smith was a liberal institution, but this was no time to indulge liberal sympathies.

Unable to reach a decision by five o'clock, the trustees delayed their final vote until Friday morning. According to Nellie Mendenhall, they remained narrowly, bitterly split into two factions: powerful businessmen, like the investment banker Frederick Warburg, who thought it would be a crime to let homosexuals, no matter how learned, influence impressionable young "ladies"; and strong, socially liberal society women, like Laura Cabot Hodgkinson, who thought it would be another kind of crime not to. Tom Mendenhall argued up to the last minute for reinstatement, but again his efforts fell short. Warburg and a majority of trustees were convinced that their concerns were vital to the college's best interests. Noting their regret at having to differ with the faculty on such an important matter, the board voted to uphold its earlier decision to release Ned and Dorius.

After the meeting, several of the trustees returned to the mansion for their suitcases. Nellie Mendenhall, who supported her husband, was appalled by their easy conviviality, as if nothing had happened. "As they parted in the front hall, I remember one of them saying, 'I'll see you at Vespers this afternoon.' They had just crucified two guys and were going off to celebrate the crucifixion of another one," she recalled.

Mendenhall himself returned from the meeting weary and disillusioned. *The New Yorker* had once written, "Mr. Mendenhall gives the impression of enjoying everything that has ever happened to him, especially the presidency of Smith." But the Affair had been a torment. "Tom had a puritanical streak in him," Nellie later said. "Lawbreaking was hard for him to understand. But he had agonized over this. He had fought right up to the end to keep their jobs, and it troubled him deeply that he hadn't been able to work it all out in a way that wouldn't lead to a great rift with the faculty. At this point he felt very strongly that he ought to resign, but couldn't for the sake of the college."

While chairman Hazel Coe wrote to Vernon Gotwals, the faculty secretary, to inform him officially of the board's decision, Mendenhall again notified Ned and Dorius. Then, five days later, on April 26, he once more addressed the faculty at its regular monthly meeting.

Reading from handwritten notes, Mendenhall first offered a brief update on the "most recent, unhappy incident" involving Robert Parks. Parks, who was married, had not yet been tried, but he had offered his resignation, and the college had accepted with "real regret," Mendenhall said. Since the facts of the case were all too clear, this was a less painful alternative than his having to appear before the joint faculty-trustee committee that, in the wake of the Affair, the board recommended should handle such cases. Mendenhall then recounted the history of the September scandal up to the trustees' last meeting. Still furious about the faculty leaks to students, he sternly warned against future "breaches of confidence and decorum."

"In an earlier time," he said, reprising his welcoming address to the students back in September, "college teaching was a calling, to be entered into primarily out of a sense of vocation. But it's now more the fashion to consider it a job, like anything else." He went on optimistically, "Salaries fortunately have increased, and should continue to do so . . . faculty are now receiving more nearly what they deserve."

But Mendenhall worried about this new trend toward academic careerism, and it was clear that he blamed it, in no small part, for Smith's current problems. "The faculty is the heart, the vital part of a unique corporate organization—the independent liberal arts college," he said. "And the very fact that the faculty's role is so vital and critical should make us jealously concerned and proud of our reputation, both at home and abroad, with our students, with those who work with us in the College, and with the world at large."

It was uncertain whether Mendenhall was criticizing Arvin, Ned, Dorius, and Parks for failing to show the proper monkish devotion to the college by indulging improper needs and risking its reputation—that somehow their homosexuality was an affront to Smith's mission—or he was more concerned with Bacon's deliberately involving the students. He seemed to be politely excoriating them both. In either case, there was little outcry. Most faculty members were either fed up with the Affair or were afraid to say anything further. Wendell Johnson had got an offer from Hunter College in New York and was planning to leave at the end of the term. Bacon herself would soon receive tenure but would take a job at Barnard. She would get the AAUP to win Ned and Dorius a full year's severance pay, but other than that there seemed little that one could do.

Arvin busied himself on his return to Northampton with small domestic matters. He reported to his probation officer and went to Pattrell's appliance shop to inquire about an aerial for his new television, a small black-and-white set that Hicks, who had purchased one in the fall so that he and Dottie could watch the presidential debates, convinced him to buy on sale.

About the same time as the faculty meeting, he wrote to John Slade asking not to be re-elected to Yaddo's Board of Directors but indicating that he hoped to stay on as a member of the corporation, a job with scant advisory duties, no pay, and no real authority. The executive committee recommended John Cheever to replace him as director, and Slade replied that he would take up with the full board Arvin's request to retain his membership.

Arvin's friends by now doubted even that reduced prospect. Yaddo was in the midst of a financial crisis. It recently had donated $25,000 to Princeton, Spencer Trask's alma mater; $10,000 to Skidmore; and $10,000 to the Saratoga Hospital fund. Together with Slade, C. Everett Bacon, the treasurer, and R. Inslee Clark, the assistant treasurer, worried that Yaddo's Wall Street and Saratoga interests would be hurt by Arvin's continued affiliation, although not, apparently, by such costly handouts. Ames resented this "Lady Bountiful role" and worried about Arvin's ability to handle a total rejection by the colony, but she recognized that she was all but alone in her support for him. "I suppose you think, as you did earlier, and as I find out many others do, that he ought not to continue in the Corporation," she wrote to Cowley on May 3.

By the May meeting, thirty-three years after he first arrived in Saratoga, Arvin was no longer a member of Yaddo.

With the last of his institutional ties severed, Arvin wondered again whether the publishing industry would follow suit and blacklist him. His name was tarnished, and while his literary friends encouraged him to plunge into some large work, he doubted that any respectable publisher could afford to have him on its list. He spent his days, he told Hicks, "reading and lying abed," and seeing almost no one. He began to feel pain when he urinated, which at another time might have caused him to worry about gonorrhea, but which he now suspected was prostatitis.

A week later, amid his deepening gloom, Arvin received an unexpected visit from Seymour Lawrence, the director of the Atlantic Monthly Press. As they talked, Lawrence, who was in town to see the Aarons, expressed strong interest in Arvin's idea for a Longfellow biography. "He insists they will publish if I write it," Arvin wrote to Hicks, "and this reassurance of course makes an immense difference to me. He might have abandoned an interest in anything I should do."

Inspired by Lawrence's offer, Arvin suddenly "got so desperate with having no real job to apply myself to" that he went to his office to see "if it was possible to do something with the problem" of Longfellow. Normally, he gathered and put on index cards all the material for his books—references, cross-references, authorities, incidental notes—before writing a single line. Now, though his research was far from done, he found himself able to get started with little trouble.

Arvin was primarily interested in how Longfellow's early influences affected his work. Longfellow was a "poet of acceptance, rather than of rebellion and rejection," he believed. This accounted for much of Longfellow's being out of favor with contemporary critics, who, including Arvin, had long demanded rebellion as a test of originality and greatness. Instead, "there was a peculiar felicity in all the circumstances of Longfellow's origin and early life; a felicity in the time, the place, the family entourage, the whole historic setting," Arvin wrote.

What fascinated him especially was that Longfellow, the scion of one of the most eminent families in Portland, Maine, a shy, bookish youth who grew up in prosperity during New England's flowering in the first half of the nineteenth century, was actually encouraged by his family to enter a life in literature. When Longfellow, swayed by what Arvin called his "inner intensities" as a teenager, told his father, Stephen, a successful lawyer, that his "whole soul burned" with wanting to become a writer, Stephen Longfellow replied that he was "happy" with the choice. Arvin noted that, in every respect, Longfellow's early influences were "mild and kindly." Yet with keen recognition and characteristic fervor, he also saw something else, something deeply familiar.

> There was a certain precariousness, even at an early date, in [Longfellow's] emotional make-up, as indeed we should expect—for was he not, with all his apparent stability, to be a poet?—and when we hear of a childhood dislike of loud noises and "rude excitements," of his having to be taken out of public school owing to his fear of the "rough boys," of "indefinite longings" and feelings of loneliness, in early boyhood, we realize that there were shadows even in a scene that was prevailingly sunny and cheerful.

For Arvin more than most biographers, subjects were surrogates, self-reflecting entities to be puzzled out at the highest level of sympathy, intelligence, and understanding. Solving "the problem" of another writer was an act of transubstantiation, an intimate convergence of two lives. As he began to write, Arvin found in Longfellow an allied spirit, someone who, like Hawthorne, Whitman, Melville, and Emerson, affirmed his own sense of separateness and, in so doing, upheld his convictions about being a writer and critic. A curious choice, especially for a New England writer as estranged from his time and place as Longfellow was comfortably a part of his, Longfellow seemed almost to have chosen *him*. As his friend the writer and *New Yorker* fiction editor William Maxwell wrote to him, "But what energy the dead have. I see him casting his eye over the field and deciding which living person is most likely to rescue him from the peculiar limbo he has been consigned to, and then the icy hand descending on your shoulder. Excellent judgment on his part."

Arvin grew more excited and hopeful than at any time since his arrest. He returned to his office the next day and the next, immersing himself in Longfellow's "shadows," trying to find premonitions of the mature poet who exalted Indians in the oddly melancholy child whose literary ardor equaled his own. "Something considerable I *must* have to occupy myself with," he wrote to Hicks on May 23, barely a week after Lawrence's visit, "and it is possible that this book will be that." He didn't know whether he could sustain a full-scale biography, or finish even a single chapter, but he was intrigued enough to try, and his tone improved sharply as he imagined for himself a future in writing books. After working longer and longer hours, he strolled home and, like other Americans that spring, turned on the television, which to his surprise provided rich cultural and political offerings. "I haven't used the set as much as I ought to," he told Hicks, "but when I have, I have been delighted with it."

Smith emptied as usual at the end of May, with a sense, overall, of sadness tinged with irritation. It had been the most troubled year in the school's history, more disturbing than the communist scandals of the early 1950s. Yet while there remained disagreement about whether a rift had opened between the faculty and trustees—Bacon and a few other professors no longer felt the college could be trusted; most of the administration, including Mendenhall, believed it had acted honorably and fairly—few doubted that it would be repaired. "They were friends when the sorry affair started," Mendenhall's assistant, Florence Macdonald, would recall, "and they were friends after it was over." As for Arvin, almost everyone, including himself, agreed that he had been treated fairly, especially in light of his "sickness."

Arvin's enthusiasm for Longfellow blossomed, although he soon suffered a setback that prevented him, temporarily, from doing more writing. Near the end of the month, he was hospitalized for his prostatitis and was operated on twice. He remained in Cooley Dickinson for the next four weeks, which, despite his health insurance, subjected him to "heavy extra expenses." Tormented by financial anxieties, Arvin again fretted about how he would survive, until Lilienthal and others rallied once again with "loans."

Yet Arvin's eagerness to get back to Longfellow not only improved his mood but spurred him to aim—and work—toward a speedy recovery. As he wrote to Lilienthal, the day after Aaron brought him home from the hospital:

I am having to take exaggeratedly good care of myself here at home for the time being—which is a little difficult, living alone as I do—but I am sure that in two or three weeks I shall be feeling practically normal again. The thing has had some very trying sequelae, some painful, some embarrassing, but I believe they will taper off as time goes on.

Ten days later, on July 8, he told Hicks proudly that he had begun to get out of his apartment twice a day. His incontinence, he thought, was diminishing, he ate meals "with a little more zest," and he expected to get back to his office within the week. Having decided to live and to write, and finding that he could do both, Arvin even expressed pity for others—surprising others—who had lost the ability to do likewise. "Hemingway's suicide knocked me for a loop when I read of it, and has haunted me ever since," he told Hicks. "Yet in a sense it was a characteristic and almost a predictable thing for him to do, wasn't it? That lifelong preoccupation with death." It was well understood that Hemingway, publicly the most masculine writer of Arvin's generation, had killed himself because he could no longer write. Arvin, who had always doubted his own manliness but found he could still put words on paper, expressed no further thought of suicide.

During Arvin's hospital stay, the Supreme Court ruled in *Mapp v. Ohio,* advancing well beyond the question of whether the pictures Cleveland police seized from Dollree Mapp's cellar were obscene. On the last day of its term, the Court held, five to four, that the Constitution forbids the use of illegally seized material as evidence in state criminal trials. "The most significant limitation ever imposed on state criminal procedure by the Supreme Court in a single decision," the *Times* heralded the ruling in its lead story. No more would prosecutors be able to use as evidence anything taken improperly during searches by state and local police.

Bill Homans was in Fall River, in the southeastern corner of the state, with a client. Sitting outside the courthouse in his car, he heard the *Mapp* ruling announced on the radio. Six-foot-four, Homans was so excited that he jumped from his seat, "came near to giving myself a concussion on the roof of my car," then "concussed myself again" when the broadcast added that the Court had also decided another case he thought would clinch Dorius's appeal. Unlike the police who raided Ned's apartment, those who searched Dorius's had had a warrant. But now the justices held that warrants that "gave the broadest discretion to the executing officer," such as the one that Regan and his men used to seize all of Dorius's letters (and, if they did have a court order, Arvin's diaries), were also illegal.

Homans believed the Massachusetts Supreme Judicial Court would have to follow suit. Dorius's case was scheduled for fall, and Homans planned to argue that leaving it up to men like Regan and Crowley to decide what was obscene was clearly a violation of due process, since even the courts couldn't define obscenity. The new ruling dramatically bolstered his argument.

Homans phoned Dorius in New Haven to tell him the news, but Dorius was too numb to take it in. Back with friends after leaving the mental hospital, he was paralyzed, he later said, with shame. Though he craved vindication, he'd already been condemned socially, and he despaired that the judgments already imposed on him could be reversed. He had become so deadened to the social world around him that legal vindication no longer promised relief. He craved acquittal, but he had entombed himself. "I didn't want to show my face to anyone. It was an impossible kind of situation to explain or apologize for, and I didn't want to do either. I started walking with a marked stoop, too depressed to care whether I held myself up or not. I felt so lousy, I just let myself go. That was the worst loss," he said. "The real loss of life, the rape of our lives."

Arvin wrote hard through the summer, finishing the second chapter of *Longfellow* on August 8, the third on August 30, and the fourth on September 29. He was writing so quickly, with such confidence, that he was almost troubled by it. He told Hicks, "There is something suspect about this, and in any case, I *don't want to finish the book too soon.*"

Longfellow proved to be the perfect subject for him. He was now writing about Longfellow's progress from sensitive, imitative teenager to major scholar and poet almost as if it were his own. After graduating from Bowdoin at the age of eighteen, in 1825, a classmate of Hawthorne's, Longfellow found that his "deepest wish" was to throw himself into "a purely intellectual, a purely literary career." But a purely literary career was practically impossible in America at the time, and Longfellow briefly followed the family tradition of studying law—until he received an extraordinary offer from Bowdoin's trustees. They established a chair of modern languages and offered it to Longfellow, who, as Arvin noted, not only was "outrageously young" but whose knowledge of foreign languages was limited to a smattering of French. Undeterred, Bowdoin sent him to Europe for three years, during which time he proved to be an extraordinary linguist, quickly mastering—as Arvin had done as a young man—French, German, Italian, and Spanish before returning to teach a field so new that he had to create his job "almost from scratch."

Perhaps because Longfellow regarded teaching as a "noble and elevated" profession, he became—unlike Arvin—a first-rate teacher, but he soon despaired of the intellectual barrenness of Brunswick, Maine—"this land of Barbarians—this miserable Down East." He got married, which temporarily allayed the "dog's life" of "teaching boys their a,b,c," but was restless to escape. So desperate was he to leave Maine in his twenties that in 1833 he traveled to Northampton in the dead of winter to discuss the possibility of taking over the experimental Round Hill School. "The spot is lovely indeed—lovely even beneath its mantle of snow," he wrote to a friend. He abandoned the idea when he was called to teach modern languages at Harvard.

Arvin wrote about this period of Longfellow's passage with barely concealed glee, as an old man who understood all too well what followed. Longfellow burned to be a writer, but, like Arvin at a similar age, had not yet found his true subject or form, and was burdened by the need to make a living. "There was a great deal of diffuse literary energy in Longfellow's mind during these years," Arvin wrote. But because of his academic duties, Longfellow had little time to write, and his prose remained derivative; Arvin described one story as "a piece of appallingly lachrymose deathbed fiction."

Was Longfellow "first of all a scholar? Or was he first of all a poet?" Arvin asked. This of course was his own lifelong conflict, and Arvin explored Longfellow's eighteen years at Harvard—"the years of his renewed productivity as a poet and the genial early summer of his great fame"—as perhaps no critic in America could have done; he brought keen insight and great fellow feeling to the question. Longfellow, a brilliant and adventurous lecturer, introduced America to Goethe and Molière and deepened its grasp of Dante, but privately he was filled with gloom and rebellion. "Perhaps the worst thing in college life," he wrote in his journal in 1838, sounding very much like Arvin in 1960, "is this having your mind constantly a playmate for boys—constantly adapting itself to them, instead of stretching out and grappling with *men's* minds." "Poetic dreams shaded by French irregular verbs!" he protested a year later. "Hang it! I wish I were a free man."

For Arvin, who had chafed under the smiling mask of threadbare academic civility all his adult life, writing with intimate knowledge about "Professor" Longfellow's physical and emotional distress provided a special catharsis, a balm. Before starting at Harvard in the fall of 1836, Longfellow had returned to Europe. There, his wife, Mary, died after a miscarriage. Thus Longfellow arrived in Cambridge alone and bereft, a sufferer whose afflictions spanned "the gamut so familiar in the lives of the poets—dyspepsia, neuralgia, insomnia, eyestrain," Arvin noted. Working slavishly and making few intimates, he suffered harrowing mood swings, a "dismal lethargy hanging about me like a darkness," alternating with "a kind of panic and wild alarm . . . which I cannot control." Disturbed about his health—he suffered crushing headaches and feared at one point that he was going blind—he eventually asked for a leave of absence and took "heroic" water cures in Europe.

Arvin could not but see in all this the familiar markings of his own past. But then Longfellow's life took a stunning, dramatic turn. In Europe, he met and married the daughter of a wealthy Boston industrialist who bought the couple a large house on Brattle Street. A warm, kindly, exuberant man, deeply in love, Longfellow easily attracted friends. As he grew content and happy, his literary energies expanded, and his gift for narrative poetry emerged. His sparkling new life culminated with a fortuitous intervention by Hawthorne, who at dinner one night urged a member of their party to repeat to Longfellow a story about two young lovers who became separated during the deportation of the Acadians from Nova Scotia. Longfellow, eager to try his hand at an epic ballad and struck by the pathos of the story, sat down and wrote *Evangeline*. The poem, which went into six editions within three months, catapulted Longfellow to the "head of our list of native poets," Hawthorne wrote. Achieving the "eminence in literature" he had long craved, Longfellow retired from Harvard soon after.

Arvin's writing about this period in Longfellow's life, more than any other factor, pushed him to embrace the possibilities of *his* new life. He, too, was now retired—"free"—which became much clearer as the fall term began. Whatever else, Arvin was no longer the "old miner . . . wearily getting in the car again to descend the shaft," as he had groaned a year earlier. Whatever else, he was "first of all a poet"—at last. His relief could hardly be overstated.

As with the turning of a switch, the tone of Arvin's letters sharply improved. On September 28, he wrote to Ehrlich: "Things are a little less bleak . . . Al [Fisher] is back, and, of course, everyone else is—not that I see much of anyone, even so. But I have long since found out that, little as one may like it, one can *live* through ages of loneliness." He told Hicks, that same day, "I now perversely have a real thirst for social relations," and even joked about a set of ill-fitting new dentures: "It feels as if someone else's mouth were in mine, and though this *might* be pleasant with another arrangement, it is distinctly uncomfortable with this."

Two days later, after finishing the chapter on Longfellow's literary ascendance and receiving an unexpected refund from his health insurer, Arvin sent Hicks a check to repay him for his gift the previous year. He wrote, "I am no longer so anxious about money as I was," and "I am now as secure as anyone has a right to expect to be." At the rate he was going, he said, he expected to finish "the whole job" of Longfellow by the following summer, and while he wanted to slow down and enjoy it, he was bristling with new ideas and offers. Louis Kronenberger, who was editing a series of critical biographies for Collier, urged Arvin to consider doing one on Hawthorne, and offered an "extravagant advance" of $1,000. Arvin feigned protest—"a *second* book about Hawthorne! . . . people might begin to discuss the question when my third book on N.H. was due," he wrote to Hicks—but in truth he was eager and happy for the work.

As the weather turned colder, Arvin reported feeling consistently "well." He made "ever-so-pleasant" overnight visits to see out-of-town friends when his probation officer approved, then returned to Prospect Street and his office to push ahead with Longfellow. His comic sense, normally donnish and dry, became sharper, more acerbic. Hearing of the demise of a loud-mouthed mutual acquaintance, he wrote merrily to Hicks, "What a relief to everybody within a mile must Mrs. Agan's death have been!" In every respect, his sense of his own powers and place in the world seemed vitally restored.

Not surprisingly, all this placed new strains on Arvin's friends, even as it made him less burdensome. Now that he was getting out more, Arvin depended almost daily on Fisher and Aaron for rides. On a day in late October, after driving him to Ashfield to visit the Linscotts, Fisher insisted on leaving "almost at once" after lunch, making Arvin feel that Fisher suspected he was being "used" by Arvin. He complained to Hicks, "[Al] is at his very best when one is in great trouble, or ill, or knocked out, and dependent on him; but under normal circumstances he is so full of crotchets, so blunt and arbitrary, so irrational in his opinions and judgments, that it takes almost more patience than I at least have, to keep on easy terms with him." Arvin had once told Fisher half-jokingly that after his crisis was over he might need a whole new set of friends, and Fisher may now have thought that was right, though he had no need to worry. Arvin ended his rant to Hicks, "Alas—for I am too deeply indebted to him to extricate myself honorably."

As the holidays approached, Arvin, half-done with his Longfellow biography, was eagerly plotting other projects. Jason Epstein, the editorial director of Vintage Books, had broached "very tentatively" the idea of Arvin's editing a series of paperbacks on American literature and writers. "If all the conditions are right," Arvin told Hicks, "I should rather like to take this on; it would keep me *affairé,* it ought not to interfere too much with writing, and it might help to keep me fed and lodged in my Senior Senior Period." Spurred by Hicks, who had begun writing his memoirs, he began assembling materials for the Secret Autobiography he had first mentioned to Lilienthal a few weeks before his arrest, although his goals for such a memoir had shifted in light of his ease and pleasure with his new life. When he had first mentioned the idea to Lilienthal, he swore such a book would be strictly "not for publication." Now, he specified to Hicks, he desired only that it not be published while he was alive. "Really, aside from the question of time," he wrote, "the only thing that deters me is the disheartening awareness of my sieve-like memory. But on the first fifteen or sixteen years I might have a few amusing things to tell."

Writing with joy, healthier than he had been in more than a decade, caring less than ever about being discredited now that he had little left to hide, Arvin sailed through the Christmas season brimming with self-resurrecting ambition and good cheer. "I hope," he wrote to Hicks, at the end of a long, chatty New Year's Eve letter, which read remarkably like a valedictory, "you are feeling as well as I am."

Chapter Fifteen

"HE WAS AT the floodtide of his energy and power," Kronenberger would write, "never more enthusiastic about what he planned to do, or more eager to set about doing it."

In late February 1962, Arvin met in New York with Jason Epstein to discuss editing the proposed paperback series on American letters. Nothing quite like it had been done before, the nearest precedent being Penguin's *Guide to English Literature,* and Arvin, though flattered to be put in charge, had reservations. The job was huge. The end-of-the-year deadline for manuscripts was onerous, and Epstein wanted the best critics in America to participate, even though he was offering only $250 per chapter.

Yet Arvin gladly agreed to take it on. Not only, he hoped, might it augment his income for as long as he lived; it would further his rehabilitation, returning him to the literary and academic worlds as a senior figure, someone like Brooks, who, at seventy-six and suffering from colon cancer, now ranked as America's most revered literary critic. Brooks, who had visited Arvin in the state hospital after his arrest, normally refused to write piecemeal, but he agreed to contribute a chapter.

The study of American writers and their work had exploded during the 1950s into a booming, notoriously fractious academic industry. Arvin loathed much of the new criticism and especially what he called "the cult of the contemporary and the native"—a scholarly obsession with twentieth-century American literature that made it hard to find a critic who had read anything else. The series promised him a raised platform from which to take aim at this new fashion. With Vintage talking about a four-volume survey, aimed at the common reader and intelligent undergraduate, it was a chance to reassert the standards of learned, *usable* criticism for the masses that Brooks and he had pioneered, while also settling scores. As a connoisseur of good writing and academic fratricide, Arvin eagerly looked forward to recruiting critics he admired and disregarding those he didn't.

He plunged into the project. Almost every day, after finishing his work on Longfellow around noon, he sat at his typewriter, writing ingratiating letters to potential contributors. A few—Leo Marx, Richard Lewis, Warner Berthoff, Irving Howe—responded "very cordially," Arvin wrote, although each had his own ideas about what he wanted to do, and Arvin quickly ran into conflicts, as when Lewis and Berthoff both asked to write about Hart Crane. "Would you have any interest at all in writing a chapter about Pound?" he cajoled a neglected Berthoff. Most others said they were too heavily committed to take on another assignment, and Arvin suspected that the fees he was able to offer were "simply inadequate."

After two months of trying to raise the Vintage Guide off the ground, he realized that the job required much more hand-holding and much less original thought than he had first imagined. He told Epstein he needed someone younger and more vigorous to join him as a co-editor. Meanwhile, he grew frustrated with the "whole subject of elephantiasis of criticism," especially of contemporary literature. "Even now," he wrote to Berthoff on April 29,

[I] am not at all sure that I am not compounding felonies, contributing to the delinquency of minors, etc., etc. . . . Now that PhD theses are being written, I suspect, on Truman Capote (whom I admire as a writer), and seminars, quite literally, being given in the work of the younger Southern writers—solemn and of course dull papers written and read on the work of Eudora Welty—one is really tempted to turn one's javelin point downward—and abdicate.

Abdicate he did. Arvin's slap at the exaltation of modern writers whose work he had earlier helped to promote betrayed his unease with the direction his field had taken. Though he loved Capote as a friend, he had never regarded him as a writer of classics, and the fact that Capote, McCullers, and Welty were now discussed heatedly by undergraduates who scarcely read Melville or Montaigne struck him as a "precursion to barbarism." The Vintage Guide was never officially abandoned, but by June 1 Arvin was out of it, divorced from any trace of the critical obsession with currency and "relevance" that would soon overtake American studies.

He was not unhappy. By then he was almost finished with Longfellow and, rooting around for another subject to occupy him, had all but decided what to do next.

On June 25, the Supreme Court held that the three "beefcake" magazines barred by Arthur Summerfield's postal inspectors in March 1960, six months before Arvin's arrest, were not pornographic and could not be banned from the mail. "Our own independent examination of the magazines leads us to conclude that the most that can be said of them is that they are *dismally unpleasant, uncouth and tawdry* [italics added]," Justice John Harlan wrote for the majority. "But this is not enough to make them obscene." By giving constitutional protection to photographs of seminude men in posing straps—pictures blatantly aimed at other men—the justices invalidated the last of the legal bases for the persecution of Arvin, Ned, and Dorius.

Coming on the same day that the Court outlawed school prayer, the ruling offered the coldest of comforts, a kind of posthumous reprieve. The Post Office had identified Arvin in the flurry of mail blocks arising from the seizure of the three magazines, *MANual, Trim,* and *Grecian Guild Pictorial,* and in the wake of Congress's stepping up its power to intercept private parcels. Regan and his men had invaded all three teachers' apartments on the grounds that they had exhibited obscene pictures. Now, less than twenty-one months later, the Court had not only decided in *Mapp* that such searches and seizures were illegal, but it had decriminalized the very items the police were looking for, overruling a lower court decision made barely two weeks before the arrests.

In truth, America was hurtling toward a new era of sexual openness and protection against government censorship, as the Court's rulings plainly—if belatedly—affirmed. Nor were the justices alone in relaxing their view of Washington's new role. Less than a month after taking office, the Kennedy administration had begun retreating from Summerfield's and Granahan's attacks on the nation's sex industry, quietly dismantling Summerfield's smut museum and returning his private collection of pornography to Post Office files. Although Kennedy would soon appoint Granahan to be the United States Treasurer, he himself had no interest in puritan moralizing. Asked at a press conference whether he planned to censor the "most dreadful stuff . . . coming into our homes and into the hands of our children," he shrugged the matter off with a statement designed to shift the burden of vigilance to parents, where he believed it belonged. "There's always been a problem of course of what is pornography and what is not," Kennedy said. "I don't think the Post Office can be expected to do anything but carry out the laws, nor can the Attorney General. And the laws which are interpreted by the courts are quite clear." With U.S. Marines arriving weekly in Vietnam and Laos, Kennedy had staked his presidency on vanquishing communism, not sin.

The hunting down of Arvin, Spofford, and Dorius thus occurred almost at the last moment it could have, at the twilight of a decade that scarcely two years later began to look hidebound, old-fashioned, and darkly repressive even to the men who ran the country.

America's unbuttoning arrived too late, of course, for Arvin. And although it may have given hope to Ned and Dorius and their friends that homosexuals would not forever be condemned as sexual criminals, it came too late for them, too. By now, both had plans to leave the country. And though their circumstances sharply differed, neither found any reason to stay.

Ned, remarkably, was soaring, apparently unscathed by the crisis that had cost him his dearest friend, his job, family, privacy, and cover. In March, the Supreme Judicial Court had reversed his conviction—the first time in Massachusetts that a higher court used the *Mapp* precedent to throw out evidence gathered illegally by police—but was still reviewing Dorius's appeal. Ned had done so well at Harvard that he'd won a coveted year-long fellowship in Italy, besting the brightest young Latinists in the country. Relieved of the strain of having to lie, his career prospects brilliant, no longer worried that he might have to go to prison, he couldn't wait to head off to the American Academy in Rome, an "embarrassingly posh" villa overlooking the city, where he would do his dissertation and return, he hoped, to an active sex life.

Dorius, meanwhile, remained "morbidly obsessed about the Affair." The Harvard critic Harry Levin had arranged for him to teach American literature at the University of Hamburg, in Germany—something that, as a convicted felon and known homosexual who'd recently lost two prestigious appointments, "I couldn't have done in America for 1,000 years at that point," he would say. After spending the year in New York, living alone in a borrowed apartment, editing in a cubicle at the *Grolier's Encyclopedia* office, so terrified of being recognized on the street that he wore a floppy brown fedora pulled down to shadow his face, he was desperate for the "false ecstasy of displacement."

By traveling to Europe, both hoped to find, as Henry James had, a discreet, civilized, *artistic* culture, a continental antidote to America that might help them distance themselves from their recent past.

It was summer when Arvin typed out the first passages of his long-considered autobiography, tentatively titled *The Past Recaptured*. Since May, when Lilienthal wrote that he was "delighted" that Arvin was "doing the autobiographical thing," and promised to send copies of the more than a thousand letters that Arvin had written to him and that Lilienthal had recently donated, along with the rest of his papers, to Princeton, Arvin had diligently gathered boxes of material and prepared chapter outlines, lists, and chronologies. Despite his "sieve-like memory," he had assembled an accounting of his early life so thorough that it was possible for him to put his finger on not only what—day by day, week by week—he had thought, felt, and experienced, but also what books and poems he'd read, discussions he'd had, and movies he had seen.

"I can hardly allege that any set of recollections I may write will ever have any exemplary value for anyone," he wrote. "Nor can I say that it gives *me* pleasure, in the usual sense, certainly unmixed pleasure, to look back over the course of my life . . . More of what I recollect, both early and late, is painful than pleasurable." But, he continued, "the purely literary motive . . . the desire to give form and verbal expression to whatever has befallen one, however distressing," demanded the effort. Characteristically, he begged the reader's indulgence, explaining that it was "painful to a writer to leave anything in this inchoate state if he can help it . . . like leaving one's living quarters untidy and disarranged—the bed unmade, one's clothes strewn about carelessly, the bathroom a mess."

As he approached his sixty-second birthday, Arvin literally was putting his life in order. In particular, he hoped to connect the events of his adult life, including his recent crisis, to "the past that James calls 'visitable'; the past to which one can reach out one's hand with some hope of touching living flesh with it." In Arvin's case, understandably, this meant starting with nineteenth-century Indiana and his own "ancestral brocade."

He had in his possession a small leatherbound daybook in which his grandfather John Hawkins kept a diary throughout 1865, the year after his mother was born. Perhaps because he knew little about his family history except that it was undistinguished, and felt both proud of and diminished by these "common" roots, no document was more precious to him than this century-old journal, "kept faithfully, day by day, often under trying circumstances, in [a] clear, neat, old-fashioned and rather elegant hand" by an obscure forebear who had died before Arvin was born and who for at least part of that year was "pathetically unemployed." Not very rugged physically and still in his twenties, Hawkins had avoided being drafted into the army during the Civil War, and, though he was a devoted Unionist and Republican, he was also "a rolling stone," who drifted from job to job, had already lost two sons to scarlet fever, and, if not for "his essential decency and his high principles, might well have been a black sheep."

In studying Hawkins's journal, Arvin found much of himself. What Hawkins had really wanted to do was teach singing. As the war shuddered that winter to a violent close, his little family struggled while he bounded among jobs—from "printing posters in a newspaper office, to 'collecting,' to the express office, back to the print shop, and so on," Arvin wrote. But his passion was the small choral classes he conducted in Valparaiso, and he despaired when they went poorly. "My singing school this evening," he wrote in January, "was a failure, so I shall give it up entirely now. There is no interest manifested." Two months later, again out of work, Hawkins moved by himself to a small town in Illinois, hoping to set himself up there, but he soon returned and finally landed a $55-a-month job as a freight handler for the railroad.

"I never had the blues worse in my life before than I have had them this afternoon," Hawkins wrote that spring, "and I hope the morrow will bring some *daylight* through the surrounding gloom."

For the rest of the year, Hawkins unloaded crops in a freight yard—and taught no more singing. Yet, as Arvin observed, there emerged in his diary "a curiously penetrating poetry"; elegant descriptions of burgeoning crop loads of oats, wheat, and corn as summer lengthened into fall, then of a harsh winter descending on the plains. Arvin felt a "strange little vicarious thrill"—and, one suspects, much more than that—as he read that on June 13, "General Grant, the Hero of the Vicksburg battle, passed thro' here this morning on his way East. He came out of the cars and shook hands with us all, and it done us good to shake him by the hand, the Savior of this country."

Here, Arvin understood powerfully, was his own past reborn, his "living flesh" of history. Hawkins, whose only brother was a prosperous hardware dealer in town, seemed to speak in some essential and profound way to the struggle that Arvin believed defined all creative life in America, including, and especially, his own. To the end of his life, Hawkins continued to be "anything but a 'good provider,'" Arvin wrote. "Yet," he added tellingly,

> I believe I do not sentimentalize when I say that he seems to me, with all his limitations, somehow an attractive and lovable character, a man by nature finer, more fastidious, more imaginative, with a deeper feeling for the arts (at least for music), than most of his fellow citizens and contemporaries. Life in a small town in the Middle West, at that time and later, as we know from too much evidence to doubt it, was crushing, sterilizing, to natures of a certain impractical sort; the Village Virus killed off two or three generations of them, and perhaps it is much to his credit that John Baker Hawkins "failed" no more disastrously than he did.

Hawkins, "like so many characters in Middle Western literature . . . a failed and frustrated poet," served for Arvin as a kind of lodestar as he began, in late August, to concentrate on his own early life in Valparaiso. Unlike Longfellow, who had enjoyed a "peculiar felicity" with his origins, Arvin had always felt deeply estranged from his, and Hawkins's example radiated caution, a lesson of the life he was sure would have befallen him had he remained near his family. In the heat and humidity of Northampton, Arvin felt tired and stultified, but he was enjoying himself, and progressing swiftly, so he kept at his desk. Fastidiously, he made notes on his journal entries from when he was thirteen and on his teenage letters to Lilienthal, filed them, then made notes on his notes. He compiled separate shorthand lists of his readings: "Jan. 1, 1914—*Seven Gables, St. Nicholas;* Jan. 5—*Master of Ballantrae*—dislike; January 8—*Blithedale;* Jan. 15—*Copperfield, The Blue Flower.*" He also read and reread the authors whose voices still echoed from his youth—"just for the sake of imparting a quasi-literary touch to my recollections," he confessed to Edmund Wilson.

Indeed, literature and life now blended so seamlessly in him that he seemed a kind of literary character himself—one so narcissistically involved in books that he had no other reflection. He reread Edmund Wilson's chapter on Ambrose Bierce in *Patriotic Gore,* an inscribed copy of which Wilson had recently sent him and that Arvin read "almost at a sitting, bulky as it is," and was stung by how much Bierce, who had grown up in northern Indiana during the same period as Arvin's father and was cold and misanthropic, resembled Fred Arvin. "These qualities of bitterness, cynicism, and emotional aridity," he wrote to Wilson, "strike me as very characteristic of the men who grew up in the Middle West in those dreary decades from say the forties on to the seventies and eighties; it was a cultural trait, a form of self-protection, an almost desperate form of indemnification." Surely it said much about Arvin's bearings in life that his chief reference point for understanding his father was a biographical essay, written by a fellow Eastern critic, about a late-nineteenth-century Midwestern writer.

Arvin worked well and rapidly through the fall, so absorbed in *The Past Recaptured* that he neglected the encumbrances of the present, which, in

October, invited a rebuke from Capote. Capote, trapped in his "imprisoning book" in the "imprisoning" Swiss Alps, hadn't heard from him in months and was desperate for news of how Arvin was doing. "Why, with people like you, must all initiation *always* come from the other side?" he complained, adding, "I'm sure you will write and tell me; you are always *meticulous* about *answering* letters."

But by then Arvin was writing to very few friends and seeing almost no one at Smith except Fisher. Aaron was traveling in Poland on a year-long fellowship, and though Arvin told Fisher that he missed him, he was now so involved in the company of his early self that he was beyond needing most companions, even those he had most relied on. Around Thanksgiving, he visited the Hickses, who thought he looked well, although they noticed he got up several times in the night to urinate and were worried that his prostate troubles weren't fully cured. Arvin reassured them. He told them that after his Hawthorne book he planned to write a history of literary ideas in America, a "magnum opus" that Hicks believed "almost nobody else could write."

Arvin had found in writing about his own life a rare self-completing satisfaction, relying on his recovered memories as he used to rely on his books and friends. Never had he seemed less needy or more at peace.

As he finished the fifth chapter, which ended with his "preposterous swoon" after the bicycle-seat incident with his father, he visited Wilson for a few days in Cambridge, where he hoped to do some research for the Harvard portion of his book. Although Wilson was ill and Arvin was reluctant to wear out his welcome, he and Wilson's wife, Elena, had a pleasant morning touring Craigie House, Longfellow's home. "It really is an extraordinary place," he wrote to her afterward, "hardly changed in any way since 1882, and numerous with the footsteps and voices of great men."

Arvin spent the Christmas season alone—not unpleasurably. He received a "charming" Christmas card from Wilson, and replied more or less promptly, on December 29, to thank him and update him on his progress:

> My book on HWL will probably be ready very soon. It will have a
> dust-jacket that Seymour Lawrence feels is highly dramatic and
> eye-catching, as indeed it is, but it suggests to me Oedipus on the

steps of the palace at Thebes or Lear in the tempest on the heath rather than the author of *Hiawatha* or *Evangeline*.

He added, almost as an afterthought,

> My doctor finds that I have acquired a case of diabetes, and this will probably hamper my movements for some weeks, but as soon as I get the thing more or less under control I hope I may come back to Cambridge again for a little visit.

Fisher wrote to Dan Aaron in Warsaw with the news:

> [Newton] came in some five or six days ago with that kind of look on his face which we have, on one occasion or other, seen: a stricken, brave, appealing expression tainted with I do not know what quality of hesitation and histrionics. It is a look that means he will, if you ask him, *say* what it means, or could mean; and/or a look that does not wish too quickly to be understood, for that might take the *story* out of the recounting . . . This time I knew that it was about to declare the diabetic.

Dr. Hugh Tatlock also knew that look. Tatlock had treated Arvin's myriad health problems for most of the past two decades. After prescribing insulin, he instructed Arvin to watch his diet and stop drinking, but instead of getting better, Arvin developed acute chest and back pains. The pains worsened throughout January, but he kept working, until Tatlock, baffled, admitted him to the Cooley Dickinson Hospital for further tests. After six hours of X-rays, which ruled out an ulcer or a gallbladder attack, Tatlock finally diagnosed him tentatively with an advanced form of diabetes resulting in nerve inflammation.

Arvin, as always, felt relieved after spending his first night in the hospital. He told Fisher the next morning that he was so much better that he planned to go home in two or three days. Fisher wrote to Aaron, knowingly: "I think, *entre nous,* that among other things he may have needed the kind of attention that hospitalization is likely, in his case, to carry with it. But that is only the psycho side of the somatism. He *has* had severe pains, and it is more than simply possible they'll recur." Yet with the cause of his pains a mystery, Tatlock's ministrations were "something like haphazard," Fisher added. Some days Arvin felt better, some nights he slept more than others, but there was no systemic improvement. The hospital refused to release him, nor did he really wish to leave.

Arvin was outwardly optimistic. Advance copies of *Longfellow* had begun circulating, and though the New York newspapers were all on strike, which meant a frustrating lag in advertising and reviews, the early response from friends had been gratifying. Capote had received a copy as he was packing to return to America after three years, his writing of *In Cold Blood* almost at an end. "It is very brilliant, and very beautiful, a fascinating book and a work of art, a real one," he wrote. Arvin had dedicated the book to Brooks, who was dying. Despite a debilitating stroke the previous August, Brooks had had his wife wheel him from the dining room, where she had placed his bed for the better light, and into his study, where he read it in his favorite chair.

When Arvin failed to improve, Tatlock suggested exploratory surgery. Arvin resisted, as did his sister Ellen, with whom Fisher discussed the matter by phone. His nearest relative, Ellen Zeigler was the sibling on whom Arvin had most depended; he'd stayed with her during his shock treatments a decade earlier. As children, they had shared a bedroom and had been sent off together to Miss Brown's kindergarten, walking ten or twelve blocks across town, "a small girl of three and a boy of five—hand in hand, with card-board lunch boxes in our free hands," Arvin recently wrote. Though Ellen lived in Cincinnati, and though he had long withdrawn from his family, she was his next of kin, and Fisher deferred to her medical judgment.

Then Arvin took a turn for the worse. His appetite began to fail. He was nauseated and was kept awake at night by excruciating abdominal pain. As the hours and days and nights passed, Arvin's doctors suspected cancer, narrowing their focus to his pancreas.

Fisher, who visited Arvin once or twice a day and was his chief link to the world, watched him decline. He was pale, weak, his face sunken. He gave up seeing other people and talked to Fisher about "practical matters"—primarily, his will—which he addressed "with remarkable good sense and quietness," Fisher told Aaron.

After three weeks in the hospital, in late February, Arvin finally agreed to the surgery. Ellen came from Cincinnati to care for him. Following the operation, the doctor came to Fisher in the waiting room and told him that Arvin had inoperable cancer of the pancreas and that there was nothing that could be done for him. Fisher was not surprised, and doubted that Arvin would be either when he was told. "Sad news about Newton, Brother," he wrote to Aaron.

With a terminal diagnosis, medicine becomes perfunctory. Arvin was put on cobalt treatments in addition to his tranquilizing shots, which nauseated him so that he could barely eat. He was moved to a private room, where he received visits from Ellen and Fisher but almost no one else. They discussed his going home if he improved, and Ellen promised to care for him as long as he needed her. He had a bell for the nurses, who shaved and bathed him. He asked Fisher to bring his diaries from his apartment, and spent his mornings reading them with an eye toward editing, clarifying certain passages, excising others with a razor blade and destroying them. He censored perhaps one in fifty pages.

Lilienthal flew in from Princeton, but couldn't stay more than an afternoon. Still taking life at a "high trot," he was leaving within days for Persia. He and Arvin had time alone, mostly to reminisce, and Arvin promised to have Ellen send him the early chapters of his autobiography. Afterward, Lilienthal told Fisher he was surprised to see Arvin looking as well as he did, and Fisher suspected he was simply trying to boost everyone's morale before returning to the airport. "So far as I can tell," he told Aaron, "there simply is no *shit* about him. On the other hand, he seems to me curiously not so much reticent as timid about his words; I feel that he is, despite everything, rather naive about certain things."

Fisher himself did not think Arvin looked well.

He is dwindling to thinness, dissolving slowly and whitely to the bone [he wrote to Aaron]. To me, he has on him the whiteness of shadows. Still, it is true that when he's not in pain, he talks with humor and even a kind of surprising vigor. His eyes wander and, at times, look a little wild or startled, as if he had seen something never before seen. His general attitude seems to be one of serenity . . . Today, he said that tomorrow he wanted to talk with me about his diet.

By early March, Arvin was failing perceptibly. Tatlock told Fisher that "he's not likely to die of a convulsion or 'racked' but of something like pneumonia [and] he will not leave the hospital." Facing death, Arvin seemed remarkably composed. He joked to Fisher that he was a "nonambulatory pharmacy," which kept down his agonies but, mingling with the ravages of his disease, also left him depleted, beyond concentration. On March 3, Fisher reported to Aaron, "For the first time in his life (he said yesterday, and without much regret, with a sense of relief, in fact) he is unable to read. He seemed astonished that such a thing could be so, rather amused by it."

No character in literature can teach a person to die, and Arvin faced his rapid dwindling fully engaged with the world around him, speaking affectionately of his friends and letting them know, when possible, how much he loved them. For the small circle that had forgiven him and remained true, the sorrow of losing him was balanced by a sense that, despite a life of suffering, Arvin had prevailed; that he had done heroic and important things. Lilienthal, who suffered Arvin's waning most keenly, was buoyed by Arvin's description of their boyhood friendship in *The Past Recaptured*. Confessing that "I find it difficult to find quite the words I want to say," he wrote, "I was moved deeply that after all these years you remembered me, 'Dave,' the chubby one with the wild hair, as a friend you could count on. When all this time I had thought of myself as the one who was a beneficiary of your friendship . . ."

Capote arrived in New York too late to visit Arvin in the hospital, as he had hoped, but not too late to talk with him by phone. Ellen had written to him and a few others to apprise them of Arvin's condition. Capote told him how sorry he was about his illness, but Arvin cut him off. "Never mind," he said, stoically. "At least I've grown up at last."

As so often, it was Wilson's timely words that perhaps meant most. With the New York newspaper strike still on, *Longfellow* and other new books were piling up unreviewed. Wilson sent Arvin proofs of his review of the book for *The New Yorker,* slated for the March 23 issue, because he was afraid Arvin might not live to see it.

"Among the writers who have really devoted their lives to the study of our literature," Wilson wrote, "I can think of only two who can themselves be called first-rate writers: Van Wyck Brooks and Newton Arvin." Citing Arvin's "charm of style—a curious kind of radiance, which is a personal emanation—and the ability to renew stale subjects," he praised his old friend for having written "a more delightful book than one could ever have believed possible."

To Arvin's friends there was no crueler irony, Hicks would lament, "than his being stricken just after a period of deep disturbance." On the other hand, "he had had one good year and made the most of it." This was the final lesson of Arvin's life; as he had written to Aaron, a decade earlier,

And I can tell you, from a fund of experience, that one can be taken down from the rack, closer to death than to life—and then still have the most exquisite joys ahead of one.

Arvin died in Cooley Dickinson Hospital on March 21, 1963. His death, like Melville's, went largely unnoticed by the public, partly because of his disgrace, partly because of the newspaper strike, but mostly because of who he was. "For better or worse," Louis Kronenberger wrote, "he lacked what is fairly enough called showmanship." In the end, no wide audience mourned him, and he stayed undiscovered by most readers. Like all writers, he feared being forgotten—unread. However, since his friends all were writers too, and of the sort like himself who left nothing unrecorded, he must have understood that they also would have their say. *The Past Recaptured* remained in files and boxes in his apartment, a quarter finished.

In Arvin's last days, Doughty wrote to Ned to tell him Arvin was dying and wanted to see him, but Ned didn't respond.

"It has been a foul winter," Fisher wrote to Aaron, "a vile and miserable time, of the sort that gives the wrong people an everlasting cold."

Arvin's funeral was held at St. John's, the gray stone church edged against the Smith campus on Elm Street. He had left instructions to have a few minutes of music to start, and the church organist, Philip Keppler, played some Bach and Mozart. After the reading of the Episcopal service for the burial of the dead, Keppler played *Ein Feste Burg*, as Arvin had also requested. The American Institute of Arts and Letters sent a wreath. There were no encomiums.

Afterward, about a dozen people returned to Arvin's apartment—Fisher, Madeleine, Robert Gorham Davis, Howard Doughty, Granville and Dorothy Hicks, Ellen, and several others—where his will was read.

Arvin left five books each "in the order named" to Ellen, Doughty, Fisher, Kronenberger, Hicks, Aaron, Davis, Oskar Seidlin, and Capote. The rest he left to his executor, Al Fisher, to keep, give away, or sell. He left his correspondence to Smith but, to Fisher's dismay, his diaries, journals, published and unpublished manuscripts, and four file drawers of notes and other materials to Barbara Pierce, a niece who had come to his aid during his crisis. Fisher worried that Pierce, a housewife from York, Pennsylvania, wasn't prepared "for the difficulties that her holding the papers could occasion," he wrote, but she satisfied him that only "duly qualified and cleared scholars" would see them, if and when interest arose.

Arvin's other bequests were small and idiosyncratic; he had possessed nothing of any great monetary value. He left to Madeleine Fisher her choice of ten of his phonograph records; to Hicks, all his remaining records; to Doughty and Aaron, small paintings by a Springfield artist, appraised at $50 each; to Ellen, a small antique salesman's sample chest and "any and all family pictures, letters, and mementos"; and to Lilienthal, a $15 pair of green Mexican pottery bookends in the shape of horses and riders.

Most of the rest of his estate he left to Ellen. He split his future book royalties among Ellen, Kronenberger, and another sister, Dorothy Hooker, with whom he rarely corresponded, and left Fisher $500. He'd had $4,421 in a checking account at the First National Bank of Northampton when he died.

A few days later, Fisher wrote to Aaron, executing one of Arvin's final wishes. "I have a copy of Newton's *Longfellow* for you (which he asked me to deliver on your return—or, if you prefer, I'll send it to you). Neither your copy nor mine is inscribed. At the time he was simply too weak. For my part it does not matter that he did not write in them. You and I know how the book grew, and that's enough."

In June 1851, Melville had written Hawthorne a long, fervent letter from Pittsfield as he approached the completion of *Moby-Dick*. "Though I wrote the Gospels in this century," he told him, "I should die in the gutter." At age thirty-two, Melville was feeling "completely done up," having been forced to lay the book aside for three weeks while he put in his crops and attended to his duties as a householder ("building and patching and tinkering away in all directions") before heading to New York in July to "work and slave" on his manuscript as it was put to press. Melville's father, a prosperous merchant, had lost everything he had, then went to pieces and died, when the author was a boy, and Melville was haunted by the "grinning" specter of catastrophic failure. "What I feel most moved to write, that is banned—it will not pay," he wrote. "Yet, altogether, write the *other* way I cannot. So the product is a final hash, and all my books are botches."

A century later, Arvin wrote of Melville's unregarded death six years after his retirement as a New York customs inspector earning four dollars a day on the city's docks:

> There is something suitable and satisfying to the imagination in the picture they present of touchily guarded solitude and rather grim obscurity . . . Melville in these years . . . suggests some almost nameless old man-of-war's man who, after a long life dutifully spent in the maintop amid tempests and sea-fights, has belayed his last halyard and slipped into obscure moorings ashore.

Finally making it to shore himself, Arvin also drifted beyond public view. Tenaciously as he had guarded his last refuge—work and friendship—he would have been gratified to know that his meager estate arrived safely in the hands of his family and the few others, mostly critics, who would be the last to remember him, and that he would soon be left alone at last.

Epilogue

THREE MONTHS AFTER Arvin's death, the Massachusetts Supreme Judicial Court reversed Joel Dorius's conviction, striking down Regan's search warrant and declaring the police raid on Dorius's apartment illegal. Dorius taught American literature at the University of Hamburg for another year and then accepted an invitation from San Francisco State College, where he taught until his retirement. He lives in San Francisco and has not been back to Northampton.

Ned Spofford also returned to America in the spring of 1964, having received an appointment at Cornell although he had not completed his dissertation. After being given tenure in 1970—still without finishing his Ph.D.—he quit and moved to San Francisco, where he lived with Dorius for two years. He was hired as a visiting lecturer at Stanford. In 1974, while at Stanford, Ned suffered the first of several breakdowns—a delayed reaction to the events of 1960. Depressed and suicidal, he was hospitalized three times during the 1970s. A decade later, he avoided being hospitalized again only by leaving the classroom. He retired in 1988 and lives alone in Palo Alto.

On Truman Capote's death, in 1984, it was learned that he had left money for the Truman Capote Lifetime Achievement Award in Literary Criticism, in Arvin's memory. Twelve years later, on a night in New York, a ceremony was held to honor its first recipient, Alfred Kazin, who noted in his remarks that Arvin hadn't thought very highly of him when Kazin taught at Smith.

Northampton remains divided between natives and newcomers, but its politics have shifted in ways Arvin wouldn't have imagined. In November 1999, seventy-five years after the Coolidge landslide, Northampton elected its first openly homosexual mayor, an Irish Catholic woman and the long-time administrator of a publicly funded day-care center. The city council president, a popular male high school guidance counselor in Amherst, also is openly gay.

Books by Newton Arvin

Hawthorne. Boston: Little, Brown, 1929.

Whitman. New York: Macmillan, 1938.

Herman Melville. New York: Sloane, 1950.

Longfellow: His Life and Work. Boston: Little, Brown, 1963.

American Pantheon (essays). Edited by Daniel Aaron and Sylvan Schendler. New York: Delacorte, 1966.

The Heart of Hawthorne's Journals (editor). Boston, New York: Houghton Mifflin, 1929.

Hawthorne's Short Stories (editor). New York: Knopf, 1946.

Moby-Dick by Herman Melville (Introduction by Arvin). New York: Rinehart, 1948.

The Scarlet Letter by Nathaniel Hawthorne (Introduction by Arvin). New York: Harper, 1950.

The Selected Letters of Henry Adams (editor). New York: Farrar, Straus and Young, 1951.

The Grandissimes: A Story of Creole Life by George W. Cable (Introduction by Arvin). New York: Sagamore, 1957.

Bibliography

Aaron, Daniel. *American Notes: Selected Essays.* Boston: Northeastern University Press, 1994.

————. *Writers on the Left: Episodes in American Literary Communism.* New York: Harcourt, Brace & World, 1961.

Allen, Frederick Lewis. *Only Yesterday: An Informal History of the Nineteen-Twenties.* New York and London: Harper, 1931.

American Psychiatric Association, Committee on Nomenclature and Statistics. *Diagnostic and Statistical Manual.* Washington, D.C.: APA-Mental Hospital Service, 1952.

Anderson, Sherwood. *Winesburg, Ohio.* New York: Huebsch, 1919.

Bergler, Edmund. *Counterfeit Sex: Homosexuality, Impotence, Frigidity.* New York: Grune & Stratton, 1958.

Berthold, Michael. "Newton Arvin," in *Dictionary of Literary Biography,* no. 100, 13–20.

Blumenthal, Sidney. "The Ruins of Georgetown." *New Yorker* 72 (21 and 28 October 1996): 222–237.

————. "The Cold War and the Closet." *New Yorker* 73 (17 March 1997): 112–117.

Bonfitto, Vincent. "The Formation of Gay and Lesbian Identity and Community in the Connecticut River Valley of Western Massachusetts, 1900–1970." *Journal of Homosexuality* 33, no. 1 (1997): 69–97.

Bradford, Gamaliel. *The Quick and the Dead.* Boston and New York: Houghton Mifflin, 1931.

Brooks, John. "A Second Sort of Life." *New Yorker* 37 (29 April 1961): 45–90.

Brooks, Van Wyck. *America's Coming of Age.* New York: Huebsch, 1915.

———. *Letters and Leadership*. New York: Huebsch, 1918.

———. *Days of the Phoenix: The Nineteen Twenties I Remember*. New York: Dutton, 1957.

Buckley, Carol. *At the Still Point: A Memoir*. New York: Simon & Schuster, 1996.

Buckley, Kerry. "The Politics of Nostalgia—The Man Nobody Knew: Bruce Barton and the Construction of Calvin Coolidge."

Buckley, William F., Jr. *God and Man at Yale*. Chicago: Regnery, 1951.

Bush, Gregory. *Lord of Attention: Gerald Stanley Lee and the Crowd Metaphor in Industrializing America*. Amherst: University of Massachusetts Press, 1991.

Capote, Truman. *Other Voices, Other Rooms*. New York: Random House, 1948.

Carr, Virginia Spencer. *The Lonely Hunter: A Biography of Carson McCullers*. Garden City, N.Y.: Doubleday, 1975.

Chauncey, George. *Gay New York: Gender, Urban Culture, and the Making of the Gay Male World, 1890–1940*. New York: Basic, 1994.

Clarke, Gerald. *Capote*. New York: Ballantine, 1988.

Cleary, Margot. "Newton Arvin's Fall from Grace." *Hampshire Life* (11–17 October 1991): 8–26.

Congressional Record. "Homosexuals in Government, 1950," vol. 96, part 4, 81st Congress, 2nd session (29 March–24 April 1950): 4527–4528.

Daniels, Jonathan. *The Time Between the Wars: Armistice to Pearl Harbor*. Garden City, N.Y.: Doubleday, 1966.

Davenport-Hines, Richard. *Auden*. New York: Pantheon, 1995.

De Grazia, Edward. *Censorship Landmarks*. New York and London: Bowker, 1969.

———. *Girls Lean Back Everywhere: The Law of Obscenity and the Assault on Genius*. New York: Vintage, 1993.

Douglas, Ann. *Terrible Honesty: Mongrel Manhattan in the 1920s*. New York: Farrar, Straus & Giroux, 1995.

Duberman, Martin. *About Time: Exploring the Gay Past*. New York: Gay Presses of New York, 1986.

Edel, Leon. *Henry James: The Conquest of London*. Philadelphia and New York: Lippincott, 1962.

Ellman, Richard. *Oscar Wilde*. New York: Vintage, 1988.

Eustis, Helen. *The Horizontal Man*. New York and London: Harper, 1946.

Everson, David, ed. *The Supreme Court as Policy-Maker: Three Studies on the Impact of Judicial Decisions*. Carbondale: Southern Illinois University, 1968.

Fitzgerald, F. Scott. *The Crack-Up*. New York: Scribner's, 1931.

Flower, Dean. "Newton Arvin," in *Dictionary of American Biography, Supplement Seven, 1961–1965*, 18–19. New York: Scribner's, 1981.

————. "Henry James in Northampton: Visions and Revisions." Northampton, Mass.: Friends of Smith College Library, 1971.

Freeman, Marsha Aileen. "Newton Arvin: A Career in American Letters." Ph.D. diss., University of Pennsylvania, 1975.

Gilbert, Clinton. *You Takes Your Choice.* New York: Putnam, 1924.

Gill, Brendan. *A New York Life: Of Friends and Others.* New York: Poseidon, 1990.

Gunn, Giles. *F. O. Matthiessen: The Critical Achievement.* Seattle and London: University of Washington Press, 1975.

Gurstein, Rochelle. *The Repeal of Reticence: America's Cultural and Legal Struggles over Free Speech, Obscenity, Sexual Liberation, and Modern Art.* New York: Hill and Wang, 1996.

Halberstam, David. *The Fifties.* New York: Villard, 1993.

Hamilton, Ian. *Robert Lowell: A Biography.* New York: Random House, 1982.

Heale, M. J. *McCarthy's Americans: Red Scare Politics in State and Nation, 1935–1965.* Athens: University of Georgia Press, 1998.

Hendrick, Ives. *Facts and Theories of Psychoanalysis.* New York: Knopf, 1935.

Hicks, Granville. *Part of the Truth.* New York: Harcourt, Brace & World, 1965.

————. *Small Town.* New York: Macmillan, 1946.

Hirsch, H. N. *The Enigma of Felix Frankfurter.* New York: Basic, 1981.

Hoopes, James. *Van Wyck Brooks: In Search of American Culture.* Amherst: University of Massachusetts Press, 1977.

Hooven, F. Valentine III. *Beefcake: The Muscle Magazines of America, 1950–1970.* Germany: Taschen, 1995.

Horowitz, Helen Lefkowitz. *Alma Mater: Design and Experience in the Women's Colleges from Their Nineteenth Century Beginnings to the 1930s.* New York: Knopf, 1984.

Hyde, Louis, ed. *Rat and the Devil: Journal Letters of F. O. Matthiessen and Russell Cheney.* Hamden, Conn.: Archon Books, 1978.

Jones, James H. "Dr. Yes." *New Yorker* 73 (25 August and 1 September 1997): 99–113.

Kahn, E. J., Jr. "Author! Author! Where's the Author?" *New Yorker* 28 (19 April 1952): 100–104.

Kaiser, Charles. *The Gay Metropolis: New York City, 1940–1996.* Boston and New York: Houghton Mifflin, 1997.

Katz, Jonathan. *Gay American History: Lesbians and Gay Men in the USA.* New York: Crowell, 1976.

————. "Hunting Witches in Massachusetts, 1960." *The Advocate* (15 August 1989): 44–45.

Kazin, Alfred. *On Native Grounds: An Interpretation of Modern American Prose Literature.* New York: Harvest, 1970.

———. *An American Procession: Major American Writers, 1830–1930.* Cambridge, Mass.: Harvard University Press, 1984.

Kurland, Philip, ed. *The Supreme Court Review, 1961.* Chicago: University of Chicago Press, 1962.

Landrum, Renee. " 'More Firmly Based Today': Anti-Communism, Academic Freedom and Smith College, 1947–1956." Bachelor's thesis, Smith College, 15 April 1998.

Latham, Earl. *Massachusetts Politics.* New York: Citizenship Clearing House, 1956.

Levenson, Leah, and Jerry Natterstad. *Granville Hicks: The Intellectual in Mass Society.* Philadelphia: Temple University Press, 1993.

Lewis, Sinclair. *Main Street.* New York: Harcourt, Brace, 1921.

Lietch, Vincent B. *American Literary Criticism, from the Thirties to the Eighties.* New York: Columbia University Press, 1988.

The Journals of David E. Lilienthal, vols. 1–4. New York: Harper & Row, 1964–1969.

Lockwood, Allison McCrillis. "Children of Paradise: A Northampton Memoir." *Northampton* (Mass.) *Daily Hampshire Gazette,* 1986.

Long, Terry. *Granville Hicks.* Boston: Twayne, 1981.

Lukas, J. Anthony. *Common Ground: A Turbulent Decade in the Lives of Three American Families.* New York: Knopf, 1985.

Mariani, Paul. *Lost Puritan: A Life of Robert Lowell.* New York and London: Norton, 1994.

Marshall, Helen. *Dorothea Dix: Forgotten Samaritan.* Chapel Hill: University of North Carolina Press, 1937.

Martin, Kingsley. *Harold Laski (1893–1950): A Biographical Memoir.* New York: Viking, 1953.

Martin, Robert K. "Scandal at Smith." *Radical Teacher* 45: 4–8.

Matthiessen, F. O. *American Renaissance: Art and Expression in the Age of Emerson and Whitman.* New York and London: Oxford University Press, 1941.

McCollough, David. *Truman.* New York: Simon & Schuster, 1992.

Mellow, James. *Invented Lives: F. Scott and Zelda Fitzgerald.* Boston: Houghton Mifflin, 1984.

Meyers, Jeffrey. *Scott Fitzgerald: A Biography.* New York: Harper/Collins, 1994.

———. *Edmund Wilson: A Biography.* Boston and New York: Houghton Mifflin, 1995.

Miller, Perry. *Jonathan Edwards.* New York: Sloane, 1949.

Moore, J. Michael, and Stan Sherer. *The Life and Death of Northampton State Hospital.* Northampton, Mass.: Historic Northampton, 1994.

Murtagh, John. *Cast the First Stone.* New York: McGraw-Hill, 1957.

Nelson, Raymond. *Van Wyck Brooks: A Writer's Life*. New York: Dutton, 1981.

Neuse, Steven. *David E. Lilienthal: The Journey of an American Liberal*. Knoxville: University of Tennessee Press, 1996.

Nichols, Elizabeth. "Paradise Lost and Regained: Experience of Refugee Professors at Smith College." Bachelor's thesis, Smith College, 1990.

Novick, Sheldon. *Henry James: The Young Master*. New York: Random House, 1996.

Parkes, Henry Bamford. *The American Experience*. New York: Vintage, 1959.

Parsons, James. *Images of America: Northampton*. Dover, N.H.: Arcadia, 1996.

Paul, James, and Murray Schwartz. *Federal Censorship: Obscenity in the Mail*. New York: Free Press of Glencoe, 1961.

Plimpton, George. *Truman Capote: In Which Various Friends, Enemies, Acquaintances and . . . His Turbulent Career*. New York: Doubleday, 1997.

Powers, William. *Enforcement Odyssey: Massachusetts State Police*. Paducah, Ky.: Turner, 1998.

"Puritan Terror—Massachusetts: 1961" (as told to John Logan by Harmon H. and Edward W.). *Mattachine Review* (April 1961): 4–26.

Rorem, Ned. *The New York Diary*. New York: Braziller, 1967.

Russell, Francis. *Sacco and Vanzetti: The Case Resolved*. New York: Harper & Row, 1986.

———. *A City in Terror: 1919—The Boston Police Strike*. New York: Viking, 1975.

Schlesinger, Arthur M., Jr. *The Crisis of the Old Order, 1919–1933*. Boston: Houghton Mifflin, 1957.

Schrecker, Ellen W. *No Ivory Tower: McCarthyism and the Universities*. New York: Oxford University Press, 1986.

Shorter, Edward. *A History of Psychiatry: From the Era of the Asylum to the Age of Prozac*. New York: Wiley, 1997.

Sinclair, Upton. *The Goose-Step: A Study of American Education*. Pasadena, Calif.: self-published, 1923.

Six Decades at Yaddo. Self-published, 1986.

Sklar, Stacey. "Scandal at Smith College: The Newton Arvin Case." Bachelor's thesis, Amherst College, 1989.

Summerfield, Arthur. *U.S. Mail: The Story of the U.S. Postal Service*. New York: Holt, Rinehart & Winston, 1960.

Sweezy, Paul, and Leo Huberman, eds. *F. O. Matthiessen (1902–1950): A Collective Portrait*. New York: Monthly Review, 1950.

Swigert, Victoria, ed. *Law and the Legal Process*. Beverly Hills, Calif.: Sage, 1982.

Talese, Gay. *Thy Neighbor's Wife*. Garden City, N.Y.: Doubleday, 1980.

Thelen, David. *Robert M. La Follette and the Insurgent Spirit*. Boston: Little, Brown, 1976.

Thorp, Margaret Farrand. *Neilson of Smith*. New York: Oxford University Press, 1956.

Timmons, Bascom. *Portrait of an American: Charles G. Dawes*. New York: Holt, 1953.

Townsend, Kim. *Manhood at Harvard: William James and Others*. Cambridge, Mass.: Harvard University Press, 1996.

Vanderbilt, Kermit. *American Literature and the Academy: The Roots, Growth and Maturity of a Profession*. Philadelphia: University of Pennsylvania Press, 1986.

Vitelli, James. *Van Wyck Brooks*. New Haven, Conn.: College and University Press, 1969.

Warren, Austin. Introduction to *The Scarlet Letter*, by Nathaniel Hawthorne. New York: Holt, Rinehart & Winston, 1947.

Wasserstrom, William. *The Legacy of Van Wyck Brooks: A Study of Maladies and Motives*. Carbondale: Southern Illinois University Press, 1971.

White, William Allen. *A Puritan in Babylon: The Story of Calvin Coolidge*. New York: Macmillan, 1958.

Wildeblood, Peter. *Against the Law*. London: Weidenfeld & Nicolson, 1955.

Wilson, Edmund. "Arvin's Longfellow and New York State's Geology." *New Yorker* 39 (23 March 1963): 174–181.

Yoder, Edwin, Jr. *Joseph Alsop's Cold War: A Study of Journalistic Influence and Intrigue*. Chapel Hill and London: The University of North Carolina Press, 1995.

Acknowledgments

I am indebted to a number of people for their help and generosity. Dan Aaron, Helen Bacon, Joel Dorius, Prudence Grand, Rick Moody, Frank Murphy, Peter Rowe, and Ned Spofford gave invaluable support. For their patience and wisdom in reviewing various portions of the manuscript, I want to thank Chris Benfey, Lisa Cholodenko, J. D. Dolan, Kathy Goos, and Bill McFeely. I am also indebted in many ways to Martin Antonetti, Vincent Brann, Susan Brynteson, Kerry Buckley, Isabelle Cardia, Stephanie Craib, Gerald Crowley, Fred Eisenstein, Richard Evans, Madeleine Fisher, Jeff Geller, Tony Giardina, Al Griggs, Dennis Grubbs, Helen Horowitz, Chris Hough, Joseph Jagodowski, William Kornegay, Karen Kukil, Leslie Leduc, Enace Lococo, Judith Lococo, Linda March, Nellie Mendenhall, Josh Miller, Marie Panik, Michael Ryan, Alan Sosne, Susan Sprung, Richard Stanley, Michael Sundell, Nanci Young, Tug Yourgrau, and John Zeigler. Gerald Clarke, Margot Cleary, Robert Martin, and Stacy Sklar provided important scholarship and insights through their published work. I owe special thanks to *The New Yorker*, especially Charles Michener, and to the Yaddo Corporation. My agent, Amanda Urban, and my editor, Nan Talese, were as ever tireless, patient, and wise, as were others at Doubleday, particularly Frances Apt, Lorna Owen, Angela Wu, and Amelia Zalcman. My family—Kathy Goos, Emily Werth, and Alex Werth—gave more than I can repay. I thank them most.

Index